Muriel S
Y Ber
Sidmouth.

With happy memories of the
Harding family.

HARDING
OF PETHERTON

HARDING
OF PETHERTON
FIELD-MARSHAL

MICHAEL CARVER

WEIDENFELD AND NICOLSON
LONDON

Weidenfeld and Nicolson
91 Clapham High St   London sw4

ISBN 0 297 7750 3

Printed in Great Britain by
Willmer Brothers Limited, Rock Ferry, Merseyside

CONTENTS

ILLUSTRATIONS

Between pages 86 and 87

MAPS

ACKNOWLEDGEMENTS

The author wishes to thank all those who gave generously of their time to talk or write about John Harding. In particular he is grateful to Viscounts Head and Boyd of Merton; Field-Marshals Sir Gerald Templer and Sir Geoffrey Baker; Generals Sir Richard O'Connor, Sir Richard Gale and Sir Dudley Ward; Lieutenant-Generals Sir Terence Airey, Sir Nigel Poett and Sir Harold Redman; the Right Honourable Malcolm MacDonald, Sir George Sinclair MP, Sir David Hunt, Sir John Clark, Lieutenant-Colonels A. Hunt and H. van Straubenzee, Mr Duncan Guthrie, Mr Joe Guthrie, Mr John Reddaway, Mr Stephen Fenlaugh, Mr Jocelyn Hambro and Mr Aubrey Greville Williams.

Thanks are also due to Viscount Head for permission to quote from his letters, to Sir David Hunt and Kimber & Co. for permission to quote from his *A Don at War*, to Clarissa Countess of Avon, her fellow trustees and Cassell & Co. for permission to quote the late Earl of Avon's letters and from his memoirs *Full Circle*, to the Viscount Montgomery of Alamein and Collins & Co, for permission to quote Field-Marshal Montgomery's letters and from his *Memoirs*, and to Brigadier Charles Turner for permission to quote from his letters.

In addition the author and publishers would like to thank the following: Cassell & Co. for permission to reproduce the map on pages 128 and 129 from Basil Liddell Hart's *History of the Second World War*. and B. T. Batsford for permission to reproduce the maps on pages 49, 97 and 103 from the author's *El Alamein* and the map on page 83 from the author's *Tobruk*.

Finally the author expresses his thanks to the staff of the Prince Consort's Army Library at Aldershot for their constant courtesy and help, to the Army Historical Branch of the Ministry of Defence and to John and Mary Harding themselves for their encouragement, help and hospitality.

ix

CHAPTER ONE

EARLY DAYS
1896–1915

On 10 February 1896, at Rock House, South Petherton, Somerset, to Francis Ebenezer and Elizabeth Ellen Harding (née Anstice), a son : Allan Francis. Had his parents been the sort of people who announced births in the newspaper, this is how the world at the time would have known of the entry into it of the infant who was to become Field-Marshal the Lord Harding of Petherton, GCB, CBE, DSO and two bars, MC, having filled all the high posts in the army, distinguished himself as Governor of Cyprus in a time of crisis, and then started a new life in industry, crowned by becoming chairman of one of the largest and most successful British companies. Yet these achievements would certainly not have formed any part of the aspirations of his parents; they might well, indeed, have disapproved on principle of every aspect of it.

Rock House is a two-storey, plain rectangular house facing onto the road on the north side of South Petherton, a few hundred yards only from the centre of this small country town just off the Roman Fosse Way between Ilminster and Ilchester, seven miles west of Yeovil in the flat, rich meadowland just north of the Dorset-Somerset border. It is built of the local stone, quarried at Hamdon near the lovely Elizabethan mansion of Montacute, itself of the same stone. Behind the house is a pleasant garden of less than an acre, overshadowed by a huge yew tree, near which, in an orchard over the wall behind, stands what some people might imagine to be a pelota wall, but is one of the very few remaining walls against which was played an early form of fives.

The Hardings and the Anstices came of a group of families, which included also the Hebditches and the Vauxes, who had lived in and around South Petherton for hundreds of years, yeoman farmers and tradesmen, hard-working, independent, God-fearing, honest and upright. They would have been for Cromwell when he defeated the Cavaliers at Langport nearby and probably sympathized with Monmouth when he was defeated at Sedgemoor a few miles to the north. Allan's (as he was christened and known until after the First World War) father, Francis, was for all his life clerk to a local firm of solicitors, Poole and Son, and a local rating officer. His father, William, had been a farmer, and his brother was the local corn merchant. Allan's mother, Elizabeth, was the stronger character of the two. Her father, Jethro Anstice, was the local draper. Both came of large families : Francis Harding was one of eight, one of his sisters being matron of a children's hospital in Birkenhead; Elizabeth Anstice one of thirteen, several of her brothers emigrating to Australia and New Zealand. They were devout Congregationalists, and Francis Harding played the organ at the chapel where all the family, Allan and his three sisters, were expected to sing in the choir at the two services they attended every Sunday, with Sunday school falling in between.

When Allan was seven or eight, Jethro Anstice bought the local stationer's shop and the Harding family moved into Bank House in the centre of the town so that Allan's mother could run the shop. At this time he attended a local dame's school at which all his fellow pupils, some fifteen of them, were cousins. Although life was strict and puritanical in many ways, it was easy and carefree in others. Allan followed the pursuits of any country boy of his time and age : haymaking on his cousins' farms, bird-nesting and playing around in the unspoilt countryside that surrounded the little town, Sunday school outings to Ham Hill by farm wagon, picnic meals looking over the glorious view to the Mendips after sliding down all the hillocks where the famous Ham stone had been quarried. One of Allan's clearest memories of this time was of going round in a trap with his uncle, Fred Anstice, the draper, taking orders and delivering orders from the previous trip in the villages round about. A special treat was when his grandfather went into Yeovil for one of the monthly meetings of the Rural District Council. The horse and trap would be left at the Mermaid Inn and Allan would window-gaze in the shops of Yeovil while his grandfather attended the meeting. This would be followed by a good lunch at the Farmers' Ordinary at the Mermaid. In the summer there would be expeditions to the seaside, usually to West Bay near Bridport. It was a close-knit community, full of vitality, life based on the rhythm of agriculture, high-principled and strict, but full of incident and with considerable personal freedom—the life depicted so graphically in the novels of Thomas Hardy.

At the age of ten Allan moved from the dame's school to Ilminster Grammar School, and at first bicycled the five miles there and back each day. The school had been founded in the reign of Edward VI and had a justifiably high reputation. Not long after he had begun to attend, he caught a bad chill, and it was decided that it was due to the journey there and back. He therefore became a weekly boarder, one of twelve who lived and had their meals in the headmaster's pleasant Georgian house next door to the lovely church and to the original school, which by then had become the girls' school. The grammar school, in which there were about a hundred and fifty pupils, was a Victorian building a few minutes' walk away. The headmaster, Bob Davidson, was one of the old school : he insisted on the highest standards and put all his talents into ensuring that these boys would benefit from the accumulated wisdom of the past and be turned out into the world with their minds and characters developed to the limits of which they were capable. He lived with his sister, and the two would dine in evening dress every day while the boarders ate at a separate table. Before dinner Harding would be summoned to his dressing-room to construe Ovid while Davidson dressed. The teaching at the school was of a high quality. Apart from the classics, the curriculum included history, geography and mathematics up to the binomial theorem, and there was a reasonably well equipped science laboratory. Among his fellow pupils there was another future General, Colin Callender. Harding worked hard, had an excellent memory and was quick to learn. He was particularly good at examination work and passed his matriculation. In retrospect he believed that two things of great value came to him from this education – the ability to teach himself, and to express himself clearly in speech and in writing, derived from the study of Latin and English.

Allan's own ambition was to be a farmer. Davidson wanted him to go for the law, while his parents would have liked him to become a Congregationalist minister. Farming and the law were ruled out on financial grounds, for his father explained that he had not the capital to start him off as a farmer and could not afford the long training for the law, although Allan had won a county scholarship which helped his father with the school fees for the last two or three years of his five years at the school. He was not drawn to religion and refused to attend communion. Although he held to the basic Christian beliefs, he had no wish to become deeply involved emotionally and regarded religious enthusiasm as a cheap and easy way of gaining admittance to heaven : it was works and faith for him.

In 1911, at the age of fifteen, owing much to the personal interest of his headmaster, he left school; the compromise found between these rival careers was for him to join the civil service in its humblest form, a boy clerk in the Post Office Savings Bank at a wage of fifteen shillings a week. His father's youngest sister had married a buyer in Waring and Gillow's. They were fairly prosperous and lived in Harlesden. Their son, Geoffrey Pether, was one of Allan's favourite cousins and attended St Paul's School as a day-boy. Allan went to live with them and worked in a small branch of the Post Office Savings Bank, which still exists, in Smithfield Square. His job was to type copies of returns. 'Now Allan, make a Chinese copy' he would be told. Lunch was usually a lentil cutlet and a banana, which could be had for a shilling at a nearby vegetarian restaurant. He had little time for leisure activities and no money with which to pursue them. Saturday afternoons were sometimes spent playing hockey for the London YMCA team. On Sundays he would go to chapel with his aunt and her family, and take a walk in the afternoon. He was an avid reader, absorbing all the standard classics, Dickens, Scott and Thackeray, and for lighter reading turning to the adventure stories of G. A. Henty, Fenimore Cooper and Marriott.

There was little outlet for Allan's excellent education in all this and, in order to work for the intermediate civil service examination, he attended night classes at King's College. He was successful, and was transferred to the main office of the Post Office Savings Bank at West Kensington near Olympia, where he worked a primitive form of adding machine. Here it was that he first became interested in military matters. Hitherto he had had no interest in them, his family regarding soldiers as brutal and licentious. They were opposed to privilege of any kind and regarded army officers as a particularly bad example of it. However, his cousin Geoffrey, who was to become a doctor, was keen on military matters, and the prospect of having something to do with them was not therefore as remote to him as it would have been if he had stayed at home. The influence came from Jimmy Maxwell, the Second Division clerk in the office, responsible for supervising

4

the group of clerks in which the young Harding worked. He had for some time been a keen member of the County of London Yeomanry and had risen to the rank of Squadron Sergeant-Major when he was offered a commission in the Finsbury Rifles, the 1/11th Battalion of the London Regiment, a battalion of the 2nd (London) Territorial Division. Maxwell and some friends used to go and practise with their rifles on the ranges near Runnymede on Saturday afternoons, spend the night camping in a stable at the back of an inn nearby and then go boating on the Thames on Sunday. It was a strictly male affair which Maxwell would invite some of the clerks to join, thus encouraging them to join the territorials. He was successful with Harding, who applied for a commission and was interviewed by the adjutant, Captain John Crosbie of the Rifle Brigade, and a week later by the commanding officer, Lieutenant-Colonel Grant, a regular from a Scottish regiment. It is to the credit of them both that they recognized 'officer-like qualities' in this eighteen-year-old clerk, and he was gazetted a Second-Lieutenant in the 1/11th Battalion of the London Regiment in May 1914.

The drill hall was in Penton Road, close to Pentonville prison, where their Old Comrades Association was still meeting at the time of writing, and they were known locally as 'The Pentonville Pissers'. Harding's company commander, Major Windsor, was very keen and worked in the City. The officers were mostly accountants, solicitors, tailors and in City business, the younger ones being solicitor's clerks and civil servants. The soldiers tended to come from the skilled artisan class, foremen, shop assistants, clerks and the like. Maxwell, the swashbuckling ex-yeoman, commanded the machine-gun platoon. The battalion was due to go to camp at Lulworth in August, and, on the Sunday before war actually broke out, they set off by train from Waterloo to Wareham. Having arrived there they were lined up on the road by the station, stood easy and then ordered to get back into the train and return to Waterloo. Before being dismissed they were warned that they would be called up in the following week. Having taken his holiday, Harding was at a loose end and joined the party that was sent down to Lulworth to pack up the camp.

On mobilization they were concentrated in the Agricultural Hall at Islington and later at the White City, where they were billeted in the exhibition buildings, training at Wormwood Scrubs, Richmond Park and Putney Common. Harding, as reserve machine-gun officer to Jimmy Maxwell, was put in charge of the machine-guns, two old Maxims on two-wheeled carriages pulled by mules. From there the battalion moved to Crowborough in Sussex for further training, which consisted of digging ditches and carrying out attacks by a process of what was called 'building up the firing line', section by section, platoon by platoon, at the end of which everyone would charge. There were no mortars and no mention of artillery. The task of the machine-guns was to follow up the attack and 'consolidate' the captured position against counter-attack. The machine-gun officer had to ride a horse, and here for the first time Harding was introduced to an activity at which he became expert and which he greatly enjoyed. Although he had lived in the country and came of a farming family, he had never before ridden a horse, apart from sitting on a farm horse bringing back the hay. The battalion marched back to London at about Christmas-time and continued training on these lines in the New Year, Harding attending a machine-gun course at the Small Arms School at Hythe. The 2nd (London) Division was now broken up: one brigade went to France and the brigade, 162, to which Harding's battalion, with its sister battalions 1/10th and 1/12th, belonged became part of the 54th (East Anglian) Territorial Division and was based at Hatfield. There it remained until the division was earmarked as a reinforcing division for Gallipoli in the summer of 1915.

Five to six thousand troops of the division embarked on the *Aquitania* at Liverpool in July 1915. The Maxims had now been replaced by four Vickers machine-guns, which during the voyage were mounted at corners of the deck as a defence against submarines. One of the guns belonging to the 1/10th Battalion was lost overboard when the ship rolled badly as a result of its anti-rolling tanks having been filled with drinking water. On arrival at Mudros, on the island of Lemnos, Harding ceased to be reserve machine-gun officer and took over command of a rifle platoon in Windsor's company. The pre-war commanding officer, Grant, had meanwhile been replaced by Lieutenant-Colonel Mudge, and the brigade was commanded by Brigadier-General de Winton. The scene at Mudros, where they were kept waiting to act as follow-up troops for the Suvla Bay landings, was one of considerable confusion and discomfort. They remained on board the *Aquitania* in cramped conditions and stifling heat with no idea of where they were going or what they would have to do.

CHAPTER TWO

GALLIPOLI
1915

The embarkation of 54th (East Anglian) Division for Gallipoli formed part of Sir Ian Hamilton's plan for a renewed attempt to capture the peninsula, following the failure of the April landings to secure more than a foothold at Cape Helles and Anzac Cove. Step by fatal step Britain had committed herself to the capture of the Dardanelles ever since the Germain cruisers, *Goeben* and *Breslau* had taken refuge in the Golden Horn at Constantinople at the outbreak of war. Winston Churchill, First Lord of the Admiralty, had been the driving force throughout. At first he had contemplated a dash by the navy through the straits to sink these ships in the Sea of Marmara. Having been dissuaded from this, he turned to the idea of seizing the Gallipoli peninsula with the help of the Greeks, although Turkey was still neutral and the principal object at that time was to win her to the allied side. However Greece insisted on impossible conditions, and matters were brought to a head at the end of September 1914 when a British squadron, off the entrance to the Dardanelles, turned back a Turkish torpedo-boat. The Turks at German instigation then closed the straits, and at the end of October sent their fleet under the German Admiral Souchon, with his ships flying the Turkish flag, to bombard the Russian Black Sea ports. Less than a week later the Royal Navy, on Churchill's orders, bombarded the forts covering the entrance to the Dardanelles and with a lucky shot blew up one of their magazines. Six weeks later a British submarine sank an old Turkish battleship in the narrows at Chanak.

Then began a minuet between Churchill, his First Sea Lord, Lord Fisher, Admiral Carden in the Mediterranean and Kitchener, Secretary of State for War, in which Fisher played an equivocal and enigmatic role. Under pressure from Churchill, the navy produced a plan for a cautious step-by-step operation to force the straits by naval action alone. The vital decision was taken at a War Council meeting on 13 January 1915, at which General Sir John French pressed hard for a renewed offensive on the Western Front. It was a long meeting, in the course of which Churchill produced his Dardanelles plan and described its prospects in glowing terms, while Fisher remained silent. In the end the War Council decided that, while provisionally authorizing a new Western offensive, for which French would have two more territorial divisions, 'the Admiralty should also prepare for a naval expedition in February to bombard and take the Gallipoli Peninsula with Constantinople as its object'. Kitchener was determined that the army should not get involved, but the disappointing results of the navy's first attempts to destroy the forts led him to change his mind. On 10 March he decided to release the 29th Division, which the War Council had sent to the Middle East with no clear task, to join the Australian and New Zealand Corps already in that area in helping the navy, and chose General Sir Ian Hamilton for the task, telling him no more than: 'We are sending a military force to support the Fleet now at the Dardanelles and you are to have Command'.

Admiral Carden, who had collapsed from worry, was succeeded by a more robust character, de Robeck, who renewed the attack on 18 March. It failed, three battleships being sunk and three crippled, with nothing to show in return. Hamilton and Kitchener both now realised that a major and deliberate operation by the army would be needed. Stormy weather and the knowledge that the army now accepted that it would have to play a major role led the navy to postpone further attempts to force the straits on their own. Hamilton and de Robeck planned a combined operation for 14 April, but the need to take his force to Egypt and reorganize it there, and to establish the elements of a forward base at Mudros, caused Hamilton to postpone this until 25 April.

In spite of great gallantry and dogged determination, the operation succeeded only in capturing the tip of Cape Helles itself, some four square miles, and a precarious foothold of about the same area around Anzac Cove, completely dominated by the heights above, which the brilliant intervention of the young Mustafa Kemal had secured for the Turks just as the Australians seemed on the point of capturing them. For the next two months, at great cost in casualties and in conditions of increasing heat and discomfort, the ground gained was pushed forward slightly, but no serious impact made on the Turkish position. A bitter controversy began over whether or not the navy should renew its attack. Roger Keyes, in charge of the minesweeping force, was strongly in favour and hoped for the support of Churchill. The other admirals were not. De Robeck, after a meeting of his admirals on 9 May, sent a signal to the Admiralty suggesting that, even if the fleet managed to penetrate the Narrows, the straits might be shut behind them and their presence off Constantinople fail to be decisive. This precipitated the famous row between Fisher and Churchill, and, later, one between Kitchener and Fisher, when the former learned that, after an old battleship had been sunk by a Turkish torpedo-boat, the new *Queen Elizabeth* had been withdrawn. The upshot of it all was the resignation of Fisher, the dismissal of Churchill as First Lord of the Admiralty and the formation of the Dardanelles Committee.

While this high-level squabbling was in train, Hamilton, still optimistic, decided to make a further attempt to break out of the restricted areas in which his troops were confined. At the beginning of June further attacks were launched at great cost and with little success. The total casualty list since the initial landings had now reached 60,000, of which 20,000 were French.

On 7 June the Dardanelles Committee met and considered a persuasive memorandum from Churchill, now Chancellor of the Duchy of Lancaster, urging a more vigorous effort at Gallipoli. This was supported by public opinion, and there seemed to be no lack of enthusiasm on the part of Australia and New Zealand. It was therefore decided to send three divisions of Kitchener's New Army, the 10th (Irish), 11th and 13th, not later than the first fortnight of July. Shortly afterwards Kitchener offered, and Hamilton accepted, two further territorial divisions, 53rd (Welsh) and 54th (East Anglian), to arrive before the middle of April, but without their artillery. Hamilton's chief anxiety at this time was about ammunition for his guns. In spite of this promise of reinforcements he allowed General Hunter-Weston, commanding 8 Corps at Helles, to go battering on without a pause through June and July, piling up casualties and exhausting his troops in the heat of mid-summer.

Hamilton now had to decide what to do with all the troops that had been thrust upon him. He was determined not to pour any more into the dead-end of Helles. Birdwood had devised a promising plan to capture the Sari Bair Ridge from the ANZAC area, but could not use more than one extra division. The obvious place was Suvla Bay, six miles to the north of the ANZAC area. There was room to deploy several divisions there, and a swift advance across the flat plain to the hills would turn the flank of the Turks facing ANZAC. This was the plan adopted. The three New Army divisions were formed into 9 Corps for the purpose, but a major error was made in the selection of the sixty-one-year-old and unfit General Stopford for command, the sole reason being that somebody had to be found who was senior to the commander of the 10th (Irish) Division, Lieutenant-General Sir Bryan Mahon, who had raised it and was a friend of Sir Edward Carson, the Ulster Protestant leader. The new offensive was to start on 6 August, a date fixed because the moon, in its last quarter, would not rise until 10.30 pm, and it was judged essential to complete the landing before the moon rose. The 10th and 11th Division were to land at Suvla, while 13th Division would be introduced into the ANZAC area and concealed there. The 53rd and 54th Divisions would not arrive in time to take part in the assault, but would be available as follow-up divisions, although Kitchener's original idea was for the 54th Division to be broken up and used as reinforcements for the other divisions.

Hamilton's aim had been clear. Stopford was to capture the low hills overlooking Suvla Bay as rapidly as possible and then push on to seize the area behind, some four miles from the shore; thereafter, as far as he was able he was to do all he could to help the ANZACs on his right. Unfortunately his chief of staff, Brigadier-General Reed, took a gloomy view of the chances of success and laid much stress on the need to get enough artillery ashore before much progress could be expected. The wording and tenor of Stopford's orders were changed, with Hamilton's approval, to stress that his primary objective was to secure Suvla Bay as a base for further operations, and to relegate progress inland and help to the ANZAC Corps to a secondary role. This was to have fatal consequences.

Stopford's plan was to land 11th Division on the night of 6 August on the southern horn of Suvla Bay, just south of the salt lake, with initial objectives the two hills, Chocolate Hill, two miles from the beach, and W. Hills, a mile further on. Originally the whole division was to land on the smooth beaches south-east of the point, but information that the defences of the hills faced south led to a change of plan by which one brigade was to be landed within the bay, in spite of the misgivings of the navy. The 10th Division was to land at dawn on the 7th on the same beaches, its tasks depending on the progress of the 11th, but generally intended to deploy on the left.

The landings south of the point went without a hitch; but, after that, everything started to go wrong. The 34th Brigade, to be landed within the bay, was put down on the wrong beach in considerable disorder. Confusion over orders and objectives led, as it always does, to inactivity. The elderly senior officers, exhausted by the heat, managed to get almost everything muddled up. The navy's plans for landing artillery, supplies and water went to pieces. The first brigade of 10th Division to arrive, with half the infantry battalions of the Division, was placed under 11th Division and at first set off to the right, as far as possible from its own division, which was then directed to land at the northern point of the bay, causing further delay.

It was this brigade of 10th Division, the 31st, with very little help from those of the 11th, which eventually captured Chocolate Hill, the rest of 10th Division by this time having established itself half-way along the ridge of Kiretch Tepe, which overlooks the Suvla plain from the north. The casualties of the corps amounted to some 100 officers and 1,600 men, roughly the same as the strength of the Turks opposing them, but they included a high proportion of battalion commanders and other senior officers. The Turkish force opposing the two divisions now ashore was still very small, although their fire had been effective. If there had been any sort of drive and energy from Hamilton downwards, it would have been possible on 8 August to have made up for the muddles and delay of the first day ashore and push quickly into the hills; but no such orders were given until Stopford, reassured by a report from GHQ that aircraft could detect no sign of Turkish forces advancing in his direction, sent a half-hearted order to his divisions to push on if they found the ground lightly held, but, in view of the lack of artillery, not to attack an entrenched position held in strength.

By this time Hamilton, whose attention throughout the previous day had been centred on the ANZAC front, became seriously concerned at the lack of any sign of energy at Suvla. It was not until 6 pm, owing to difficulties in getting hold of a ship, that he reached Suvla Bay. Half an hour before, prompted by Brigadier-General

Aspinall of Hamilton's staff, who had arrived about midday, Stopford gave orders for an advance by both divisions on the following day, the 11th to be reinforced by a brigade of 53rd Division which would land during the night. The timing of 10th Division's advance was to be dependent on the action of the 11th. Hardly had these orders been issued when Hamilton finally met Stopford and insisted on a night advance that very night to the further objective of the Tekke Tepe ridge to the east of the Suvla plain, some three miles on from the forward positions of 11th Division. Leaving Stopford, whose knee was giving him trouble, still afloat, the Commander-in-Chief went ashore to the head-quarters of 11th Division and, in spite of repeated objections by the divisional commander, General Hammersley, another sick man, insisted that, even if only one battalion was used, a night advance to Tekke Tepe should be attempted. Orders to this effect were given to 32 Brigade, which could have carried them out with good hopes of success if the two battalions best placed to do so had been used; but the brigade commander decided to concentrate his whole brigade first. Precious time was thus lost, in the course of which Turkish reinforcements from Bulair reached the objective and also the area north of the W.Hills, the objective of the brigade on its right. The attacks of both brigades completely failed and they were pushed back by strong Turkish counter-attacks, suffering heavy casualties in the process.

The newly-arrived 53rd Division was employed to extend the line northwards towards 10th Division, which had had a disappointing day. Although the Turkish forces opposing them numbered no more than a few hundred, such progress as was made eastward along the ridge of Kiretch Tepe, supported by naval gunfire, was forfeited when the troops returned to the line from which they had started suffering from extremes of heat and thirst, having begun the day with empty water bottles. In an exchange of letters at the end of the day, Hamilton urged Stopford to make a further attempt to secure the Tekke Tepe ridge, while the latter complained that lack of water and artillery severely restricted what could be achieved by his troops, who were not trained for what he called 'field manoeuvring', but only for trench warfare. He had however ordered 53rd Division in the centre to attack the Anafarta spur, south-west of Tekke Tepe, next day, 10 August. There were the usual muddles, battalions got lost, there was no time for reconnaissance and the attack was a total failure. On the same day the

ANZAC Corps on the right, having received no help from Suvla Bay, was thrown off the position it had gained with great difficulty at Chunuk Bair, once more by the brilliant intervention of Mustafa Kemal.

It was on this day that 54th Division, in whose 162 Brigade Lieutenant A. F. Harding was commanding a platoon of the 1/11th London Regiment, began landing. They had been transferred from the *Aquitania* to smaller ships at Mudros and then to lighters in Suvla Bay. Hamilton was anxious that the division should not be dispersed piecemeal as all the other divisions had been, but should be kept intact for a further attempt to secure Tekke Tepe. 9 Corps was therefore told that it was the last available reserve and was not to be used without the previous approval of GHQ. But this order came too late. At about 10 pm that night the first six of its battalions to land, from three different brigades, were rushed up to fill a gap in the front between the 53rd and 10th Divisions. The guides lost their way and the battalions spent the night aimlessly marching and counter-marching. Harding's memory of the day was of hanging about for a long time on the beach, receiving a sudden order that the battalion was to move up to the front, followed by a night march, the purpose and destination of which remained a mystery. When they finally halted and dossed down for some sleep, the stench was dreadful. At dawn the cause was revealed, as they had slept among a heap of Turkish corpses. They were then withdrawn again to the beach, no explanation for their apparently useless manoeuvre being given. It was a frustrating first day in action for a keen nineteen-year-old officer, full of patriotic enthusiasm.

Early next day, 11 August, Stopford received an order from GHQ for 54th Division to launch an attack to capture the Tekke Tepe ridge from Karah Tepe on the left to Anafarta on the right, a frontage of nearly two miles involving an advance of three miles from the existing front line over a plain overlooked on both flanks by Turkish positions. It was a tall order, and hardly surprising that the laggard Stopford did nothing but write a letter which did not arrive at GHQ until the late afternoon, complaining that the two territorial divisions, one of which, the 54th, had not even been in action, were 'sucked oranges'. This brought Hamilton back to Suvla that evening, insisting that his orders be obeyed. It was clearly not now possible to launch the attack on the 12th. Hamilton demanded that the attack must take place at dawn on 13 August, 10th and 11th Divisions on either flank giving what support they could. Stopford's objections were that, even if the division succeeded in reaching the Tekke Tepe ridge, they would not be able to clear the scrub-covered area over which they would have passed; that Turkish snipers would be left behind in it and that runners and mule parties would then be prevented from maintaining communications with, and supply to, the division. Hamilton promised to send a hundred trained marksmen from ANZAC to deal with this threat.

On 12 August Stopford held a conference of his divisional commanders at which it was decided that a preliminary operation would take place that afternoon, in which one brigade of 54th Division (volunteered by its GOC, General Inglefield, as 53rd Division appeared reluctant to carry it out) would secure the start line in the middle of the plain betwen 53rd and 10th Divisions. 163 Brigade was detailed for the task and suffered heavily, failing to reach its objectives. As a result Stopford signalled to GHQ on the morning of the 13th that 54th Division would not be ready to mount its attack until the 15th. His telegram had only just been sent when news arrived from the GOC of 53rd Division that, owing to Turkish shelling, one of his brigades was 'so exhausted that it was finding it very hard to hold on' and 11th Division reported that one of 53rd's brigades was 'very shaky'. Stopford panicked at this, and sent an alarmist signal to GHQ saying that the Turks were 'inclined to be aggressive' and, in the event of the worst happening, he had only the 54th Division to replace the 53rd, 'which are only a danger and may bolt at any minute'. Not surprisingly this brought the C-in-C back to Suvla. Stopford insisted that the 53rd Division was finished and the 54th incapable of carrying out an attack, a totally unwarranted judgement considering that the one had seen little action and two brigades of the other none. However Ian Hamilton felt that he now had to bow to the inevitable and at midnight a signal was sent to Stopford postponing for the present any thought of a further general advance.

But Harding was, at last, to see some action, for Stopford's reaction to Hamilton's signal was surprising: he ordered General Mahon to push eastwards with his 10th Division along Kiretch Tepe ridge, and orders to this effect were issued at 8.40 am on 15

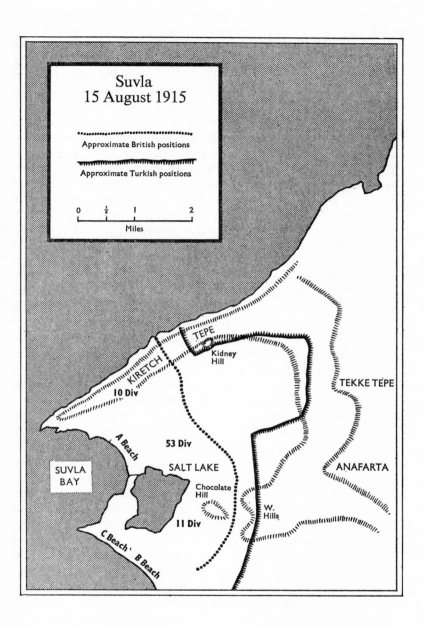

Suvla
15 August 1915

Approximate British positions

Approximate Turkish positions

0   ½   1   2
Miles

TÉPE

KIRETCH

Kidney Hill

10 Div

TEKKE TÉPE

A Beach

53 Div

SALT LAKE

SUVLA BAY

Chocolate Hill

ANAFARTA

W. Hills

11 Div

C Beach

B Beach

August. To help him with this, he was given 162 Brigade from 54th Division, then resting back at A Beach, which included 1/11 Londons. The objective was Kidney Hill, three quarters of a mile into the Turkish position. The main attack was to be made by 31 Brigade from the west along the ridge, while Brigadier-General de Winton's 162 Brigade was to approach it from the south. Opposition was not expected to be heavy, neither corps nor division apparently appreciating the considerable Turkish reinforcements that had arrived from Bulair in the previous twenty-four hours. The attack was to start at 1 pm, which gave little or no time for reconnaissance or the issue of orders. 30 Brigade on the north side of the ridge, helped by naval bombardment, made good progress, but 31 Brigade on the south side lagged behind. 162 Brigade had reached its position on the right flank of 31 Brigade on time at 1 pm. They had had no opportunity to see the ground or learn much about the enemy. It was thought that they would merely act as a flank guard to 31 Brigade and that little opposition would be met. However, soon after they had started, 1/5 Bedfords, the leading battalion, came under increasingly heavy fire and the advance began to lose cohesion as elements of the other two battalions, 1/10 and 1/11 Londons, were dribbled forward.

Harding was the leading platoon commander of C Company 1/11 Londons, which was brigade reserve. He and all his men were keen as mustard to prove their worth at last. They carried three days' rations – three tins of bully beef, a bag of biscuits and three tins of tea and sugar, packed in their mess tins. Their water-bottles were full, but these had to last all day in stifling heat, pestered by clouds of flies. As an officer, Harding carried a revolver and an alpenstock. Late in the afternoon the brigade commander, who shortly afterwards was gravely wounded, called the company commander up to the head of the wadi in which the company was halted. Harding went with him and heard the orders : 'Take your company forward, carry the firing line with you and capture the position', which was in fact the southwest slope of Kidney Hill. The ground in front was very broken and covered with scrub up to knee height. His company commander, Major Windsor, told Harding to advance, whereupon he formed his platoon into line and went forward, having no idea where the Turkish position was. He soon came upon some frightened-looking soldiers from another battalion lying down, and asked them if they were the firing line. 'I suppose we are' was the reply. 'Well, you've got to come forward with me' said Harding. But they stayed where they were, so his platoon went on by itself, some men being hit as they advanced. He then halted his men and opened fire at what he thought was the Turkish position. More of his men were hit and a runner sent back to report the situation was shot dead. His platoon sergeant was next to be hit.

Harding stayed there until it was dark and then picked up the wounded, left six of his men dead on the field and moved back a few hundred yards to the 'firing line' of 1/10 Londons and spent the night there. Next morning their position was shelled by the Turks and Harding was hit in the left leg by a piece of shrapnel. He was taken by stretcher to a casualty clearing station on A Beach and thence by boat to a hospital ship. Here he lay on a stretcher in the sun until a well-meaning sailor moved him into the shade. There he was forgotten about and went to sleep. Eventually, however, he was found, taken to a bunk and treated. This was not a proper hospital ship, but only a casualty carrier. It was grossly overcrowded and understaffed, the general impression being of a shambles strongly reminiscent of the Crimea. The ship sailed for Alexandria and there, in a general hospital at Sidi Bishr, he was at last properly cared for.

When he returned to his battalion in October, he found them in the ANZAC area, as 54th Division had meanwhile changed places with the 13th on the extreme left of the ANZAC front. In the two months he had been away the military situation had not changed. At Helles, Anzac and Suvla the allies were hemmed into their restricted areas, overlooked and dominated by the Turkish positions on the high ground. Only the Turks' shortage of artillery ammunition made the allied position tenable and their supply possible at all. The conditions the soldiers lived in were terrible, and disease, particularly dysentery, was rife. There were no days or weeks out of the line, as there were in France.

Harding's return coincided with the decision to replace General Hamilton with General Monro, who came to the conclusion soon after his arrival on 28 October that the only answer lay in evacuation. None of this was known to Harding who, on arrival back at Mudros and, while waiting to return to his battalion, had been given a short course in catapulting bombs made of jam tins, a hazardous form of warfare. He found the battalion, which was at the head of the wadi known as the Aghyl Dere, in very poor shape, only two hundred men strong, riddled with dysentery and jaundice and thoroughly demoralized. Among the many casualties they had suffered in his absence was Jimmy Maxwell, who had been killed a few weeks after Harding had been wounded. Windsor, his former company commander, had taken over the battalion and Harding returned to the machine-gun platoon, being also made responsible for instruction in 'bombing', as grenade-throwing was then called. It was while engaged in this that he nearly brought to an end the promising career of General Monash, at that time commanding a brigade in the New Zealand and Australian Division. Harding had found what he thought was a quiet place in which to practise bombing and was thus engaged when an important-looking Australian staff officer appeared and summoned him to see his brigade commander. Monash picked up a bit of a bomb that had come through the window of his dugout and quietly and politely made it clear to Harding that he had better find somewhere else to use as a bombing range.

Most of the activity of the battalion at this time consisted of night patrols towards the Turkish positions on the higher ground. These were a 'nightmare' experience. If one lay down or crawled along, one could see nothing in the low scrub. If one stood up, one was an easy target. The battalion just held on day after day in a depressing atmosphere, made worse by the dreariness of the food, which was hardly ever fresh. Some Welsh miners, whose task was to mine towards the enemy positions, went on strike, saying : 'No fresh rations, no mines.'

Monro's recommendation for abandonment of the enterprise and evacuation stirred up a hornet's nest. The enthusiasts for pressing on, like Churchill and Keyes, were aghast. Lloyd George and Bonar Law were for evacuation. Monro was supported by his staff and two of his three corps commanders; but the third, Birdwood, and Maxwell in Egypt, opposed it on the grounds of the repercussions it would have all over the Middle East. Kitchener, horrified at Monro's recommendation, switched to the side of Keyes, who was once more urging a naval assault on the Narrows, but the Admiralty would not contemplate this unless accompanied by a major operation on the peninsula. Kitchener then signalled direct to Birdwood while Monro was away consulting Maxwell. He said that he would not order evacuation, that Birdwood was to replace Monro, who would be switched to the Salonika front, that a plan was to be made for a major landing at Bulair, at the neck of the peninsula, in conjunction with a naval assault, and that he, Kitchener, was coming out to Gallipoli to see things for himself. Birdwood was appalled both at the suggestion of a landing at Bulair and also at the summary dismissal of Monro, whom he admired, for giving unpopular advice, and begged Kitchener to think again. This produced a volte-face in a further message which said : 'I fear that the navy may not play up ... The more I look at the problem the less I see my way through, so you had better very quietly and secretly work out any scheme for getting the troops off.'

Kitchener arrived at Mudros from Marseilles on 9 November shortly after Monro from Egypt, who learned then for the first time of the telegrams that had passed between Kitchener and Birdwood. By 15 November Kitchener had come firmly round to recommending evacuation and to the opinion that it could be carried out with fewer losses than he had feared. The Cabinet considered this on 23 November, by which time Churchill had left the government to serve with the army in France. Curzon argued strongly against evacuation, mainly on account of its repercussions elsewhere, and painted a lurid picture of the ghastly scenes it would probably involve. The navy, especially Admiral Wemyss, sided with him. The weather had now turned stormy and the urgency of a decision became even greater. Monro protested strongly to Kitchener when there was still no decision by 1 December, Kitchener appearing to swing back to the decision to stay, bringing the four divisions from Salonika to Suvla to attack again there. It was not until 7 December that the final decision to evacuate was made, but orders had already been given to withdraw the infantry of 54th Division to Mudros to rest on 8 December. Harding had already left. He had fallen ill and, after spending a few days in a field hospital on the beach, was evacuated to Egypt and back to the hospital at Sidi Bishr.

CHAPTER THREE

EGYPT AND PALESTINE
1916–18

While Harding was in hospital 54th Division arrived from Gallipoli and was stationed in reserve in the Nile Delta. Rejoining his battalion, Harding took over the machine-gun platoon again in a camp not far from the hospital at Sidi Bishr. Not long after he had returned, his life was enlivened by the detachment of his brigade to form part of the force under Major-General Peyton, dealing with the Senussi in the Western Desert, which included Major the Duke of Westminster's armoured car squadron.

This squadron had originally been raised, as had all armoured cars at that time, by the Royal Naval Air Service to protect their airfields in the Low Countries in support of the Royal Naval Division at Antwerp. The Duke of Westminster's squadron had been sent to Egypt to join the force, known as Western Frontier Force, formed at Mersa Matruh in November 1915 to deal with the Senussi under Sayed Ahmed, who, supported by the Turks, were co-operating with German submarines operating off the Egyptian coast. The main reason for the formation of the force was to rescue the survivors of two ships, the *Tara* and the *Moorina*, torpedoed by a German submarine, who had been handed over to the Senussi and whom Sayed Ahmed refused to release.

After some indecisive operations near Matruh at the turn of the year, the tide turned shortly after General Peyton had relieved Major-General Wallace. On 26 February 1916 Sayed Ahmed was decisively defeated in a battle near Sidi Barrani in which the Dorset Yeomanry distinguished themselves in a gallant cavalry charge. On 15 March Sollum, which had been evacuated by the Egyptian coastguard in November, was reoccupied, the armoured cars pursing the Senussi westwards above the escarpment west of Halfaya pass. It was then discovered that the survivors of the *Tara* and *Moorina* were 120 miles further to the west in an isolated encampment at Bir Hacheim. At 1 am on 17 March the Duke, with 45 vehicles, half of them armoured cars and the remainder ambulances, set off across the unknown and unmapped desert, almost every track and cairn in which was to become familiar to Harding a quarter of a century later. The Duke reached Bir Hacheim fourteen hours later to find 91 famished survivors, four having died in captivity. Having plied them with bully beef, tinned chicken and condensed milk, he brought them safely back to Sollum, spending a night in the desert on the way, an exploit which received wide acclaim at the time. Harding's brigade did not accompany the main force in these exploits, but remained guarding the delta of the Nile from the remote threat of an incursion from the desert. His chief memory of this period was of playing endless games of poker with two Roman Catholic chaplains and Walter Clutterbuck, the new adjutant of 1/10 Londons, who had won a Military Cross in France and was to become a great friend.

After this interlude the battalion moved to a camp near the Pyramids, which gave Harding and his fellow officers the opportunity to enjoy the amenities of civilized life in Cairo. Later in the year the division was moved from the Cairo area to man the defences of the Suez Canal; the sector allotted to 162 Brigade was in the area of El Kubri, north of Suez. It was at this time that it was decided to concentrate the machine-gun platoons of all the battalions into a brigade machine-gun company, and Harding was given command, bringing him the acting rank of captain.

At this time also a circular from the War Office offered Territorial Army and other wartime officers of certain ages and ranks the opportunity to apply for regular commissions. Harding was now enjoying life as an army officer and did not relish the prospect of returning to the Post Office Savings Bank as a clerk when the war was over. He therefore decided to apply for a commission in his county regiment, the Somerset Light Infantry, and was recommended by his commanding officer. Somewhat to his surprise and greatly to his pleasure, his application was successful and he was gazetted a lieutenant in the Somerset Light Infantry on 22 March 1917, being granted the wartime rank of a captain in the Machine-Gun Corps on the same date. One of the machine-gunners of 1/11 Londons who remembered Harding well and met him again for many years at old comrades' reunions was Joe Guthrie. Seven years older than Harding, he was a lance-corporal in the machine-gun platoon when Harding joined the battalion. 'A lovely pink-faced little lad; always very mannerly; very nice chap; never lost his temper; the boys liked him' was Guthrie's description sixty-three years later. He remembered Harding's return to the platoon in the Aghyl Dere (Guthrie by then was the platoon sergeant). 'Show me round, Guthrie,' were Harding's first words. As they went up the communication trench, Harding jumped up onto the parapet to have a look round. No sooner had he done so than a Turkish sniper's bullet hit the sandbag a few inches away from his head, and Guthrie pulled him down. It was not the last time that Harding would startle his companions by his total disregard of danger. The soldiers often gently teased him for his youth and small size. Guthrie recalls a time later when Harding on horseback was leading his company on the march up to Gaza and they began to sing a hymn which included the line 'and a little child shall lead them'. Harding turned round and added 'but on a bloody big horse.'

At the beginning of 1916 in Egypt it had been expected the Turks would launch a large-scale expedition in the spring against the Suez Canal from their base in Palestine. In 1915 General Maxwell had asked for twelve divisions to meet this threat, and after the evacuation from Gallipoli this was the force that he had in Egypt, although it was regarded as an Imperial Reserve for the Middle East and not just for the defence of Egypt alone. But in January 1916 the Russian Grand Duke Nicholas attacked Turkey from the Caucasus and in February captured Erzerum. Turkish reserves that might have been devoted to an expedition against Egypt were switched to meet the Russian invasion and the threat to the Suez Canal was accordingly much reduced. However, the demands of other theatres on British and Commonwealth manpower were high. The Mesopotamian campaign was not going well and the 13th Division was sent there to strengthen the force trying to relieve Kut. Great hopes were placed by some on the Nivelle offensive on the Western front and every other available division from Egypt was sent there. All that was left by the end of June was a force of four territorial divisions, 42nd (Lancashire), 52nd (Lowland), 53rd (Welsh) and 54th (East Anglian) and the ANZAC Mounted Division.

In March General Sir Archibald Murray assumed overall command in Egypt from General Sir John Maxwell, and the whole force was renamed the Egyptian Expeditionary Force. His task was a purely defensive one, but he pointed out that it would be much more economical to defend Egypt with a mobile force based on El Arish near the coast of Sinai than by stringing forces all along the Canal. He was allowed to take the first step towards this by building a railway forwards to Katia on the coast some forty miles east of the Canal, covering its construction with a mounted Yeomanry brigade. The Turks, under Kress von Kressenstein, reacted to this, and in a successful raid on Katia in April gave the brigade a very bloody nose, subsequently withdrawing. The recently formed ANZAC Mounted Division then took over the covering force with two of its brigades, and by July the railway was nearing Romani, a few miles from Katia. In August the Turks struck again with a larger force, but 52nd Division had by this time been moved up there and the 42nd moved up also to support it. The infantry on both sides got stuck in the sand in extreme heat, and the brunt of the fighting was taken by the ANZAC Mounted Division. The Turks suffered heavy casualties and withdrew unmolested to El Arish. This battle of Romani turned the tide on the Sinai front and removed any direct threat to the Canal. During the rest of the year the railway was pushed gradually eastward to within twenty miles of El Arish. The force protecting it, known as Eastern Force, was commanded by Lieutenant-General Sir Charles Dobell, and the main part of it, which led the way and was known as the Desert Column, was under Lieutenant-General Sir Philip Chetwode. They entered El Arish unopposed on 21 December 1916, the enemy withdrawing to Rafa and Maghaba, thirty miles further on and some twenty miles west of Gaza.

The attitude in Whitehall to the EEF now changed. The high hopes for 1916 on the Western Front had not been fulfilled and casualties had been very high. The Russian offensive led by Brusilov had petered out. On 7 December Lloyd George had succeeded Asquith as Prime Minister and looked to the east for hopes of victory. General Murray, who had moved his headquarters back from Ismailia to Cairo in October, said that he would need two more divisions if he were to operate into Palestine east of El Arish. He was told in December that he could not have them : his primary task was the defence of Egypt and he must be as aggressive as he could with the troops he had. This was followed in January 1917 by a telegram stating that he was to defer any large-scale operation until the autumn; meanwhile he was to give up the 42nd Division to go to France. Its place at El Arish was taken by the 53rd, and the 54th moved up behind it, now commanded by Major-General Hare, whose granddaughter nearly fifty years later was to marry Harding's only son.

On 5 March, when the railway was approaching Rafa, Kress withdrew to a position running from Gaza to Beersheba, to the disappointment of General Dobell, who had hoped to engage his forces in their position on the Wadi Ghuzze. This withdrawal created the impression in the minds of the British that the Turks would not stand on the Gaza-Beersheba line either. Dobell proposed to Murray that he should attack the Gaza position at the end of March, and Murray agreed. The main problem was supply, especially as Dobell wished to employ his whole force. The final concentration took place between 20 and 25 March, the 54th Division finishing up round In Seirat, about two miles west of the Wadi Ghuzze and seven southwest of Gaza. Harding's machine-gun company consisted of four sections, each of four Vickers machine-guns. Their transport was provided by mules brought from the Argentine, while the supply transport was provided by camels. The mules greatly disliked the camels and, to avoid trouble, were normally kept up wind of them. On the final night march they found themselves downwind of a supply column going in the opposite direction. Chaos ensued as the mules scattered over the desert, but they were eventually reassembled and 162 Brigade had its machine-guns in time for the start of the battle.

The plan was a bold one. The ANZAC Mounted Division, reinforced by the Imperial Camel Brigade and the 5th (Yeomanry) Mounted Brigade, was to encircle Gaza from the east while 53rd Division, with a call on 163 Brigade of the 54th, was to attack the Ali el Muntar ridge on the eastern outskirts of Gaza. The 54th Division, less the brigade made available to the 53rd, was to cross the Wadi Ghuzze and occupy the Sheikh Abbas ridge about four miles southeast of Gaza, protecting the right rear of the 53rd and acting as a backstop to the cavalry. The 53rd Division had a difficult task. First a night march of four miles to the Wadi Ghuzze, and then an approach of five miles across an open plain, covered with knee-high crops of barley, to attack the Turkish positions round Gaza among cactus hedges on slightly higher ground. To everyone's consternation, a sea fog came swirling in at 4 am on 26

March, the day chosen for the attack. It did not lift until 7.30 and then not completely. This held everything up and after that things moved very slowly. It was not until midday that the artillery opened fire for the start of 53rd Division's attack on the Ali el Muntar ridge. General Chetwode, whose mounted troops had by this time penetrated well to the northeast of Gaza, was becoming intensely impatient and decided to attack Gaza itself from the north with his own troops. Meanwhile 163 Brigade was wandering about trying to find its place between 54th Division, established on the Sheikh Abbas ridge without incident, and the 53rd struggling to secure the Ali el Muntar ridge. Harding's 162 Brigade machine-guns in the earlier stages had been supporting the advance of 53rd Division from the ridge to their right.

During the afternoon Dobell and Chetwode agreed that, if Gaza had not been captured by nightfall, the attack should be called off. There were two principal reasons for this : water, which would only be available for men and horses alike if Gaza itself, with its wells, were captured; and the approach of Turkish reinforcements, which were already beginning to bring pressure to bear on the widely scattered arc of mounted troops encircling Gaza from the east. As a first step in reorganization, at 5.30 pm Dobell ordered 54th Division to move to the Mansura ridge, two miles to the west of them, in order more closely to support the 53rd when night fell. Unfortunately General Dallas, commanding the 53rd, did not know of this. His gallant troops finally secured the Ali el Muntar ridge at 6.30, but by this time Dobell had ordered the Mounted Division, which had not watered its horses all day, to withdraw all the way to the Wadi Ghuzze, and at 7 pm he ordered Dallas to withdraw his right in order to join up with 54th Division. Not knowing that the latter had moved, Dallas protested vigorously and, when he was overruled, withdrew further than intended, almost to the line from which he had started his main attack. The Turks, who were on the point of abandoning Gaza, were astonished at the turn of events and quickly reoccupied the Ali el Muntar ridge.

It was 5 am on 27 March before Dobell realized what had happened, and he immediately ordered Dallas to reoccupy the ridge, 160 and 161 Brigades being ordered back. Some of them actually reached the ridge, but were driven off it by a Turkish counter attack. When daylight came 53rd and 54th Divisions found themselves back to back on the Es Sire and Mensura ridges about a mile and a half south of the Turkish position south of Gaza, the 53rd facing west and the 54th east, while a further Turkish force, one of the reinforcing formations from the centre of the Gaza-Beersheba line, had occupied the Sheikh Abbas ridge where the 54th had been the day before. It was an uncomfortable position and impossible to hold for long. It was abandoned during the night of 27 March and the whole force withdrawn to the Wadi Ghuzze, Harding himself having been hit in the lower right leg by either a piece of shrapnel or a bullet. He was evacuated to a hospital in the fort at Alexandria and was away for two months.

He therefore missed the Second Battle of Gaza on 19 April, in which 54th Division played a major part in the unsuccessful attack on the much strengthened Turkish positions. Both 1/10 Londons and the machine-gun company of 162 Brigade distinguished themselves on the extreme left of the division's line on the Wadi el Makkademe, a mile east of the Ali el Muntar ridge, by penetrating further into the Turkish positions than any other unit. The battle was a result of the combined over-optimism of General Murray himself and of Whitehall. Murray's report on the First Battle of Gaza had been complacent, giving the impression that it was only a temporary setback, and the War Council was anxious to exploit the combination of General Maude's capture of Baghdad on 11 March and the hopes raised by the agreement of the Russian Grand Duke Nicholas to advance from Eastern Turkey to Mosul, in spite of the outbreak of the Russian Revolution on 9 March – indeed it was thought that a major victory against Turkey could affect it. Murray was therefore told in a telegram on 30 March that his immediate objective was Jerusalem, an order which startled him. However he accepted it and expressed himself hopeful of capturing Gaza and developing operations into Palestine itself. In his remote headquarters in Cairo he failed to appreciate the strength of the Turkish positions between Gaza and Beersheba and the practical difficulties in dealing with them. The result of the direct assault on the strong Turkish positions on 17 April was failure, and it is to the credit of General Dobell that he did not persist into a second day. The British suffered six thousand casualties, half of which were in the 54th Division. It was perhaps fortunate for Harding that he missed the battle. Given his propensity for disregarding danger, he might well not have survived it.

When Harding returned to his company in May, considerable

changes were afoot. General Chetwode had replaced Dobell as commander of the Eastern Force, General Chauvel taking over command of the Desert Mounted Corps. Back in London it had been decided that Palestine was now to be given high priority. This was partly because of failure elsewhere : Russia had collapsed, the spring offensive in France had proved a costly failure, and the force at Salonika was serving no useful purpose. Although the United States had now joined the war, her forces would not be able to contribute for a long time and there was clearly no hope of ending the war in 1917. Furthermore, with other threats removed, Turkey was planning the recapture of Baghdad. The best way of preventing it, and at the same time achieving a victory which would have some popular appeal, such as the capture of Jerusalem, seemed to be by an offensive in Palestine. But for this both a new commander and more forces were needed. Most of the latter were to be provided by transfer from the force at Salonika, including the 10th and 60th Divisions. A further division, the 75th, was formed from troops drawn from Aden and India. The choice of a commander fell on General Sir Edmund Allenby, commanding the Third Army in France, which had recently distinguished itself in the Battle of Arras.

Allenby arrived in Egypt on 27 June 1917 and quickly made his presence felt, one of his most significant decisions being to move his headquarters from Cairo up into Sinai at Rafa. He was a 'no nonsense' man, full of energy, and his arrival, with the promise of reinforcements and the vigorous preparation for a renewed attack that he set in train, had the same effect, as Harding clearly recalls, as the arrival of Montgomery to command Eighth Army twenty-five years later. Murray had seldom, if ever, been seen by his troops, and to Harding and his fellow-officers he was thought of as the man who insisted that officers visiting Cairo on leave from the front must wear collars, ties, breeches and puttees or field boots. Allenby bustled around and Harding recalls that one day, when his company was on the move on a wire-netting road across the sand, a large car flying a Union Jack passed them. His orderly said 'Gawd, who's that?' to which Harding replied that it must be the Commander-in-Chief. It was the first time they had seen a general other than the divisional commander. Better equipment soon came along, tanks were seen and a feeling of confidence that things were on the up-turn and that the end of the war might not be too far off penetrated through the ranks down to the private soldier. Plans were now put in hand for the Third Battle of Gaza, and Harding was transferred to the headquarters of 54th Division as the divisional machine-gun officer, responsible for preparing and coordinating the machine-gun support for the part the division was to play. This appointment brought him promotion to the rank of major at the age of twenty-one.

While Allenby had been building up his force, the enemy had been doing the same. A special force including Germans, had been created, called *Yilderim,* or Lightning, with the aim of recapturing Baghdad. General von Falkenhayn had been appointed in overall command of the whole theatre, Kress von Kressenstein retaining command of the forces west of the Jordan, and Djemal, harried by Lawrence and the Arabs, to the east. The Turkish defences running east from Gaza had been strengthened and reinforced, but there was a gap of some fifteen miles between the eastern end of the defences at Hareira and Beersheba itself, which was defended by the Turkish III Corps. Allenby's plan in essence was to attempt to deceive Kress into thinking that the major attack was to be renewed on the defences of Gaza itself, a preliminary attack on Beersheba being merely a diversion, designed to draw his forces away from the main defences of Gaza. In fact he intended to launch the main attack against the eastern end of the line near Hareira, after a preliminary attack by the Desert Mounted Corps had secured Beersheba and its important water supplies.

Much therefore depended on the success of the deception plan, which was developed with great ingenuity and thoroughness. 54th Division, with one brigade also of the 52nd, was to play the major part in General Bulfin's 21 Corps attack on Gaza itself. The timing of this would depend on the progress of events at Beersheba, and would precede by twenty-four or forty-eight hours that of the Desert Mounted Corps and 20 Corps on the eastern end of the Turkish line. The plan was to attack the west and southwestern defences of Gaza, approaching across the soft sand dunes along the coast. This posed difficulties of movement and direction finding. Much of Harding's task in the planning stage consisted of personally reconnoitring and surveying positions among the sand dunes, from which the machine-guns of the division would give overhead covering fire to the initial attacks and then move forward with the assaulting troops in order to help them meet the inevitable counter-attacks. His outlook was signifi-

cantly broadened by having to work at divisional level and coordinate his plans with artillery, engineers and all the other arms
and services, a useful experience for a young officer whose vision
had not hitherto extended beyond the level of a brigade. General
Hare's plan was for his four brigades to attack by night in succession from the right, 156 Brigade capturing a Turkish position
immediately west of the road leading into Gaza before midnight;
163 and 161 Brigades would then advance across the dunes and
swing right to attack the western edge of the defences, which on
the right were about 750 yards and on the left some 1,200 yards
from the British front line. Finally, before dawn, Harding's old
brigade, 162, would pass through 161 and push along the coast for
another 2,000 yards, dealing also with the defences on their right as
they did so – not at all an easy operation to plan or execute,
especially as it was all over soft sand dunes in which movement of
any kind was difficult and slow.

Allenby's original intention had been to launch the attack in
September, but it was clear that the administrative preparations
could not be completed in time, and eventually 31 October was
selected as the date for the opening attack on Beersheba, the
preliminary moves being made at night over the preceding few
days while the artillery bombardment opened against the defences
of Gaza. Chauvel's attack on Beersheba was brilliantly successful,
and although there were anxieties about whether or not the captured water supplies would suffice to enable the main attack to be
launched on 3 or 4 November, Allenby gave the order to Bulfin
to launch his attack on Gaza on the night of 1/2 November. The
attack went more or less according to plan, although several battalions went astray in the dunes and casualties were heavy.
Harding was awarded the Military Cross for his part in both the
planning and execution of 54th Division's successful assault.
Turkish casualties were also severe and Kress was forced to send a
division from his reserve to reinforce the town. Water difficulties
and an attempt by the Turks to recapture Beersheba caused a
postponement of the main attack on the Turkish left until 6
November, 21 Corps renewing its attack on Gaza that night, on
this occasion with 75th Division on the right. By dawn the
Turkish garrison had withdrawn northwards. 54th Division, having borne the brunt of the attack, remained at Gaza, while the
52nd was sent forward to pursue the enemy up the coast towards
Jaffa and the Desert Mounted Corps made for Jerusalem. 54th

Division stayed at Gaza until it was moved up to join the ANZAC Division north of Lydda to protect the north flank of the forces attempting to make their way up through the mountains towards Jerusalem. Here they were counter-attacked by the Turks on 27 November at Wilhelma, 162 Brigade distinguished itself by firmly defeating a strong Turkish thrust.

Jerusalem fell on 9 December and the only other operation in which 54th Division took part before winter set in was the Battle of the River Auja, north of Jaffa, on 21 and 22 December. The main attack on the left across the flooded river was made by 52nd Division, 54th subsequently crossing further upstream. Both divisions were successful, and the aim of pushing the enemy back, out of artillery range of Jaffa, was achieved.

In February 1918 the Supreme War Council at Versailles had decided to stand on the defensive in the west and to finish off Turkey by an offensive in Palestine; but the German offensive in March, which threw the allies back to Amiens, changed all that, and Allenby found himself having to send divisions to France and postpone his plans for a renewed offensive until the autumn. In April Harding left 54th Division and joined General Bulfin's staff at 21 Corps headquarters as the corps machine-gun officer, responsible for the same sort of task at corps level as he had been at division. It ranked as a grade two general staff appointment, a further feather in the cap of the twenty-two-year-old major. He found the work of great interest. Bulfin was, in his words, 'a good, steady file'. The staff was headed by Brigadier-General Salt, a man of lively mind who corresponded weekly with his opposite numbers in the other two corps, one of whom, at 20 Corps, was Brigadier-General Wavell. These letters were circulated round the staff, and did much to educate them and make them aware of all the factors that had to be taken into account in planning. Harding found the work of wider interest, and the whole atmosphere was invigorated by the elation of success and a feeling that the end of the war could not be far away.

Allenby's plan was again bold, although simple in concept. Bulfin's corps, which had four of the six infantry divisions under command, was to break through the Turks on the coast, creating a gap through which the Desert Mounted Corps would pass and make straight for the passes through the hills running southeast from Mount Carmel, which divide the plain of Sharon from that of Esdraelon. Once through the hills, they would seize and hold the railway at El Affule and Beisan. Meanwhile 21 Corps would swing eastwards into the hills past Tulkarm to seize Mesudiye junction, the other nodal point of the single-track railway on which the Turks depended for all their supply. East of the Jordan, Lawrence and Feisal's Arabs would pose as much of a threat as they could to the other vital point of the railway system, Dera'a. Again deception was to play a major part, every step being taken to make the Turks believe that the Jordan valley itself was to be the main area of operations. Once the planning was completed, and before it was put into effect, Harding left corps headquarters and took over command of 161 Brigade machine-gun company. The machine-guns of 54th Division had now been grouped together in a battalion, known as 54 Machine-Gun Battalion. The deception plan was successful and Liman von Sanders, who had now replaced von Falkenhayn, had no suspicion that by mid-September four divisions, the 60th, 7th Indian, 75th and 3rd Indian had been concentrated in the coastal area west of the Jaffa-Tulkarm railway, with 54th and the French to the east of it. Zero hour was 4.30 am on 19 September, and by midday the Turkish Eighth Army was fleeing in disorder. 54th Division, acting with the French as the hinge of the door, had some tough fighting before capturing all their objectives near Bidieh, some four miles into the hills from their start line. The cavalry quickly passed through the gap made for them and the leading brigades were through the passes and into the Plain of Edraelon by 2.30 am on 20 September, Nazareth, Liman von Sanders's headquarters, being reached by dawn. All organized resistance by both the Seventh and Eighth Turkish Armies ceased next day, 21 September, the last day of active fighting for the infantry divisions.

Damascus was captured on 1 October and 21 Corps had an unopposed march up the coast, led by the 7th Indian Division, which reached Beirut on 8 October. They were replaced there by 54th Division at the end of the month, and it was there that Harding took part in a victory march after the armistice in November at which Allenby took the salute. Joe Guthrie remembered a conversation between Harding and himself in Beirut. 'What are you going to do now, Guthrie?' said Harding. 'Well, I've had enough of these b – – – s and I'm going home', was the reply. 'I've nothing to go home for', said Harding, 'and I'm soldiering on.' His battalion was then moved further north to the south of Tripoli, but not so far from Beirut as to prevent the officers from going there to enjoy a good meal.

In July Harding's commanding officer, Lieutenant-Colonel Pigot-Moodie, went back to England, and at the age of twenty-two Harding was appointed to command the battalion, yet another and a very bright feather in his cap. The year he was to hold this command gave him a self-confidence and assurance of his own ability to deal successfully both with men of all ranks and ages and with the manifold problems of command. It was an experience that he relished, and it did much to give him a maturity beyond his years and to mould his character into the shape it was ever after to bear. At the end of the year the division moved back to Alexandria, Harding's battalion much reduced in strength, and in July 1919 Harding himself sailed on leave for England, a very different man from the green Territorial Army subaltern who had sailed four years before for Gallipoli.

CHAPTER FOUR

BETWEEN THE WARS
1919–40

In September 1919, after his leave, Harding, now reduced to the rank of captain, joined the 12th Battalion of the Machine-Gun Corps which was forming as a regular battalion at Shorncliffe, due to go to India. Harding was second-in-command of a company and one of the subalterns was Lieutenant Richard Gale, also destined, after a long period in the doldrums in the Worcestershire Regiment, for a distinguished army career, succeeding Harding as Commander-in-Chief of the British Army of the Rhine in 1952 and Montgomery as NATO Deputy Supreme Allied Commander Europe in 1958. Gale remembered Harding at this time as a lively young officer, very ready to take part in jaunts to London, dances in Folkestone and other festivities with which they celebrated the change from war, financed by their war gratuities. One very significant incident now took place. When Harding reported on arrival to the adjutant, Mulholland, he was asked what his Christian name was. When Harding replied 'Allan', Mulholland said: 'Oh, you can't be called that: we'll call you John' and, as far as the army and finally everybody else was concerned, John he became and remained thereafter. Before the end of the year they sailed in the P and O liner *Mawla,* used as a troopship, and Harding recalled the arrival at Bombay, he and Gale leaning over the ship's rail as they entered the harbour and Gale saying: 'Ah, the glamorous East.'

The battalion went first to Kirkee, near Poona, and the group photograph of the officers, almost all decorated with the Military Cross, shows a very determined-looking Captain Harding at the end of the front row. One might have thought that, not having come from at all the sort of background from which regular army officers at that time normally came, he might have some difficulty in adapting himself to the typical life of a regular army officer in India. This was clearly not so. Only the more senior officers had served with the regular army before the war. Most of them, like Harding, had become regular officers by the chance of war. They were keen to accept what their seniors told them were the standards and habits of the pre-war army, both professionally and socially, and Harding set out to be as successful and typical an army officer as any. Gale remembered him as very determined, very capable and ruthlessly efficient, but at the same time keen on the social life and on making a success of it.

Social life centred on the garrison Gymkhana Club, where one played either tennis or polo, the smarter set, such as the Indian Cavalry, the gunners and the smarter British infantry regiments, tending to concentrate on polo. Harding, although his knowledge and experience of horses derived solely from his army service, enjoyed riding and had a definite flair for it. It was to polo that he turned in India, and he therefore gravitated towards the smarter set, where he certainly gave no sign of his puritanical background. In the club he was usually to be seen with a girl, although he was not one of those who flitted from flower to flower. Professionally the officers of the machine-gun battalion had an advantage over those whose service had been limited to that of an infantry battalion. They had at the least seen things from the level of a brigade, with the need to cooperate and coordinate with artillery and other arms. Harding had the added advantage that he had also experienced planning and battle at the level of division and corps, and finally, at the age of twenty-two, had achieved the soldier's great ambition, command of a battalion. He therefore not only had a wider experience than most officers of his age, but had acquired a wide measure of self-confidence also.

After a time at Kirkee the battalion moved further north to Jabalpur, and from there two companies, including Harding's, were sent to Chaman, on the Northwest Frontier with Afghanistan, where it is crossed by the road from Quetta to Kandahar. They formed part of a force which included an Indian cavalry regiment and an infantry brigade, sent there because of the possibility of hostilities against Afghanistan. In the event they did not materialize and the battalion returned first to Quetta and then to Jabalpur. By this time the War Office had decided that machine-guns were to revert to being part of the armoury of the infantry battalion itself and that the Machine-Gun Corps was to be disbanded, much to the regret of the officers of the 12th Battalion, which had been a very happy one under the command of Lieutenant-Colonel Cyril Porter.

So, on 9 July 1921, Harding joined the 2nd Battalion of his own county regiment, the Somerset Light Infantry, into which he had been gazetted as a regular officer in 1917, but with which he had not yet served. They were at Lucknow. Here he was well received, especially as he was a polo-player and had brought two ponies with him. The first reaction of the subalterns, almost all of whom had passed through Sandhurst, was to resent the intrusion of an unknown outsider, very little older than them and coming in over their heads as a captain, when their own prospects of promotion were then so poor; but this feeling was very rapidly dissipated when they got to know him, like him and respect his professionalism. The commanding officer, a mean and crotchety bachelor by the name of Bowker, was a great change from Porter. He slept on a stretcher rather than buy a bed and would invite his officers to go for a walk with him in the afternoon, invariably finishing up at the club, where his companion would find himself paying for the colonel's tea. Harding thoroughly enjoyed the life.

On one occasion he had a narrow escape. He and several other officers had been invited by the Maharaja of Bharatpur for a week's polo, pig-sticking and shooting. Driving back one evening with the Maharaja at the wheel of his Rolls-Royce, the coupling of the trailer, in which Harding and seven others were travelling, broke when it was travelling at more than forty miles per hour. The trailer careered off the road. Fortunately nobody was killed, but several bones were broken and Harding was badly concussed.

After the battalion had moved to Agra, about a hundred miles south of Delhi and site of the famous Taj Mahal, in February 1922, Harding was made adjutant. This prevented him from taking home leave, but gave him the experience of having to deal with the communal riots which broke out in Agra in August 1923. Hindu-Muslim antagonism was widespread in northern India at that time. In reaction to Muslim attacks, a Hindu movement, known as Mahasabha, had developed, to unite all Hindu communities with the aim of improving their conditions of life and to defend themselves against the Muslims, who were further provoked by this. The event that sparked off the general rioting in northern India, of which the Agra riots formed part, was a decision to restrict Indian immigration into Kenya.

One of his duties as adjutant was to run a tactical course for young officers, a novelty in those days. Harding, a great believer in careful planning, made them write an appreciation to produce a plan for one day in which they would complete the job they had to do, have a day's hunting, dance with the girl they were fond of and be back in barracks in time for the next day's work. His own philosophy was that, with careful planning, one should be able to work hard and enjoy oneself as well. He did this himself, and showed no sign to his brother officers of his puritanical upbringing.

The battalion formed part of the Delhi Infantry Brigade, commanded by Brigadier Wigram, brother of Sir Clive Wigram, private secretary to King George v. On his annual inspection Wigram encouraged Harding to aim for the staff college, a thought that had not hitherto entered his head. When he completed his tour as adjutant in September 1925, he found that he was entitled to a year's leave and decided that most of this should be devoted to working for the staff college examination. In preparation for it he had done some reading and been attached to brigade headquarters in Delhi, which had the added advantage of widening his experience of polo also. His first attempt at the examination in February 1926 was not successful, and before he tried again his attention was directed into a different channel, that of matrimony. George Rooke was one of the subalterns in the Somerset Light Infantry and, when Harding was planning his leave, Rooke suggested to him that he should look up his mother and give her news of her son. She lived with his stepfather, Charles Fry, and his two sisters at Long Ashton near Bristol. The opportunity occurred when Harding was staying with another brother-officer, Basil Whicher, whose father was a doctor in Clifton. Mrs Fry had asked him to come and play tennis and he had explained that Harding was staying with him. He was therefore included in the invitation. Unfortunately it poured with rain and both sisters found their guest silent and rather heavy on their hands. Then a game of bridge was suggested, at which Mary, the elder sister, was a complete novice. Harding willingly undertook her instruction and livened up when he did so.

He was immediately attracted to this small, pretty, lively and vivacious girl, eight years younger than himself, and he soon found opportunities to call in on his way back to South Petherton from London, where he was studying for the staff college. Before his leave was up he invited her to come up to London, have lunch with him and go to a matinée. Suitably chaperoned, she was allowed to accept the invitation, although the chaperone disappeared after lunch. After the matinée Mary told John that she was meeting a cousin for a thé dansant at the Piccadilly Hotel. He was indignant at this and, to her embarrassment, the cousin was put off and John himself took her there instead. Soon after this, at Long Ashton, in spite of a wager with his brother officers that he would not get engaged during his leave, he asked her to marry him, revealing his own family background of which Mary, and indeed his brother officers, had hitherto been ignorant. As he had arrived with the battalion with two polo ponies and lived the same sort of life as themselves, they had assumed that his background was very similar to their own.

Mary accepted the proposal without hesitation, but her mother and stepfather, when told, both had strong reservations, feeling that the difference of background and John's lack of private means were obstacles.

Mary's father's family had originally been Quakers from Cumberland, and her father, alone of his family, had abandoned his Quakerism, to the disapproval of his relations. He had been a solicitor in Manchester and had acquired a large house near Knutsford in Cheshire, where he hunted regularly with the Cheshire Hunt, among whom he was known as a lively and amusing man. Her mother was the daughter of Sir Thomas Sowler. He came of a wealthy northern family, his brother having been a well-known QC and he himself proprietor and editor of the *Manchester Courier,* Tory rival of the Liberal *Manchester Guardian.* He had been offered a peerage, but preferred a knighthood. He died young, leaving a considerable fortune, which was dissipated by his sons, chiefly on horses and hounds. Fearful that money might attract an adventurer, he had only given Mary's mother, his only daughter, half of what he gave each of his sons. In spite of this she was fairly well off, and when Mary's father died she was married again, to one of the famous chocolate-manufacturing family of Fry, and moved to Long Ashton. Mary's stepfather, Charles Harrington Fry, had, like her father, been brought up as a Quaker, but had joined the Church of England when he grew up, and, also like her father, enjoyed hunting and fishing, sports which would have been strongly disapproved of by his Quaker forebears. His son and only child by his first wife, Leslie Fry, had been killed on the last day of the First World War, serving with the 19th Hussars, to which he had transferred from the North Somerset Yeomanry. Charles Fry was well off and both he and Mary's mother played a full part in the public life of North Somerset.

Mary had therefore been brought up in affluent surroundings, and her mother and stepfather were very much concerned that she might find it difficult to adapt herself to the life of an army officer, with nothing but his pay as a captain and much of that devoted to horses. However, after they had met John's mother and been charmed by her, they overcame their scruples and it was decided that the wedding would take place when John's battalion returned to England the following year, 1927, which they were due to do after a period in Khartoum. It was there that he rejoined them in September 1926 in command of a company, deciding that not only had he lost five pounds but that he would also have to give up polo.

The battalion returned to England in January and went to Tidworth to form a motor machine-gun battalion in the new 'Experimental Armoured Force', the command of which had been offered to Boney Fuller, but which he had refused when he realized that it would also entail command of Tidworth garrison, and that the experimental aspects of the force would be very limited. Command went instead to Colonel Collins, a cautious man known within his brigade as 'no advance without security'. The role was one which naturally came easily to Harding with all his machine-gun experience. However the shortage of men and weapons made it a frustrating time. There were only enough men in the company to provide one full platoon and the only weapons available were rifles. On exercises the other two platoons, the light machine-guns and anti-tank rifles had to be represented by men with flags. In Khartoum he had passed his captain-to-major promotion examination by re-fighting the Battle of Omdurman, and in February he took the staff college examination for the second time, on this occasion successfully.

In April came the wedding at Long Ashton, after which the newly-married couple moved into a bungalow flat in Tidworth, where Mary for the first time in her life had to turn her hand to cooking. Harding had an old soldier batman called Spurgeon, who after a time suggested to Mary that he should take over the cooking. 'Oh, can you cook, Spurge?' she said. 'Well, madam,' came the reply 'I can do as well as you and there'd be a lot less mess for me to clear up afterwards.' However she persevered. In January 1928 Harding went to the staff college and Mary went home to Long Ashton for the birth of their first and only child. It was a boy, and he was christened John Charles. His father had found a rather sordid little house in Blackwater, a far from fashionable appendage to Camberley. Mary was appalled when she arrived with the baby to live there. The change in her life-style was stark, and she took some time to adjust.

Many of Harding's future colleagues were among his fellow students, including Gerald Templer and Dick McCreery. The commandant was Major-General Gwynne and both Dick O'Connor and Montgomery were members of the directing staff. Harding found Montgomery a brilliant teacher of tactics. He would pose the problem and then encourage the student to develop his own answer without interruption. 'Ah, that's interesting,' he would say at the end, 'very interesting.' It would end in only one way : a scene of intense military confusion.' He would then proceed to expound his own solution with perfect clarity. It was a two-year course, the first year being devoted to staff work at divisional level and the second to the level required at corps and army headquarters. In Harding's opinion, both at the time and later, the second year was a waste of time. Neither the Hardings nor the Templers were well off, but both kept horses and were keen followers of the staff college drag hunt and rode in point-to-point races. Having, in company with McCreery, become a whipper-in to the drag, Harding had to buy a second horse, his only mount up to that time being his army charger. Mary complained that she was kept on starvation diet in order that his two horses should be well fed. The future Field-Marshals, Harding and Templer, were not regarded by the directing staff as among the fliers, although their qualities of intelligence, hard work and energy were recognized. Among his fellow students were 'Bomber Harris, Neil Ritchie and 'Dixie' Redman, who remembered Harding as a very smart, well turned out officer.

At the end of the course, in 1930, Harding returned to his battalion once more to command a company, until, at the end of the year, he was posted to the headquarters of Southern Command at Salisbury as the general staff officer concerned with training. The general was Sir Cecil Romer, and Bernard Freyberg was a lieutenant-colonel on the administrative staff, obsessed with the need to improve army food and, in order to promote this, in the habit of taking his own meals in the soldiers' dining hall. The Hardings lived at Longhedge farmhouse near Old Sarum, just north of Salisbury. This was a time when there was much controversy over the mechanization of the army and the form it should take. Fond as he was of horses, Harding was fully in favour of the complete mechanization of the army, but was not of the school who believed that tanks could fight on their own. In May 1933 he was posted to Catterick as brigade major to 13 Infantry Brigade, the commander of which was Brigadier Forster, a religious sapper, Oxford Groupist and anti-bloodsport. However the divisional commander, Major-General Humphreys, was particularly keen, as was Forster himself, who had a good tactical sense, on TEWTS, tactical exercises without troops. Harding managed to persuade Forster that hunting on his army charger was an essential method of finding suitable parts of the country in which to hold these exercises, and was not therefore prevented by his brigadier's scruples from following his favourite sport. General Humphreys took Mary aside one day and said : 'Do you realize that your husband is a brilliant young man and will go far? You must therefore help him.' This was a great surprise to Mary, who was not an ambitious army wife and had never realized that her husband was 'brilliant'. She asked the general how she could help, to which his reply was : 'By working hard at all the chores expected of an army wife' – a somewhat daunting prospect.

The main event of this period was the selection of the brigade headquarters and two of its battalions as the British contingent for the international force to supervise the plebiscite to be conducted in the Saarland in January 1935 in order to decide whether or not it should be returned to Germany. The force, under the command of General Brind, assembled in December 1934 and consisted of Dutch, Swedish and Italian contingents as well as British, a special force of German-speaking British Military Police proving invaluable. Their task officially was merely to maintain law and order while the plebiscite took place, but in the end they found themselves organizing and running it. The force was not welcomed by the Saarlanders, who seemed a glum lot. Harding's impressions of the other contingents were that the Italians made a great show in their cloaks, hung about with weapons, the Dutch were dour and the Swedes, although all part-time soldiers, were more professional. He found it an interesting experience, to be of value many years later when dealing with Alexander's polyglot army group in Italy and exercising international command himself in Trieste after the end of the Second World War. As a result of his work there, he was specially commended by the Commander-in-Chief in an official letter to the Military Secretary.

In January 1935 he returned to his battalion, which was then in Colchester, and commanded a company yet again, leaving them in April 1936 for the War Office, where he took over the post of general staff officer grade two in the directorate of military operations, dealing with disarmament negotiations, the League of Nations and similar subjects. Mary and he and John Charles, now eight years old, together with a dog, moved into a flat on the south side of Battersea Park. Neither War Office work nor London life were to his liking, although the subjects he dealt with were not without interest. The international scene was darkening, with both the Italo-Abyssinian war and the Spanish civil war in train. Harding's work involved him in monitoring the effect of sanctions on Italy and the arms embargo on the Spanish civil war.

Halifax's visit to Goering and Hitler in 1938 resulted in the establishment of a joint service committee on the qualitative limitation of armaments on which Harding represented the army; the navy member was Tom Phillips, who was to die as an admiral when the *Repulse* and the *Prince of Wales* were sunk by the Japanese off the coast of Malaya in December 1941; the air force was represented by the future Marshal of the Royal Air Force Jack Slessor. Most of the arguments raged about the effects of air bombardment, and Harding found himself the pig in the middle. Later that year, when disillusion set in after Munich and rearmament was put in train, Harding was much involved as secretary of a War Office committee concerned with rearming potential allies, including France, Romania, the Balkans and the Low Countries. The chairman of this large and unwieldy committee was Brigadier Akerman, and Harding learnt much about committees, what to do and what not to do, particularly not letting any member reopen the subject after the decision had been reached, as the chairman was liable to do. This work brought him into contact not only with the other services but also with other departments of state, including the Foreign Office, and he attended meetings of the Committee of Imperial Defence – all this was to be of value to him when he became CIGS. The impression he

gained was that the navy could get away with anything: whereas
it was the King's army, it was the People's navy. In one of his
confidential reports while he was at the War Office, the Director of
Military Operations wrote of Harding: 'Has the power to reduce
a complicated case to a statement of the salient facts in an exceptional manner.' Redman, his future VCIGS, confirmed that he had
this reputation at that time. He remembered him as always being
accessible, welcoming, and ready to discuss matters in a cooperative spirit; but that he never wasted time and took hard work in
his stride.

In July 1939, at the age of forty-three, Harding was to achieve
the great ambition of a regular soldier, command of a battalion of
his own regiment, this time the 1st Battalion, twenty-one years
after his first lieutenant-colonel's command. They were in India,
at Poona, and due to move shortly to Multan in the plains of what
is now Pakistan. With war clouds clearly gathering, it was decided
that Mary and John Charles, who was at boarding school at
Folkestone, should stay behind, and they moved to join her
mother at Long Ashton when he sailed. Soon after he had taken
over command, the battalion was moved to the Northwest Frontier
to be the British battalion in the brigade at Kohat south of
Peshawar. Here they set about training in mountain warfare before being sent up in March 1940 into the Ahmedzair salient,
covering the construction of a road to Darzale. It was traditional
Northwest Frontier fighting, picketing the heights and being
sniped at by Waziris: not too dangerous, but a sharp enough
operational situation to keep everyone up to the mark in their
duties.

Harding threw himself with great enthusiasm into the task of
training his men and sharpening them up. He set an example,
rare in India, of an officer sharing work with his men, when they
were engaged in laying a water pipeline. Stripped to the waist he
led his officers in taking part in the work of carrying the pipes and
digging the trench for them in the heat of the day. A further
example of his enlightened attitude to command is recalled by
Tony Hunt then his adjutant. Harding overheard one of his
officers rebuking a soldier who had fired on the wrong target on
the range. 'Why did you do that, you silly idiot,' said the officer,
to which the soldier began to reply: 'But I thought...' The

officer broke in with the classic army remark : 'You're not paid to think,' when he in turn was interrupted by the CO, who said that was exactly what he *was* trying to train his men to do and that he must never use that expression again.

In May, having earned a mention in despatches, he brought the battalion back to Multan, after arranging to get out of a posting as GSO 1 to Northern Command Headquarters at Rawalpindi. He threw himself with equal enthusiasm into the task of training the battalion for mechanized warfare, but was horrified to find little or no support for this in higher quarters. The excuse given was that no motor transport was available to replace the battalion's mules, and that, in any case the war would be over before the Indian Army could be equipped, trained and moved to take part in it. Harding, who wished to train his battalion in the principles of surprise, speed and simplicity, was extremely frustrated. He saw himself spending the war in the military backwater of India. When out shooting, reservists of the Indian Army would come up and ask when they were going to be called up, and he found it galling to put them off with an equivocal answer. Command, instead of being the highlight of his career, was proving to be a depressing experience, as every excuse and obstacle was raised to what he wished to do to train his battalion.

Release came when Wavell in the Middle East decided in the autumn of 1940 that he needed the skeleton staff for an additional divisional headquarters. Harding was replaced as commanding officer by a newly-married officer for whom service in India would be more congenial, and he sailed from Bombay in a troopship full of Australians, posted as the GSO 1 of the skeleton division. The ship was attacked by Italian aircraft as it entered the Red Sea, but nothing in the convoy was hit and they arrived safely at Suez in October. When Harding arrived in Cairo, nobody seemed to know why he had come. The divisional commander designate, Major-General Gambier-Parry, was in hospital and Harding was given odd jobs to do in GHQ by the brigadier general staff (operations), an ex-fellow student at the staff college, Brigadier Jock Whiteley.

When Harding left his battalion at Multan, Mary's brother George Rooke, who was serving as a major in it at the time, wrote to her :

Well, your gallant husband has been taken away from us at last.

Why a man of his ability was left here so long I can't imagine. He certainly woke this battalion up in the year he commanded it and he woke *me* up during the last couple of months! They all admired him very much, I think. He expected a lot of us all but he never asked anybody to do anything either physical or mental which he wasn't prepared to do himself. There aren't many COS who'll come and dig trenches with the men, stripped to the waist. I thought he took a lot out of himself but then he always did and always will do and he seemed perfectly fit if rather thin. I expect the sea voyage will fatten him up much to his fury. He eats and drinks so little of course. He had a splendid send-off here and at Dalhousie. I described it all in my last letter to Mother so won't do it again. He made very good farewell speeches on parade and in the mess. He told us he had always longed to command one of the regular battalions and that this last year had been the happiest time of his soldiering career. He paid special tribute to the help received from Bee Line, Tony and Farmer the Quartermaster and said that he longed to take the battalion on service but such was not to be. He said it was very galling for us to be left here but he felt sure we'd see service before the war was over. I wonder! One does feel terribly out of it all and we long to be doing something more active to help our country. However I'm afraid some British troops *must* be left in India. Life is so easy out here of course compared to yours. No air-raids, no black-outs, no rationing!

Mary felt very cut off back at Long Ashton, John Charles away, except for holidays, at his preparatory boarding school which had moved to Marsh Court at Stockbridge in Hampshire. She occupied herself, as she did throughout the war, by working, mostly on night shifts, in the canteen for servicemen passing through Temple Meads station in Bristol run by the YMCA. She never forgot the sight of the soldiers returning from Dunkirk, utterly exhausted, falling asleep at the tables. Bristol had its fair share of air raids, aimed at the docks there and at Avonmouth, and she often had to take refuge and continue to serve tea to the weary servicemen in the tunnels below the station. As an important rail junction there was never a shortage of customers and there were times when it was not easy to get to or from her work in the black-out.

CHAPTER FIVE

O'CONNOR'S VICTORY
1940–1

When Harding arrived in the Middle East both sides were taking stock after the dramatic events of the summer of 1940. The very small force, mainly 7th Armoured Division, which had operated against the Italians in the Western Desert of Egypt, had established a moral supremacy over its opponents, but its activities had worn out its vehicles and led to a need to husband its resources. When in September 1940 the very much larger Italian Tenth Army under General Berti lumbered forward the sixty miles from the Libyan frontier to Sidi Barrani, they had not been seriously opposed and the main British force had been withdrawn to the area of Mersa Matruh, armoured car patrols and 'Jock columns' of field guns and motorized infantry maintaining contact, harassing the enemy and dominating the open desert in the forward area. The forces in the desert were under the command of Headquarters Western Desert Force, formed in June from the headquarters of 6th Infantry Division, which had been in Palestine, its commander, Major-General Richard O'Connor, being promoted lieutenant-general when the change took place.

But the Western Desert was not Wavell's only preoccupation nor, in the eyes of the Chiefs of Staff and the Defence Committee in London, was it the principal one. The Italian forces in Ethiopia, posing a threat both to the Sudan and to the use of the Red Sea, as well as to Kenya, had to be taken into account; but it was the intentions of the Germans and means of countering them which, in the eyes of London, were of prime concern. Hitler had met Mussolini in the Brenner Pass on 4 October 1940 and had offered the help of mechanized and specialized troops in the form of 3rd Panzer Division to reinforce the Italian Fifth and Tenth Armies under Marshal Graziani in Libya. Mussolini rejected the offer, confident that Berti would be able to capture Mersa Matruh on his own, although he accepted that he might need them for a subsequent advance to Alexandria. Meanwhile General von Thoma had been sent to Libya to report on the situation. He was very unfavourably impressed, particularly by the logistic difficulties, and recommended that no German troops should be sent until the Italians had captured Mersa Matruh. His advice was accepted, and the 3rd Panzer Division was then earmarked for an attack on Gibraltar, which Hitler hoped that Franco would agree to when he met him at Hendaye on 23 October, the day that Mussolini informed him that he had decided to go to war with Greece, which he did five days later.

It was this latter event which preoccupied the attention of Churchill and the Chiefs of Staff, both militarily and politically. They were anxious to erect barriers to further Axis expansion in the Balkans and placed their hopes on both Greece and Turkey as the pillars to support them. They were also concerned at the threat from the Italian Dodecanese Islands, primarily Rhodes, particularly if the Luftwaffe were to be deployed there. The first action of the Commanders-in-Chief Middle East was to send a small force to Crete to reconnoitre and prepare for the establishment of a naval base at Suda Bay. This was agreed by London, who also told Wavell to offer the help of a brigade and some Royal Air Force squadrons to Greece. Eden, Secretary of State for War, was on a visit to the Middle East at the time and was available to discuss the problems all this posed. Wavell's view was that the security of Egypt must take priority. Only if it was secure could offensive measure against Italy and support to Greece and Turkey be provided. All three services were operating on a shoe-string. Anything that could be spared for Greece could not have any significant effect on events there and would put the security of Egypt at risk. It would certainly jeopardize the plans, of which Wavell had made no mention to London, to strike a blow against the Italian army which had established itself inside Egypt round Sidi Barrani. These plans were now revealed to Eden, who supported Wavell and his fellow Commanders-in-Chief. For the moment therefore assistance to Greece was limited to three Royal Air Force squadrons and some anti-aircraft artillery and the relief of some Greek troops in Crete by British.

Eden returned to England on 6 November, three days before the highly successful fleet air arm attack on the Italian navy at

Taranto, but the argument about priorities continued as a result of fears of a German occupation of Bulgaria. Wavell was informed that help to Turkey must be first priority, if necessary at the expense of all activity except a strictly defensive policy in Egypt. Wavell's view was that Germany could not afford to see Italy defeated or even just held in Greece, and would be bound to intervene, even if only with air support. She probably did not wish at this stage to antagonize Bulgaria or Yugoslavia, although she might be forced to do so. Being able to act on interior lines, she could always bring forces to bear to attack Greece or Turkey before we could support them. This was in fact what Hitler proposed to do, but he had told the Italians that he could not move until March and that he hoped to gain the acquiescence of Yugoslavia and Turkey and persuade the Russians to turn their attention elsewhere.

Harding personally was not directly concerned in these high-level discussions. Whiteley had put him on to examining a plan proposed by Wingate for a force, based on West Africa, to advance to capture Tripoli from the south. Harding worked out that it was feasible only if a huge fleet of ten-ton cross-country lorries and also of transport aircraft were available, as neither were. He reported this verbally to Major-General Arthur Smith, Wavell's Chief of Staff, who sent him in to see Wavell himself. The latter's laconic response to Harding's explanation was 'I see. I suppose we'd better stick to the LRDG' (Long Range Desert Group). There was a danger that he would be posted to head the army element of the reconnaissance sent to Crete, but he managed to avoid this, and opportunity knocked when Brigadier 'Sandy' Galloway, the brigadier general staff of Headquarters British Troops in Egypt, General 'Jumbo' Wilson's headquarters, fell ill at a crucial stage of the planning of what was to become the Battle of Sidi Barrani, the counter-offensive in the desert about which Wavell had been so secretive.

Knowledge of the plan, and that such an attack was contemplated, was restricted to a very small circle. Harding now found himself one of the initiates, and one of his first tasks was to be present at a meeting between Wilson and O'Connor, who came under his command, to discuss it. Berti's Tenth Army showed little sign of planning a further advance and had settled into a series of fortified positions or 'camps', running south from Sidi Barrani. Three divisions, two Libyan and one Italian, were disposed in four of these camps, one at Sidi Barrani itself, one on the coast fifteen miles east, known as Maktila, and two, Tummar East and Tummar West, ten miles south, with General Maletti's armoured group at Nibeiwa, a few miles further south of them. South of this again there was an unoccupied gap of some ten miles, known as the Bir Enba gap, before another group of camps was reached on the eastern end of the main escarpment which ran northwest from there, impassable to vehicles except at a few places, all the way to the frontier at Sollum. Ever since the Italians had settled into these camps, the patrols of 7th Armoured Division had been active in the Bir Enba gap and ensured that the two groups were not joined together by any defensive system.

Wavell's plan was for a rapid operation which would last not more than five days. He saw this as being, first, an attack on the four isolated camps on the escarpment, at Sofafi and Rabia, followed by an envelopment of the Tummar and Sidi Barrani group, after which O'Connor's force would probably withdraw back to the area of Matruh. The 7th Armoured Division had been reinforced by two regiments from 2nd Armoured Division in England, 3rd Hussars with light tanks and 2nd Royal Tank Regiment with cruisers, and 7th Royal Tank Regiment with Matilda 'I' tanks had also arrived, all having been sent round the Cape in August despite the fact that the invasion of Britain still seemed a serious threat. O'Connor was also given the recently arrived 4th Indian Division, but not told that one of Wavell's reasons for limiting operations to five days was his plan to switch the division to join the 5th Indian in attacking the Italians in Eritrea. This increase in his force was welcome, but it accentuated the problems caused by a severe shortage of motor transport. O'Connor's main force was back south of Matruh, the rail- and roadhead for supplies from Alexandria. Thus an advance of some seventy miles would have to take place before he could get to grips with the enemy. Any premature move would give the game away and there was not enough transport both to move everyone forward and bring supplies up to support them at the same time. The first step therefore was to create carefully dispersed and concealed forward dumps of supplies, protected only by the presence of 7th Armoured Division's screen of armoured car patrols and columns.

O'Connor had decided that the original plan could not be completed within five days and that a preliminary attack on the Sofafi group of camps would forfeit the advantage of surprise in

The Eastern Mediterranean

ARTHUR BANKS

49

dealing with the more important group around Sidi Barrani. He therefore proposed to exploit the Bir Enba gap by passing through it the assaulting troops, 4th Indian Division supported by 7th Royal Tanks, while 7th Armoured Division operated to the south and west of them, masking the Sofafi group, preventing any reinforcement from Sollum along the coast and completing their encirclement. The Sofafi group were not so essential and could be dealt with later. The Royal Navy was to help by naval bombardment of Sidi Barrani and Maktila, and the Royal Air Force by operations against the Italian Air Force and targets further to the rear. Two exercises were carried out on 25 and 26 November to practise 4th Indian Division and its supporting troops in the tactics required to assault the camps, and two days later Wavell modified his five-day concept by telling Wilson to be prepared to exploit success up to the frontier. 'I do not entertain extravagant hopes of the operation,' he wrote, 'but I do wish to make certain that, if a big opportunity comes, we are prepared morally, mentally and administratively to use it to the fullest.' A few days after this he told Generals Platt and Cunningham, who had come from the Sudan and Kenya respectively to confer about plans to deal with the Italians in Ethiopia, what was afoot, promising Platt to send him the 4th Indian Division, which he assumed would have completed its task in the Western Desert by the middle of December, taking advantage of a convoy returning down the Red Sea at that time to move it to Port Sudan. He planned to relieve it in the Western Desert with the recently arrived 6th Australian Division, then training in Palestine : one brigade in mid-December and the rest by the end of the month.

By this time Galloway had returned to work as Wilson's brigadier general staff, and Harding was lent to O'Connor to act as a personal liaison officer to ensure that the triangular and awkward relationship, Wavell-Wilson-O'Connor, did not get its wires crossed and that all three knew what was in each other's minds. It was a help that both Galloway and the brigadier responsible for operations at GHQ, Eric Dorman-Smith, were well known to Harding. All of them had been present at a conference held at O'Connor's headquarters at Ma'aten Bagush, just east of Matruh, after the two 'training exercises' designed as rehearsals. At this conference the detailed tactical plan had been agreed by which the assaults on each camp would be made in succession from the northwest, the Matildas of 7th Royal Tanks making use of the entrances in those sectors used by the Italians themselves in order to avoid mines. The general plan was that both 7th Armoured and 4th Indian Divisions would move forward from the Matruh-Siwa road on 8 December, making the final approach march during the night. The assault on Nibeiwa was to be made at dawn, each brigade of 4th Indian Division then attacking the camps further north in succession, the support of the tanks and the artillery being switched to them. It was no easy task for Lieutenant-Colonel Jerram's 7th Royal Tanks to reorganize rapidly and support one attack after another, especially after a long approach on their tracks. While this was going on, Brigadier Selby's 16th British Infantry Brigade was to make a feint attack on Maktila.

In spite of the presence of an Italian reconnaissance aircraft over the area through which the advance was made on 8 December, surprise was complete. The very strict measures to keep planning secret, which had annoyed Churchill and caused some confusion among the staff, had paid off. O'Connor had decided to set up a small tactical headquarters at the start of the battle not far from Bir Enba with Harding in charge. Here he was not far from both divisional HQs and was able to keep in personal touch both with General Beresford-Peirse, the GOC 4th Indian Division, and with Brigadier 'Blood' Caunter, temporarily in command of 7th Armoured Division in the absence through sickness of General Creagh, Colonel Horace Birks taking over command of Caunter's 4th Armoured Brigade, which was effectively cutting off the Italians from the rear. The whole plan had worked almost like clockwork, the Nibeiwa and Tummar camps being successfully captured for very small loss. No news had been received of what was happening on the coast road, but O'Connor was confident and ordered Beresford-Peirse to continue the attack to capture Sidi Barrani itself on 10 December, while 7th Armoured Division was to push further north, giving support to the attack on Sidi Barrani, cutting off any attempt at withdrawal and preventing any reinforcement from Buq-Buq, the reserve position on the coast.

O'Connor and Harding were up early on 11 December, their high spirits dampened by the receipt of a signal telling O'Connor that 4th Indian Division and 7th Medium Regiment Royal Artillery were to be withdrawn as soon as possible to move to the Sudan, to be replaced, as described, by 6th Australian Division, which would not be complete for several weeks and was deficient in artillery. In the interval the only infantry formation available would be Selby's 16th Brigade. Not only would the loss of the fighting troops prevent any rapid exploitation, but considerable use was being made of 4th Indian Division's transport for supply as well as troop movement. The haul of prisoners, already some 20,000, further complicated matters. They had to be guarded, fed and transported back to railhead. Fortunately most of their own transport, excellent Lancia ten-ton lorries, had also been captured and they proved to be docile and often cooperative prisoners. A further large bag of prisoners was taken late in the day when 7th Armoured Brigade reached Buq-Buq. After a sharp encounter, where the coastal track passed through a salt marsh, another 15,000 of the enemy surrendered, bringing the total 'bag' for the three days to 38,300 prisoners, 237 guns and 73 tanks, while our own casualties had only amounted to 624 killed, wounded and missing.

O'Connor, helped by Harding, now had to think quickly. He protested against the withdrawal, but Wavell was insistent, although he relented to the extent of allowing 7th Medium Regiment to remain. He defended what to many, then and since, seemed a failure to be prepared to adjust himself to a change in the situation, in a letter he wrote to O'Connor in 1945. In it he stated that, if he had missed the chance of moving the division to the Sudan by the convoy, whose sailing he could not delay, he would not have been able to attack from the Sudan that winter. He had to decide either to remain entirely on the defensive in the Sudan for some time to come or accept the delay in the pursuit in the Western Desert, while the Australian division replaced the Indian. He said his decision was a difficult one, but he was sure he was right. In retrospect one must be inclined to agree with him. The principal cause of such delay as there was was logistic, although of course the changeover of divisions accentuated this. It is possible that the week or two that might have been saved could have led to a longer gap between the collapse of the Italian army in Cyrenaica and the intervention of the Germans, which might have made it both possible and acceptable to London that O'Connor should have made a dash to Tripoli before the Germans got there and before Metaxas died and his opposition to British reinforcement of Greece was removed; but the odds are long, as they are that such a dash would even then have been successful and secured Tripolitania. Wavell knew that London's eyes were primarily on the Balkans, although O'Connor's victory had brought about a change of tune.

Where Wavell was not quite honest was in pleading pressure from London over fears for the Sudan. This had never been the case, and both Churchill and the Chiefs of Staff were consistent in putting low priority on dealing with the Italians in Ethiopia, who, in their justifiable view, could be left to wither in isolation. This view was reiterated in a message to Wavell received on 17 December from Churchill in which he said:

> Your first objective now must be to maul the Italian army and rip them off the African shore to the utmost possible extent. We were very glad to learn your intentions against Bardia and Tobruk and now to hear the latest captures of Sollum and Capuzzo. I feel convinced that it is only after you have made sure that you can get no further that you will relinquish the main hope in favour of secondary action in the Sudan or Dodecanese. The Sudan is of prime importance, and eminently desirable and it may be that the two Indian brigades can be spared without prejudice to the Libyan pursuit battle. The Dodecanese will not get harder for a little waiting. But neither of them ought to detract from the supreme task of inflicting further defeats upon the main Italian army.

Meanwhile O'Connor had been doing the best he could with the meagre resources at his disposal. His order to Caunter during the night of 10 December to withdraw 4th Armoured Brigade back through the Bir Enba gap and to encircle the Sofafi group of camps from the south and west on 11 December was not acted on, owing to a misunderstanding, and by the time patrols of the Support Group reached them early in the morning, the Cirene Division, which had occupied them, had withdrawn. O'Connor's orders were now for 4th Armoured Brigade to pursue them south of the escarpment and encircle Bardia while 7th Armoured Brigade pressed along the coast, 16th Brigade taking over the task of dealing with the mass of prisoners round Sidi Barrani. Logistic problems loomed large, principally the supply of water and petrol, and for the first and almost only time in the desert campaign the daily ration of water was reduced to half a gallon per man, and that was so salty that it was barely drinkable even as tea. With help from the navy a crisis was averted, and by 26 December, in the face of some severe attacks from the Italian air force, 7th Armoured Division had cut the road from Bardia to Tobruk, four days after Sollum itself had been secured.

The move of Major-General Mackay's rough, tough 6th Australian Division was now in train, and O'Connor moved his own headquarters nearer to the front. When he did so, he took the opportunity to replace his BGS, Brigadier Rupert Hobday, by Harding, on whom he had now come to rely strongly for advice and to get his intentions translated into action. The two men complemented each other, both diminutive in stature, lively, quick and clear in thought and decision, bold and impatient of delay: they were like two cheerful, chirping, active little birds. O'Connor had been dissatisfied with Hobday and had made a special request to Wavell personally that Harding should replace him. Wavell, who thought O'Connor was being hard on Hobday, said there would be difficulties on account of Harding's lack of seniority. However, strongly pressed by O'Connor, Wavell overcame them. So, on 20 December 1940 Harding assumed the temporary rank of brigadier and, as BGS, was the equivalent of Chief of Staff, the logistic and administrative side remaining in the hands of Brigadier Nares.

In the absence on leave, fortunately for himself, of General Berti, Lieutenant-General Bergenzoli, commander of 23rd Italian Corps, known to the British as 'Electric Whiskers', was in command of Tenth Army. Marshal Graziani, supported by Mussolini, told him to hold Tobruk and Bardia, the latter now defended by five divisions, totalling some 45,000 men with 400 guns, double the number estimated by British intelligence. By 21 December Mackay was able to take over the Sollum area and begin to plan the attack on Bardia. O'Connor advised him to base his plan on exploiting to the maximum the power and moral effect of Jerram's Matildas, which had impressed Harding as being the decisive factor in bringing about the swift collapse of the Italian defences south of Sidi Barrani. They could only make twenty-three tanks available, but this was considered enough, and Mackay was given additional artillery, including 7th Medium Regiment.

A number of factors delayed the date of the attack: one was believed by 7th Armoured Division to be the over-zealous celebration of Christmas and the New Year by the Australians, but the late arrival of ammunition is recorded as the true one. Finally 5.30 am on 3 January was fixed as the time for the opening barrage. By 7 am the Matildas of 7th Royal Tanks were inside the perimeter, and by 8.30 16th Australian Brigade had captured almost all of its objectives and taken some eight thousand prisoners. Three hours later 17th Brigade began its attack which was not so successful and ran into some difficulties. It did not complete the seizure of all its objectives until 1 pm on 4 January. By this time the garrison was surrendering everywhere, their losses adding up to over forty thousand men, more than 400 guns, 13 medium and 117 light tanks. Bergenzoli himself got away. In less than a month O'Connor, with a force of only two divisions, had completely destroyed eight Italian ones.

On 1 January Western Desert Force was renamed 13 Corps and Harding's appointment renamed accordingly. As it moved out of Egypt into Libya, it ceased to be under command of Wilson and HQ British Troops in Egypt and came directly under Wavell's GHQ. This was hailed with relief by O'Connor and Harding, who had found dealing through Wilson as an intermediary a cause of needless misunderstanding and delay. No time was lost in pressing on to Tobruk, and on 5 January 7th Armoured Division, now reduced to only 69 cruiser and 126 light tanks, was on its way to El Adem, the important airfield above the escarpment fifteen miles south of Tobruk. Very soon afterwards it had completed the encirclement of the garrison of about 25,000 under General Manella, commander of the 22nd Corps. With half the number of men that had held Bardia, he had a perimeter of double the length, some thirty miles, to defend. O'Connor's plan was to repeat the formula that had proved so successful at Bardia, using 6th Australian Division, supported by 7th Royal Tanks, who could now provide only sixteen Matildas fit for action. O'Connor's principle problem, with the slender resources of motor transport available to him, was the logistic one of moving the Australians forward with the supplies to support both them and 7th Armoured Division, when they were so far from the railhead at Matruh. Without the captured Lancias, the fortnight's pause before Tobruk could be attacked would certainly have been longer.

At dawn on 21 January 1941, 16th Australian Brigade, with all Jerram's Matildas, broke in through the southeastern sector of Tobruk's perimeter between the Bardia and the El Adem roads. Three hours later 19th Brigade passed through them and had a fierce fight to reach the northern escarpment overlooking the town and harbour by nightfall. During the night the sound of explosions made it clear that the Italians had given up hope and were

C

engaged in demolition. General Mackay gave orders for a final push northwards to start at dawn on the 22nd. When it came, it led immediately to the collapse of all resistance and the surrender of 23,000 soldiers, 2,000 sailors, 208 field and medium guns and 87 tanks. O'Connor's total casualties were 400, 355 of whom were Australian.

Even before this remarkable victory, which accounted for all Italian forces east of Derna, was complete, Harding found much of his time taken up in dealing with GHQ over what was to follow. The pendulum in London was swinging back again. The reverses suffered by Italy both in Libya and on the Albanian-Greek frontier were making German intervention more likely, and there were definite indications that she was making preparations in Romania for an attack on Greece through Bulgaria, which was expected before the end of January. Support for Greece became top priority again : not only might it strengthen her resolution to stand up to German threats and perhaps deter an attack, but it would have a significant effect on the attitudes of Turkey and the USA. On 10 January the Chiefs of Staff told Wavell and his colleagues that, as soon as Tobruk had been captured, help to Greece was to take priority over all operations in the Middle East, although this should not prevent an advance to Benghazi 'if the going was good'; but once more they were told that help to Greece must come from within the resources already available to them. Wavell and Longmore were to go to Athens and discuss these matters with General Metaxas.

The meeting took place on 15th January, Wavell offering, as he had been told to do, several regiments of artillery and one of tanks while Longmore offered three squadrons of aircraft. This was not at all to the taste of Metaxas. He took the view that the dispatch of these units would serve as a *casus belli* to both Germany and Bulgaria and stated that he had assurances from Yugoslavia that they would resist any German attempt to cross their territory, provided that Germany had not been provoked by a British presence in Greece. Metaxas wanted the British to prepare to land a force strong enough to act offensively in the area of Salonika, but it should not actually land unless and until the Germans had crossed the Danube into Bulgaria. Wavell was told by the Chiefs of Staff to warn Metaxas that, in such an eventuality, intervention would be too late and that we might then feel impelled to send help to Turkey instead. No preparations were to be made to send British forces to the area of Salonika other than three RAF squadrons.

When he returned to Cairo, having visited Crete on the way, Wavell warned London that they were in danger of falling between two stools. The help we had offered would not be sufficient to swing the balance if the Germans were really intent on gaining Salonika : if it were sent and the Germans did not attack, it would be serving no useful purpose; but its dispatch would prejudice the chances of securing Benghazi and the 'Bulge' of Cyrenaica, which would have great advantages for naval and air operations in the Mediterranean and effectively prevent any Italian attempt to regain what they had lost. His own view was that Germany might well hesitate to violate Bulgarian neutrality, as it would invite retaliation against the Romanian oilfields on which they relied. He recommended that Metaxas's refusal to accept help should be accepted : that plans should be drawn up for sending a force to the Salonika area, but that nothing should be promised. Wavell and his colleagues received an answer to his signal on the day of the attack on Tobruk. The Chiefs of Staff agreed that Benghazi should be captured and converted into a naval and air base. Optimistically they believed that it could immediately be used as O'Connor's supply base, maintained by sea from Alexandria, thus greatly reducing the demands of his long land line of communication. They were equally keen on the capture of Rhodes, fearing the threat of it becoming a base for the Luftwaffe. They also placed high priority on giving help and encouragement to Turkey. Nearer the end of the month they got excited again about information that Germany was about to invade Bulgaria and pressed for speed in implementing these divergent priorities, especially the capture of Benghazi which would, in their view, release forces, especially RAF squadrons, to help Turkey and Greece. On 29 January General Metaxas died and was succeeded by Mr Koryzis, who reaffirmed the line that no British troops should be sent to Greece unless the Germans entered Bulgaria.

O'Connor and Harding now had a clear mandate to capture Benghazi as quickly as possible. In addition to the ever-present logistic problem, they faced two others, the state of 7th Armoured Division's vehicles and the nature of the country. The former had already made it necessary to 'dismount' two of the division's tank regiments and share out the remaining fit tanks between the other four. The country to the west of Gazala changed from the flat open desert which had favoured O'Connor's 13 Corps hitherto : the 'Bulge' or Jebel was a hilly cultivated area, through which movement east to west would in many cases be limited to roads and tracks. The desert to the south of it was unreconnoitred and inadequately mapped. There was reason to believe that it might not be as easy to move over as that over which 7th Armoured Division had already passed. But this change in the terrain did not occur immediately west of Tobruk, and O'Connor decided that he would press on at once, his first aim being to isolate and destroy General Babini's armoured brigade near Mechili, while pushing forward along the coast road towards Derna. The first task was given to 7th Armoured Division, reinforced by one of the Australian brigades, while Mackay made for Derna, relieving 7th Armoured Brigade on the coast road only two days after the fall of Tobruk, 24 January. Unfortunately Babini made off on 26 January, eluding the grasp of 7th Armoured Division, much to O'Connor's chagrin.

Three days later the Italians abandoned Derna, with the result that O'Connor faced a fairly formidable force, which showed signs of being prepared to stand and fight in country which did not favour his reduced mobile forces. His mind therefore turned to a much wider and more ambitious turning movement. He proposed to move 7th Armoured Division nearly a hundred miles southwest from Mechili to a spot on the map called Msus. If the enemy remained in Benghazi, it would then continue westwards, cut the coast road and attack Benghazi from the south. If the enemy had begun to withdraw, it could continue southwest and try to head him off. The problems would be logistics and the state of the tanks, now down to only fifty and all of them on their last legs. Both of these factors favoured a pause, the latter because by about 8 February two fresh tank regiments could reach O'Connor from the newly arrived 2nd Armoured Division. Hardly had he decided to pause until then, when air reports began to come in of significant westward movement on the roads in the western part of the Jebel leading to Benghazi. By the afternoon of 2 February it appeared that a major withdrawal was in progress. O'Connor, fully supported by Harding, decided that he could not afford to wait. Every device must be employed to make it logistically possible for 7th Armoured Division to set off with every tank it could muster as soon as possible. On 3 February the division was ordered to start its move at dawn the following day, with orders both to prevent any reinforcements from Tripolitania reaching Benghazi and to prevent the withdrawal of Italian forces in the opposite direction. Meanwhile the Australians were to push on as fast as they could through the Jebel. Wavell flew up to O'Connor's headquarters at Tmimi on 4 February and gave his full approval to the plan.

The previous two days had been hectic ones for Harding, who had to organize a major and complicated operation at very short notice, the resources to support it being stretched far beyond normal limits. As always, the key factor was transport : units and formations had to be moved to new locations and their orders changed; supplies of petrol, ammunition, food and water sufficient to support several days of operations over long distances had to be brought up from the rear and distributed; equipment under repair had hastily to be got ready; some units had to be reorganized, their equipment being worn out; and new maps and air photographs had to be obtained and distributed. All this had to be done when the force was widely scattered. Wireless communication over these distances, particularly at night, was uncertain and unreliable. If surprise was to be obtained, communication had to be entirely in the form of enciphered written messages, which involved long delays. Few logistic units in any case had wireless sets below the level of company, if that. The alternative was to send off a despatch-rider into the desert, armed with a useless map of Italian origin and very limited aids to navigation. The pace of advance had been so fast that telephone lines and marked tracks had not caught up. It was mid-winter. The wind blew and the rains came and it was cold. Western Desert force was still wearing summer uniform – if one could grace the clothes it wore by that name – as winter clothing had been low in logistic priority and had not yet left the Delta of Egypt. Fortunately everybody rose to the occasion, worked flat-out all round the clock, and broke all the rules in improvising what was needed. Harding's combination of energy, will-power, clear headedness and charm were never more needed and were employed to the full.

The desert over which 7th Armoured Division had to pass turned out to be very rocky and slower for the tanks to move over than had been expected. When the division was refuelling at a dump which had been placed well in advance of all but the foremost armoured car patrols two days before, it was decided to send a wheeled force ahead of the tanks under command of Lieutenant-

Colonel John Combe, the commanding officer of 11th Hussars, the armoured car regiment which was leading the way. This consisted, in addition to his own regiment and a squadron of the 1st King's Dragoon Guards, of a field battery of 4th Regiment Royal Horse Artillery, three Bofors guns of 155th Light Antiaircraft Regiment, eight guns of 106th Anti-tank Regiment and 2nd Battalion The Rifle Brigade, commanded by Lieutenant-Colonel Callum Renton. By 3 pm this force had reached Msus, driving away a small Italian garrison, and by nightfall the leading armoured cars were thirty miles further on towards Antelat.

The rest of the division, delayed by 'thermos' bombs (small mines the size and shape of a thermos) dropped by the Italian air force, continued to move through the moonlit night and by dawn on 5 February was just to the east of Msus. Further air reports had come in during the 4th making it clear that the Italians had already started to withdraw from Benghazi, and Major-General Creagh, who had been about to go on sick leave to Cairo when 7th Armoured Division's move had been ordered, decided to continue movement southwest to Antelat on the 5th, a significant decision for which O'Connor gave him full credit. Soon after midday armoured cars of 11th Hussars were observing the coast road between Beda Fomm and Sidi Saleh some thirty miles west of Antelat, and, not long after, the first Italian column appeared heading south. Combe's guns opened fire and threw them into confusion. This gave time for Renton's motor battalion to come up and establish a position between the coast road and the sea at Sidi Saleh before a large column of enemy tanks appeared, which they immediately engaged. By 4.30 pm, 4th Armoured Brigade, with almost all of 7th Armoured Division's remaining tanks, had reached Antelat and was directed towards the flank of the Italian column in the area of Beda Fomm, which it reached just as darkness was falling.

O'Connor and Harding had both been on the move separately during the day. O'Connor, accompanied by Brigadier Dorman-Smith, set off by car from Mechili, to which he had moved his headquarters, escorted by an armoured car with a wireless set. The armoured car and the spare staff car both broke down in the area of the rocky desert which had delayed 7th Armoured Division, and O'Connor and Dorman-Smith continued in a single staff car with no wireless, finally catching up with Creagh in the afternoon. Harding had meanwhile flown to the Australians to put Mackay in the picture and give him orders to push on as fast as possible by every possible means and route towards Benghazi. He then flew on, found Creagh's headquarters and landed beside it. When Creagh explained his intention to continue to move southwest instead of west, Harding had no hesitation in assuring him that O'Connor would approve. He then flew back to Mechili, while O'Connor, when he eventually joined up with Creagh, decided it was best for him to stay there as he would both be in touch with events and by wireless with Harding back at his own headquarters. The 6th of February saw the total defeat and final elimination of the Italian army in Cyrenaica, the Rifle Brigade and Combe's force firmly holding the stopper at the southern end against repeated attacks, all 7th Armoured Division's remaining tanks under 4th Armoured Brigade repeatedly attacking the flank of the column near Beda Fomm, and the Support Group, closely followed by the Australians, coming up in their rear. Soon after dawn on 7 February, after one final attempt to break through the Rifle Brigade, the enemy began to surrender. Twenty-five thousand men, including General 'Electric Whiskers' Bergenzoli, were taken prisoner, and over 100 guns and 100 tanks were counted on the battlefield. General Tellera, who had recently succeeded General Gariboldi as commander of Tenth Army, was mortally wounded. British casualties were very small. In the whole campaign they amounted to 500 killed, 1,373 wounded and 55 missing. They had captured 130,000 prisoners, 180 medium and over 200 light tanks and 845 guns, their two divisions destroying ten Italian. O'Connor and Harding had good reason to be as proud of themselves as they were of the troops under O'Connor's command.

But there was no time for reflection. The problem was what to do next. O'Connor's natural reaction was to press on, and, at the time, Harding supported him. Already, at the end of the day of 7 February, O'Connor had asked Dorman-Smith, returning to GHQ, to propose to Wavell that he be allowed to advance as far as Sirte and, if it proved possible, all the way to Tripoli. Meanwhile the armoured cars of 11th Hussars pushed on to Agedabia, El Agheila and some fifty miles beyond into Tripolitania without meeting opposition.

Dorman-Smith did not reach Cairo until the early hours of 12 February, by which time the decisions had been taken. On 10 February Wavell had signalled the CIGS, Dill, saying that it seemed possible that Tripoli might yield to a small force 'if dispatched without undue delay', but making it clear that he had not fully considered all the implications and that it was likely to meet opposition from the navy and air force. Meanwhile he was provisionally planning to advance to Sirte and asked for views, including the possible effect on the French in North Africa. When Dill put this to a War Cabinet meeting on the evening of the 11th, suggesting that no troops were available for Greece, Churchill saw red and, as he was to do on several further occasions, complained of the number of men at Wavell's disposal, so few of whom appeared ever to reach the front line. The result was a long signal from Churchill to Wavell of which the third paragraph read :

> We should have been content with making a safe flank for Egypt at Tobruk, and we told you that thereafter Greece and/or Turkey must have priority, but that if you could get Benghazi easily and without prejudice to European calls so much the better. We are delighted that you have got this prize three weeks ahead of expectation, but this does not alter, indeed it rather confirms, our previous directive, namely, that your major effort must now be to aid Greece and/or Turkey. This rules out any serious effort against Tripoli, although minor demonstrations thitherwards would be a useful feint. You should therefore make yourself secure in Benghazi and concentrate all available forces in the Delta in preparation for movement to Europe.

On the day, 12 February, that this signal was received, Rommel and the leading elements of the German 5th Light Panzer Division, later to become 21st Panzer Division, landed at Tripoli. Four days later their first troops had taken up positions at Sirte and Rommel had submitted a plan to General Gariboldi, who had replaced Graziani in overall command in Libya on 11 February, to defend Tripolitania in that area.

In retrospect O'Connor came to feel that he should have pressed harder to be allowed to push on and take the considerable risks involved, which could possibly have resulted in Tripoli falling into our hands before the Germans had disembarked, with all that that could have meant for the future of the war in North Africa and the Mediterranean. Harding in retrospect took the opposite view : that without strong air and naval support, which would not have been forthcoming, we would not have been able to maintain a force there even if, as was not likely, Tripoli had surrendered without a struggle. The forces there, having been reinforced in the meantime, were considerably larger than the one division assumed by 13 Corps intelligence.

For his contribution to the victory Harding was both mentioned in despatches and created a Commander of the Order of the British Empire. He and O'Connor had made a powerful team, both frank, straightforward men, sharing their thoughts so that each could predict the reaction of the other. Harding had developed a strong admiration for O'Connor, for his foresight, his agility of mind and his drive. His own contribution had been to draw out and then formulate O'Connor's thoughts and concepts, and transform them into clear and definite orders. In particular he was always concerned to see that the next step ahead was thought out, planned in detail and that the orders to execute it had been issued in advance, so that only a codeword was needed to implement them. As a result there had been no delay in moving forward to Tobruk as soon as success at Bardia was assured, to Mechili as soon as Tobruk was about to fall, and on from Mechili to Derna and beyond.

One of Harding's main tasks in this respect had been to bring all the resources of the staff together to see that as many as possible of the Matildas of Jerram's 7th Royal Tanks were available for each successive operation. He had been greatly impressed by the decisive effect which these tanks, small in numbers as they were, had produced on the battlefields of Sidi Barrani, Bardia and Tobruk. After each operation he had devoted much of his energy to seeing that Jerram had the support of all branches of the staff in getting his tanks repaired and refurbished for the next battle. His other main task had been to shield O'Connor from worry about the increasing load of problems arising from behind, from the pressure of GHQ and from all the difficulties of communication and logistics caused by the rapidly extending line of communication, devoid of all but the slenderest of resources. These threw a heavy load on the chief of staff. O'Connor was the first to appreciate this and his gratitude to his chief of staff was as great as his admiration for him.

CHAPTER SIX

TO AND FRO IN THE DESERT
1941–2

O'Connor, who was suffering from stomach trouble, now returned to Cairo and took over command of British Troops in Egypt from Maitland Wilson, who assumed command of all troops west of the Libyan frontier with a much reduced and less operational headquarters called Cyrenaica Command at Barce, with which Headquarters 13 Corps was merged. Harding transferring to it as BGS. 13 Corps Headquarters was originally replaced by 1st Australian Corps Headquarters, but the latter was soon removed and sent to Greece. 6th Australian Division was replaced by the partially trained and equipped 9th Australian, while 7th Armoured Division's place was taken by the 2nd, a division only in name, as half of it went to Greece and the remainder had already been mulcted in advance to keep 7th Armoured Division up to strength. Wavell believed that no serious threat to Cyrenaica could develop until May, by which time the two divisions should be better trained and equipped and two more divisions and supporting troops would be available. Harding did not relish the change from O'Connor to Wilson, whom he regarded as little more than an expert in minor infantry tactics. However Wilson did not stay long and was sent to Greece, to be replaced by Lieutenant-General Philip Neame, who was GOC Palestine, having commanded 4th Indian Division beforehand, although not in action.

By this time the Luftwaffe was beginning to make itself a nuisance, in particular preventing the use of Benghazi as a port and supply base for the troops in Cyrenaica. The logistic difficulties that this created, so much of the motor transport having been removed for Greece, meant that the Australians had to be held back at Tobruk. The best position from which Cyrenaica could be defended, at El Agheila, could not be occupied, and the much reduced 2nd Armoured Division was tied to operating and training within reach of a number of supply dumps round Msus. After a visit by Dill and Wavell in the middle of March, during which Neame, prompted by Harding, pointed out the weakness of his position, he was told by Wavell that, if attacked, he was to fight a delaying action from his forward positions near Agedabia, not hesitating to give ground as far as and even beyond Benghazi if necessary, making his stand on the escarpment to the east of it. It was more important for him to preserve his force against a serious reverse than to hold ground. Benghazi had little military importance and it was not worth risking defeat in order to hold on to it. These orders were confirmed on 26 March and three days later, Neame received one reinforcement, 3rd Indian Motor Brigade, which was positioned at Martuba in the centre of the eastern part of the Jebel. Wavell told Neame that he could expect no further significant reinforcement for two months and that his task was to delay the enemy for that time. Neame replied that his task was clear and that he would do his best to carry it out. On the same day, 30 March, Harding, as BGS, issued an operation instruction which stated that, since the enemy had occupied El Agheila on 24 March, there had been no sign that he planned to advance further. It did not appear that he intended to launch a major offensive, or was likely to be able to do so, in the near future.

Had Neame and Harding been able to 'see the other side of the hill', they would have found both Gariboldi and Rommel in agreement with them. The plan that Rommel put to Gariboldi early in March and to OKH in Berlin late in the month was for an offensive to be launched in May to reoccupy Cyrenaica and then to invade Egypt, finally capturing the Suez Canal. Considerable German army and air force reinforcements would be needed in addition to 15th Panzer Division, which was due to reach him in May. Berlin's response was not enthusiastic. He was told that he would get no further German reinforcements after 15th Panzer Division. Once they had arrived, the Agedabia area was to be taken as a jumping-off point for the recapture of Cyrenaica. Not until the British reaction to this operation had been judged would it be possible to determine whether more Italian forces would be needed to get as far as Tobruk. There was no hurry, and Rommel was to report in a month's time what he and Gariboldi had decided. On 30 March, a week after his return, Rommel ordered

General Streich, commanding 5th Light Division, to capture Mersa Brega next day, Gariboldi insisting that no advance beyond there should take place without his permission.

2nd Armoured Division's Support Group held a position about eight miles wide astride the road to Mersa Brega, its 3rd Armoured Brigade being some five miles away to the left rear. At 10 am Streich, after a lengthy reconnaissance, delivered a cautious attack, which was held. In the afternoon Brigadier Latham, the Support Group commander, asked for 3rd Armoured Brigade to attack the enemy's right flank, but Major-General Gambier-Parry, the divisional commander, thought it was too late to put in an attack before dark, and instead the Germans at 5.30 pm attacked the end of the Support Group position nearest the sea and furthest from the armour. Fearful of being outflanked and cut off, Latham withdrew to southwest of Agedabia and the armoured brigade kept station with him. In retrospect these decisions can be seen to have been fatally mistaken, giving Rommel the idea that, whatever happened, the British would withdraw. However these decisions were in line with Wavell's orders to Neame. There was no contact between the two sides on 1 April, but enemy patrols were in touch with the Support Group again early on 2 April. On this day Neame told Gambier-Parry that his Support Group was to continue to block the road but not to risk being overrun; that the armoured brigade was not to be committed without his permission (way back in Barce, with very unreliable communication between the two); and that he was to be prepared to move it back some sixty miles to Sceleidima on the escarpment west of Msus, from which it would be able to operate against the enemy's flank whether he went north to Benghazi or straight across the desert towards Tobruk.

At this point everything began to go wrong. Streich attacked the position covering Agedabia and by the afternoon Gambier-Parry was withdrawing, having asked Neame to let him keep his division together, if necessary uncovering the road. He only had twenty-two cruisers and twenty-five light tanks left and forecast a breakdown rate of one every ten miles. This message reached Neame just as Wavell, disturbed at the course of events, arrived to see him. Reversing the guidance he had given a fortnight before, he said that the armoured division's task was to impose the maximum delay on the road to Benghazi and that it should operate as a whole to effect this as far north as El Magrun, half way between

Agedabia and Benghazi. If, as Wavell, who appreciated the problems Rommel would be facing, hoped would not be the case, the division was forced as far back as this, the Support Group would continue to impose delay along the road while the armoured brigade would move right back to El Abiar, half way between Benghazi and Barce, to guard the flank of the 9th Australian Division, which had been brought forward to that area.

Harding was far from happy at the way Neame was handling things and took an opportunity to talk to Wavell personally and beg him to send O'Connor back to replace Neame. Wavell agreed and sent an order for O'Connor, accompanied by Brigadier John Combe, to come immediately to Barce. When they arrived on 3 April, Wavell had a private talk with O'Connor, who had known and admired Neame at the staff college and suggested that for him to take over in the middle of a crisis, when he knew and was known to none of the subordinate commanders, might not be a good idea and would certainly be hard on Neame. Wavell, after some hours' reflection, decided to leave Neame in command, but attach O'Connor to him as an adviser. By this time both Neame and O'Connor thought that the enemy would make for Mechili, repeating in reverse O'Connor's own stroke.

By the time Wavell's order had got through to Gambier-Parry on 3 April, everything had gone wrong. Rommel had got the bit between his teeth and, in spite of protests from Gariboldi and from those of his own subordinates who were running out of supplies, split Streich's division up into four task groups, one making straight for Tengeder, forty miles south of Mechili, one to Msus, one up the coast road to Benghazi and one branching off it near El Magrun to Sceleidima and Msus. 2nd Armoured Division was thrown into confusion, compounded by the destruction of its main petrol supply at Msus by the Free French company guarding it because of the rumour of the enemy's approach. Some elements of the division had intercepted the orders mentioning El Abiar and had set off in that direction. Gambier-Parry, fearing that the Support Group would be cut off on the coast road, wished to withdraw it and to concentrate his whole division south of El Abiar. Wavell was still with Neame when his request was received. He was told that he was no longer required to cover the road, but must hold the escarpment, protect the left flank of the Australians and guard the supply depot at Msus, which it was not realized had already been abandoned. On receipt of this, Gambier-Parry tried to reorganize his disorganized division in order to send a force back to Msus, but he was not successful and by dawn on the 4th most of it, in a very disorganised state, was south of El Abiar.

It was clear that Benghazi could no longer be held, and Neame decided to move the Australians back to the line Derna-Tmimi. Harding had to set in train the complicated orders for the demolitions to be effected in Benghazi and the withdrawal through the Jebel, while at the same time moving the headquarters itself, which had not been designed for mobility, and trying to get 2nd Armoured Division together as a viable operational formation. On 5 April order followed counter-order. When a large force was reported moving east of El Abiar, Neame ordered Morshead to withdraw 9th Australian Division that night and Gambier-Parry to move his division to Mechili; but when the report was thought to be false Neame countermanded the orders, so late that Morshead had already started to move and had to turn his units back in the dark. Next day, 6 April, it was clear from air reports that there were enemy all over the place, some near Mechili and others moving in different directions through the desert. Neame had left his headquarters to visit Gambier-Parry. O'Connor, appreciating that the enemy had started the movement which he had feared – to outflank the Jebel – decided that there was no time to be lost in starting the withdrawal and gave orders for the whole of 2nd Armoured Division to move to Mechili, to which in fact Gambier-Parry was already heading. Rimington decided that his 3rd Armoured Brigade had not enough petrol to get there and moved instead through the Jebel, becoming entangled with 9th Australian Division's withdrawal to the Derna-Tmimi line. Neame returned, having failed to find Gambier-Parry, and at 8 pm he, O'Connor and Combe set off to the site near Tmimi to which his headquarters was moving.

Harding and Nares remained until later at Marawa in order to ensure that communication was maintained until the headquarters was functioning again at the new site. They then set off together in a staff car. When they found that the track to Martuba, which avoided the descent down the escarpment into Derna, was blocked with vehicles of the Australian Division, they decided to take the road through Derna and, by doing so, may have avoided the fate which overtook Neame and O'Connor. At one point they were shot at but they finished up safely at the headquarters near Tmimi, just as a scratch collection of troops were engaging a small German raiding party nearby. There was no sign of the generals and, after he had tried several times to contact them by wireless, Harding was forced to the conclusion that they had probably been captured and sent a message to GHQ to warn Wavell of this. During the day the RAF reported that they had seen what looked like a party of British prisoners near Martuba and Harding decided that his fears were confirmed. He tried to organize their rescue by a strong fighting patrol, but it could not reach them. He had by this time moved the headquarters back into Tobruk and joined up with General Morshead. Between them they decided to hold Tobruk and organize its defence with every man they could muster. Harding got through on the telephone to Wavell, reported the situation and asked Wavell to come up, which he said he would do next day.

Wavell set off at 7 am on 8 April in an RAF Hudson accompanied by Major-General Lavarack, commander of 7th Australian Division, Colonel de Guingand and Colonel Gairdner. A severe dust-storm blew up but, in spite of the local RAF pronouncing it impossible to land, the pilot managed to get in to El Adem, where Morshead met them and brought them to the headquarters which Harding had set up in the Municipio in Tobruk, chosen because the telephone exchange there was intact. When Harding had explained the situation as he knew it, Wavell said: 'I see, I see. Do you think you can hold Tobruk?' Harding said that it could be done, provided that the German did not produce a mass of tanks and the navy could continue supply by sea. 'Well, if you think you can hold it, you'd better,' replied Wavell, who then wrote out in his own hand a directive to Lavarack to take overall command and hold Tobruk.

It was late in the afternoon before he set off back. The dust-storm was still raging and one of the brakes of the aircraft seized up as he was about to take off. It took an hour to repair and, soon after taking off again, failure of the oil pressure on one engine forced a return. After an attempt to cure it, they took off once more, but it failed again and the pilot was forced to land in the desert in the failing light not far from Capuzzo, the faulty brake then swinging the aircraft, which lost a wingtip and tail as a result. Fortunately the Commander-in-Chief was found by a detachment of Sudanese troops. Meanwhile GHQ had rung Harding to find out why Wavell had not arrived in Cairo. Harding was horrified and immediately began organizing search parties, and was relieved when Wavell got through to him on the telephone, having been unable to contact GHQ. Harding ordered an RAF Lysander to pick Wavell up at first light. GHQ remained in a state of anxiety, as Harding could not get through to them either.

When Captain Dent, O'Connor's ADC, who had not been with O'Connor when he was captured, returned to England in September 1941, he wrote to Mary :

> John gave me your address when I left him at Tobruk and told me to call if I was near your part, but I am afraid I shall not be for some time so I feel I must write to tell you about your most excellent husband. I am the dug out ADC to General O'Connor, so saw a great deal of your husband and I just cannot tell you how grand he was at Tobruk. We were all retreating over long distances and no one knew where anyone else was and then came that dreadful affair when both Gen. Neame – who was commanding in Libya – and Gen. O'Connor who flew out a few days before in an advisory capacity, were captured in the middle of the night, and our BGS took over command. He was simply wonderful and everyone there was full of admiration for the way he got people and units together, got out his orders clear and concise *and* so sound, sent people off to collect stragglers and others to make a hasty defence of Tobruk with Tank Corps men without tanks, RASC drivers without lorries, gunners without guns, signallers and sappers all collected and given jobs of defence and it is entirely due to John that we still hold Tobruk today.
>
> The two photographs were taken just after the conferences to decide the attack on Tobruk, in the one John – in a typical attitude of his is talking to Gen. Dickie Creagh and Gen. O'Connor is sitting on the table.[1] John is probably not quite as neat as when you saw him last but he had had the same pair of trousers and jersey for over a month.

By 11 April Rommel had surrounded Tobruk and immediately began preparations for an attack. Harding, under the direction of Lavarack, worked closely with Morshead on the plan for defence. It was based on the infantry standing firm and on flexible and concentrated use of the artillery, the exiguous tank force being the sole mobile reserve with which to counter-attack. It succeeded in defeating two penetrations of the perimeter by the Germans, the

[1] See plate 8.

more serious one on Easter Day, 14 April. Harding then left Tobruk to join Headquarters Western Desert Force, resurrected on its old site at Ma'aten Bagush east of Matruh, still as BGS. Here Beresford-Peirse had been appointed to command all the available forces: 9th Australian Division, now shut up in Tobruk, and a force hastily formed from 7th Armoured Division's Support Group and 22nd Guards Brigade, commanded by Brigadier 'Strafer' Gott, on the frontier, while 7th Australian Division worked on the defences of Matruh itself and Wavell turned his attention to Greece.

Rommel was not the man to give his opponents any breathing space. He made a further attempt to penetrate the defences of Tobruk on 16 April and again on the 25th, on which day his force in the frontier area under Colonel von Herft also attacked 22nd Guards Brigade and forced them off Halfaya Pass, thus removing a potential threat to the attack on Tobruk he was planning at the end of the month in spite of the misgivings of his superiors, German and Italian. The latter was carried out by the newly arrived 15th Panzer Division and was defeated by 26th Australian Brigade. The presence of this division had been instrumental in persuading the Defence Committee in London to take the risk of sending a convoy, called 'Tiger', through the Mediterranean carrying 295 tanks and fifty-three Hurricane fighter aircraft, of which all but fifty-seven tanks and ten aircraft arrived safely at Alexandria on 12 May. The fact that these tanks were on their way persuaded Wavell to tell Beresford-Peirse to use all the tanks he had to recapture the Capuzzo-Halfaya area as a preliminary to the counter-offensive which the tanks of 'Tiger' convoy should make possible. Accordingly Brigadier Gott's force, supported by twenty-nine cruiser tanks and twenty-four Matildas, launched Operation *Brevity* on 15 May. Rommel reacted strongly, and all that Gott succeeded in achieving was the recapture of Halfaya, which was lost to a German attack with 160 tanks on 26 May.

While this bickering on the frontier had been going on, events of great significance were taking place in the rest of Wavell's large and scattered command. Rommel's first attack on Tobruk had coincided with German entry into Belgrade; his last, at the end of April, with the evacuation of the last British soldier from Greece; the second loss of Halfaya with the final evacuation from

Crete. During May, Rashid Ali's revolt in Iraq had taken place, with the threat of Luftwaffe deployment there and to Syria. All this time Malta had been under attack, and the inability to use airfields west of Matruh was of great significance to the navy and air force, all the more so with the Germans now established in Greece and Crete. On the credit side, however, 19 May had seen the final surrender of the Italian forces under the Duke of Aosta in Ethiopia.

Under constant pressure from Churchill to do something to redress the depressing picture and to exploit the successful passage of the 'Tiger' convoy, Wavell on 28 May issued his orders to Beresford-Peirse for Operation *Battleaxe,* a counter-offensive in three phases : first to secure the Bardia-Capuzzo area; the second, Tobruk-El Adem; and the final, Derna-Mechili. The Tobruk garrison was to play an active part. Beresford-Peirse's plan was for Messervy's 4th Indian Division to recapture Halfaya with his 11th Indian Brigade and twenty Matildas, while 4th Armoured Brigade, with some eighty Matildas and 22nd Guards Brigade, both under Messervy, would advance above the escarpment to capture Capuzzo and Bardia. Creagh, with 7th Armoured Division's one hundred cruisers and Gott's Support Group, was to move wider round the flank of the enemy position at Hafid and Sidi Omar. Beresford-Peirse and Harding were to move the headquarters up to Sidi Barrani, as far forward as they could go and still keep in touch with the RAF, but sixty miles and a long difficult drive from the battle area.

Unfortunately the secrecy which had been so successful a feature of the battle of Sidi Barrani was not achieved for *Battleaxe,* and from wireless intercept and other sources Rommel was aware at least that an attack was planned and was ready to meet it when it came on 15 June. By the end of the day 11th Indian Brigade had failed to capture Halfaya and 7th Armoured Division had been reduced to forty-eight tanks, partly casualties from the German 88mm – in use for the first time – and 50mm anti-tank guns, partly from breakdowns to which the newly arrived Crusaders were prone. The 4th Armoured Brigade's Matildas had penetrated north of Capuzzo, but the Guards had been unable to follow them. Beresford-Peirse's plan for the 16th was to leave to Messervy the task of clearing up the Capuzzo-Halfaya area and pressing on to Bardia, while switching 4th Armoured Brigade to Creagh to deal with the German tanks and positions between Sidi Omar and Hafid; but a strong counter-attack by Neumann-Silkow's 15 Panzer Division round Capuzzo prevented this plan from being put into effect, leaving Creagh's reduced cruiser force to face von Ravenstein's 5th Light Division on its own. Again on the 17th the same plan was ordered, but Gatehouse's Matilda force was now down to eighteen and the cruisers to twenty-eight. A double enveloping movement by 15th Panzer Division from the north and 5th Light Division from the west threatened to cut off the remaining tanks as well as the Guards and the Support Group. Withdrawal was therefore order-ed, leaving sixty-four Matildas and twenty-seven cruiser tanks knocked out or broken down in the hands of the enemy, who himself had lost only twelve tanks.

Reflecting on *Battleaxe,* Harding laid a large share of the blame on faulty intelligence. The Director of Intelligence at GHQ, Brigadier Shearer, had advised Wavell that the German supply system was inadequate to enable them to resist an attack or to pursue an offensive. Neither Harding nor Beresford-Peirse had been keen to launch *Battleaxe* at that time. The 'Tiger' convoy tanks were new, and there had not been time fully to re-equip 7th Armoured Division either in numbers or to see that the tanks they did receive were fully fit for battle. The capability of the Germans had been underestimated, and too optimistic a view taken of our own. Harding found Beresford-Peirse gallant, quick and decisive, but, apart from his experience with 4th Indian Division at Sidi Barrani, he had had no experience of armoured warfare. He liked Harding to accompany him everywhere, which left no senior officer in charge of operations in the headquarters when they were away. Wavell, when he flew up towards the end of *Battleaxe* and found them both absent, was angered by this. It was a sad occa-sion. The failure of the attack on which his hopes had been based, coming on top of all the strains and stresses of Greece and Crete, not unnaturally upset him. Harding had never seen him so dis-tressed and angry, on the verge of tears from his one eye.

It was not only to Wavell that this failure had come as a bitter blow, and heads began to fall. On 22 June Wavell was replaced by Auchinleck and at the same time Creagh handed over to Gott. Beresford-Peirse himself remained until the reorganization in October connected with the formation of the 8th Army. Auchin-leck's refusal to be hurried prematurely into launching another counter-offensive to regain contact with Tobruk gave Western Desert Force a breathing space in the hot summer days.

Harding's first DSO was awarded to him at this time. The citation read :

> As Brigadier General Staff Cyrenaica Command, on the capture of his Commander, and due to the dispersion of other forces, Brigadier Harding in fact exercised command for several days of the withdrawal from Cyrenaica. The sound decisions which he took and the firm control which he exercised in circumstances of the greatest difficulty had great effect upon the stabilization of the enemy advance, and the restoration of control and morale amongst our own forces. His services were invaluable and have had a marked effect upon the subsequent course of the campaign. During the offensive of May and June 1941, his services as Brigadier General Staff, Western Desert Force, have been of outstanding merit.

When General Creagh returned to England shortly afterwards, he wrote to Mary :

> A line to tell you that 6 weeks ago I saw your John and that he is in cracking order and a great chap. You won't know who I am but I commanded the 7th Armd Division and am now about to land in England for another job at home. John has done sterling work and in a very delightful way : everyone has the greatest respect and affection for him. Wrapped up in that small exterior is a very stout heart and very sound sense, and you can be very proud of him.

While Western Desert Force was being built up both in forces and in the logistic backing needed to support a counter-offensive, 9th Australian Division in Tobruk, at the demand of the Australian government, was replaced by Scobie's 70th (ex-6th) British Division and the Polish Carpathian Brigade. The frontier area was looked after by a force drawn from 7th Armoured and 4th Indian Divisions, the only incident being a foray by Rommel in September, the result of which was to persuade him that Auchinleck was making no preparations for an offensive which might interfere with his own plan for a renewed attack on Tobruk.

In fact however Auchinleck's plans were well advanced, although he was not prepared to give in to Churchill's pressure to launch his offensive in August or September, Auchinleck taking the line that he must have two, preferably three, armoured divisions before he could start an operation designed to recapture the whole of Cyrenaica and its airfields, which were of such importance to bring help to Malta. To command the force he was building up, Auchinleck decided that he needed an army headquarters in the desert and, below this, two corps headquarters, one to command the infantry divisions operating in the coastal area, the other the armoured divisions in the open desert. Alan Cunningham, who had commanded the forces that had invaded Ethiopia from East Africa, was chosen for the army command, designated 8th Army. HQ Western Desert Force provided the framework for his headquarters, but threw off also a resurrected Headquarters 13 Corps, of which Harding again became the BGS, General Godwin-Austen, who had commanded the 12th African Division under Cunningham, arriving to command while Beresford-Peirse went to the Sudan. The armoured corps headquarters, 30th, was formed from scratch in a few weeks, largely from officers who had served with 7th Armoured Division. General Vyvyan Pope was flown out from England to command it, but unfortunately he was killed when the aircraft in which he and some of his senior staff officers were flying from Cairo to 8th Army Headquarters crashed soon after taking off. His place was taken by General Willoughby Norrie, who with his division, 1st Armoured, was on his way out by sea round the Cape.

The plan for the offensive, called *Crusader,* the first aim of which was to relieve Tobruk, was a repetition on a large scale of all that had gone before : an assault by a primarily infantry force on the defences in the coastal area, while the armour made a wide sweeping movement through the desert. The essence of the argument that developed in the planning stage, and continued throughout the battles which followed, was the extent to which these two should be closely linked, particularly the degree to which the movement and operations of the armoured forces should be linked to those of the infantry. The issue was brought to a head in characteristically blunt fashion by Freyberg at the operational conference on 6 October. His New Zealand Division's task was to outflank and roll up the frontier defences from Sidi Omar northwards, while 4th Indian Division attacked them. To support both these divisions Godwin-Austen had Watkins' 1st Army Tank Brigade of 132 Infantry tanks, two regiments of

Matilda and one of Valentine tanks. Gatehouse's 4th Armoured Brigade had been re-equipped with American Stuart cruiser tanks and was to play much the same 'pig in the middle' role that it had done with its Matildas in *Battleaxe*. In Cunningham's original plan it was to start the battle under Godwin-Austen, its task to entice any enemy armour that attempted to interfere with 13 Corps away to the south into the jaws of Norrie's 30 Corps. By 6 October, although its task was unchanged, he had been persuaded to place it under command of 30 Corps throughout. It was this that Freyberg did not like, fearing that the protection it would afford him as he moved round the enemy's flank might be removed if Norrie needed it elsewhere. Norrie disliked both the restriction placed on 4th Armoured Brigade and the concept that his armour should move to an intermediate position midway between the frontier and Tobruk and pause there until the enemy's reaction was seen. He wished to concentrate all the armour, except the infantry tanks which he thought provided 13 Corps with all the tank support they should need, in one straight thrust to El Adem and there join up with a sortie by the Tobruk garrison. Harding sympathized with Freyberg and Godwin-Austen argued that Gatehouse should remain under his control 'until the armoured threat was removed'.

It was not until 29 October that the issue was finally settled. 4th Armoured Brigade was to be under Norrie's command, but remain initially close to the flank of the New Zealanders, who would not be launched round the frontier defences until the outcome of the main armoured battle was known, nor would the sortie from Tobruk take place before then. At the time the plan was being formulated, Rommel's forces were widely split : his eyes were fixed on plans for attacking Tobruk between 15 and 20 November, and 21st Panzer Division, held in reserve south of Gambut, was considered sufficient to back up the Italian Savona Division in dealing with any attempt by 8th Army to interfere in the frontier area. 15th Panzer Division was on the coast close to the eastern sector of the Tobruk perimeter. These divisions had not moved when 8th Army moved forward on the night of 17/18 November, 13 Corps with two infantry divisions and 132 tanks, 30 Corps with an armoured division of three armoured brigades, totalling 491 tanks, and three infantry brigades, two of them in 1st South African Division. In Tobruk Scobie had four infantry brigades and 32nd Army Tank Brigade with sixty-nine Matildas, twenty-eight old cruisers and twenty-five light tanks. To deal with this formidable force Rommel had 174 German tanks in two panzer divisions, 146 Italian in one armoured and one mobile division, a light German infantry division (later to be called 90th Light) and five Italian infantry divisions. On the balance of numbers of tanks there were good reasons for expecting victory.

Rommel had not changed his dispositions, designed for an attack on Tobruk, when 8th Army crossed the frontier in the early hours of 18 November. At first all seemed to be going according to plan, the only serious clash being between 22nd Armoured Brigade on Norrie's left and the Italian Ariete Armoured Division at Bir Gubi, south of El Adem. Rommel seemed to have been taken by surprise, and there was no sign of his main armoured forces. At midday on 19 November Cunningham agreed to let Norrie go ahead with his thrust towards Tobruk, but insisted that Gatehouse must still stay near Godwin-Austen's left flank. The result was to split 7th Armoured Division into three groups, Davy's 7th Armoured Brigade and Jock Campbell's Support Group moving swiftly forward to Sidi Rezegh, while Scott-Cockburn's 22nd Armoured Brigade was engaged at Bir Gubi and Gatehouse, tied to 13 Corps, sent one regiment off to chase a German reconnaissance unit northwards west of the frontier defences. At this stage 4th Indian Division had moved a battalion round behind Sidi Omar and the New Zealand Division was some ten miles to the southwest of them and fifteen southeast of Gatehouse.

During 20 November it was learnt from wireless intercept that Rommel was concentrating his two panzer divisions to attack Gatehouse and concern was shown by both Godwin-Austen and Cunningham for the safety of the New Zealanders. In fact 21st Panzer Division had not succeeded in joining up with 15th when the latter clashed with Gatehouse late in the day in an inconclusive encounter in which both sides thought erroneously that they had effectively incapacitated the other. By this time Scott-Cockburn had arrived from Bir Gubi to join Gatehouse, and Gott with Davy and Campbell had secured the airfield at Sidi Rezegh. Cunningham's plan seemed to be working out and, pressed by Gott and Norrie, he agreed to order Scobie to start his breakout from Tobruk to join hands with Gott near Sidi Rezegh next day, 21 November. Soon after dawn Gott ordered Gatehouse to attack the panzer divisions, which were now concentrated north of him, from the east while Scott-Cockburn engaged from the south; but before his orders had been acted on the two panzer divisions moved off to the northwest in response to orders from Cruewell, the Afrika Korps commander, to deal with the situation round Sidi Rezegh. Unfortunately not only were Gatehouse and Scott-Cockburn slow to follow up, with both in difficulties over fuel supply, but the German move was interpreted as flight and a sign that the defeat of the enemy's main armoured force had been achieved. Prompted by Norrie, Cunningham spoke to Harding on the telephone and gave orders for Godwin-Austen 'to advance as he pleased, but not to take undue risks', an order which Auchinleck, when he was informed, approved. While 4th Indian Division attacked Savona's southernmost post at Sidi Omar, Freyberg moved round behind the defences and by the end of the day was established behind them, a warning having already been given that Cunningham might wish to transfer him to Norrie's command in order to help the latter to join hands with Scobie.

The day was one of crisis at Sidi Rezegh, where a fierce battle raged between the concentrated Afrika Korps and 7th Armoured Brigade and the Support Group, Scobie's sortie from the north making only limited progress. Neither 22nd nor 4th Armoured Brigade were involved, but by the end of the day they were close at hand. There seemed good reason to believe that the concentrated resources of 7th Armoured Division should on the morrow be able to finish off the estimated sixty tanks erroneously believed to be all that Rommel had left in the area. The South Africans from the south and the New Zealanders from the east could then safely move up and join hands with Scobie, who was told to defer any further attempt to break out until the afternoon. Harding and Godwin-Austen however did not take quite such a rosy view, and were concerned at the isolated and vulnerable position of the New Zealanders if the enemy's armour had not, after all, been eliminated from the chessboard, particularly as the enemy's frontier defences were still intact and any supply to Freyberg had to get round them. Their anxiety was justified by the events of 22 December. Davy and Campbell fought a gallant action all day to beat off the concentrated assaults by the Afrika Korps, while Gatehouse and Scott-Cockburn failed to intervene effectively and Scobie, under orders not to press his attacks, had merely improved the position of the salient he had developed towards Ed Duda. But 13 Corps had had a good day, Freyberg capturing Capuzzo and Musaid and isolating Bardia, while the Indians captured Sidi Omar.

Cunningham was now more than ever concerned that there should be enough infantry to secure a link with Tobruk, particularly as Norrie seemed to be slow in getting his South Africans up to meet Scobie's thrust. But at midnight, still without a clear picture of what had happened at Sidi Rezegh during the day, he gave orders for Freyberg to move west towards Tobruk. Godwin-Austen's task was to contain the enemy in the Bardia-Capuzzo area with the minimum forces necessary. Norrie was to complete the defeat of the enemy's armour and help the New Zealanders if they were attacked by tanks. He was to remain responsible for joining hands with Scobie; but when Cunningham visited Godwin-Austen early in the morning of the 23rd, he agreed that Godwin-Austen should become responsible for 'the infantry operation against Tobruk' at a time to be decided mutually between him and Norrie. 6th New Zealand Brigade had been ordered to start its move west the day before and by this time was not far east of Sidi Rezegh, having unknowingly spent the night cheek by jowl with Cruewell's headquarters, most of which they succeeded in capturing when dawn broke.

The day of 23 November, the German *Totensonntag,* was a bad one. Little was left of the forces that had fought so gallantly at Sidi Rezegh, which was now in enemy hands. 4th Armoured Brigade had been thrown into confusion by getting mixed up with 15th Panzer Division during the night. Cruewell, acting independently of Rommel, decided to break clear of this entanglement, join up with the Italian armour near Bir Gubi and return to attack Norrie's forces from the southwest. He succeeded in doing this without interference, until he attacked 5th South African Brigade southwest of Sidi Rezegh in the afternoon and overran them completely within an hour and a half before darkness fell. Before this had happened, the true outcome of the previous day's fighting had become clear to Cunningham. It appeared that 7th Armoured Brigade had no tanks left, 22nd only thirty, and nobody could say what had happened to the 4th. Far from the defeat of the enemy's armour having been achieved, it looked as if the boot was on the other foot.

Cunningham was deeply anxious and his BGS, Galloway, was worried at the degree of his chief's anxiety. Both separately sent messages to GHQ suggesting that Auchinleck should come up quickly. Around midday Galloway, with one of Norrie's staff (the author), met Godwin-Austen to decide details of the transfer of the main battle to him from Norrie. Godwin-Austen gained the impression that Cunningham was considering breaking off the battle for a time south of Sidi Rezegh, and was horrified. He felt that his corps was largely intact and that, once it had joined up with Tobruk, it need not worry about its long desert line of communication, but could rely on supply through Tobruk. He spoke by wireless (in clear, that is to say without any code) with Norrie shortly afterwards and formed the view that, although Norrie was dealing adequately with the forces in the desert, he no longer had the capability to link up with Tobruk. Godwin-Austen felt that he himself had. In a letter to Freyberg that evening he said that he refused to consider withdrawal and that he was confident, and was sure that Freyberg would agree, that with the infantry, tanks and guns he had they could meet and destroy the enemy's tanks; he was absolutely determined to relieve Tobruk.

Auchinleck reached Cunningham's headquarters late in the afternoon and soon put an end to any idea of breaking off the battle or withdrawing, in spite of the gloomy news that arrived while he was there of the fate of 5th South African Brigade. At 10.30 pm orders were issued for 13 Corps to assume responsibility from midnight for 'operations against enemy forces investing Tobruk, taking Scobie under command'. 30 Corps was to give all possible protection to the rest of 1st South African Division against tank attack and be prepared to go to the assistance of the New Zealand Division 'in the event of a concentrated enemy tank attack during advance'. From being in a backwater a few days before, 13 Corps was now in charge of the main operation, which was to be controlled from Godwin-Austen's advanced headquarters which Harding had moved round behind the frontier defences to Bir Hariga, ten miles west of Sidi Azeiz. When Harding got through to Cunningham to tell him of Godwin-Austen's intention to do this, Cunningham started to say that the headquarters must remain where it was, but Harding quickly told a junior staff officer to disconnect the line. Freyberg, leaving his 5th Brigade to look after the frontier area, had now moved the rest of his division to join his 6th Brigade about fifteen miles east of Sidi Rezegh, some twenty-five miles from Scobie's nearest troops.

The 24th of November started peacefully, and nothing much had happened by the time that Cunningham flew up to see Norrie, whom Godwin-Austen had already contacted, while

Auchinleck remained at 8th Army Headquarters drafting a new directive. But while Cunningham was with Norrie at Gott's headquarters, alarming news came in of enemy moving towards them. Norrie bundled Cunningham away just in time before Norrie's main headquarters and most of the corps supply transport was swept eastwards by the incursion of all Rommel's armour, which, regardless of Cruewell, had set off in a bold dash for the frontier, south of almost all of Norrie's remaining forces, most of Norrie's headquarters eventually joining up with Godwin-Austen's near Bir Hariga. Cunningham had flown to see Godwin-Austen there that afternoon. Both had agreed that Rommel was making a last desperate fling and that there was no need to alter 13 Corps' task. But the reports from 30 Corps, and what Cunningham saw himself as he flew back to his headquarters over the area in which Rommel's columns were putting hordes of vehicles to flight, did not reassure him. He found Auchinleck as unruffled as ever, taking the view that Rommel's action placed 8th Army in a favourable position. But as the latter flew back to Cairo next day, he decided to relieve Cunningham and sent Ritchie up on the following day to take over command.

Meanwhile, undeterred by the presence of Rommel's forces astride his rear in the frontier area, Godwin-Austen got on with his task, Freyberg having replaced the absent Afrika Korps at Sidi Rezegh, continuing his advance towards Tobruk next day and reducing the gap between himself and Scobie to less than ten miles. Godwin-Austen therefore ordered Scobie to attack southeast to join Freyberg, once the latter had secured the high ground which dominated the area between them round Belhamed, El Duda and Sidi Rezegh itself. One of Harding's principal difficulties at this time was to coordinate the action of the two divisions, see that they did not fight each other by mistake, and make sure that the RAF could support them – not easy when the situation was so confused, the enemy sandwiched between the two and communications both with the divisions and with the air force unreliable and insecure. The presence of Rommel in their rear now began to make Godwin-Austen and Freyberg think of the object of linking up with Tobruk not so much in terms of letting Scobie out as of getting themselves in. This feeling was reinforced when the headquarters of Hargest's 5th New Zealand Brigade, still at Sidi Azeiz, was attacked and captured by 15th Panzer Division on 27 November.

Had Headquarters 13 Corps remained at Bir Hariga, Harding might have suffered the same fate. Over the previous two days columns of vehicles, some of them almost certainly enemy, had been seen moving west, to the south of the headquarters, and there had been constant rumours of impending attack. Harding had calmly organized the defence of the headquarters, swollen by the unwelcome guests from HQ 30 Corps, had organized patrols of bren carriers to try and identify the columns which approached them, and by his example had removed the jitteriness which afflicted everybody in the rear areas at that time.

Feeling isolated and unprotected, and determined that Godwin-Austen should above all be able to control the operations of both Freyberg and Scobie effectively, Harding moved the headquarters on the afternoon of 26 November twenty miles further west to Bir Chleta, in order to be nearer to the main body of the New Zealand Division. Here he was only just to the west of the battle that developed late that day, when 15th Panzer, hurrying back to deal with the situation caused by Freyberg's and Scobie's attacks, clashed with 4th and 22nd Armoured Brigades. Unfortunately these brigades moved away during the night, leaving nothing between 15th Panzer and both Godwin-Austen's and Freyberg's headquarters. There was now nothing but some armoured cars of 11th Hussars between the headquarters and 15th Panzer Division a few miles away. Although they were shelled, they were not physically attacked. Harding moved again in the morning of 27 November a further ten miles to the west and tucked the headquarters into the edge of the escarpment south of the Trigh Capuzzo, prepared once more to defend itself from any direction. The vulnerability of a corps headquarters virtually in the front line persuaded Godwin-Austen that he should move it into Tobruk through the narrow corridor that had been established when contact was made between Freyberg's and Scobie's forces on the night of 26 November.

As they had no secure communication with Scobie, Harding decided that the only way to fix matters up with Scobie was actually to fly into Tobruk. He had a strip cleared and ordered a Lysander of 208 Squadron RAF to come up and take him in. The red-headed pilot's only remark, when given his destination, was 'Oh, Christ!' Harding manned the rear Lewis-gun while they flew low, shot at by Germans whom they could see clearly for most of the way. They arrived safely in Tobruk, where Harding made

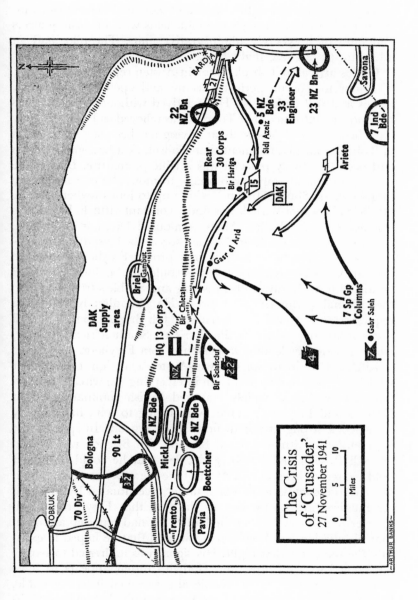

The Crisis
of 'Crusader'
27 November 1941

Miles
0   5   10

~ARTHUR BANKS~

arrangements for the night's move and remained to meet Godwin-Austen as he came through the minefields with his headquarters and most of Freyberg's administrative units. The pilot had an adventurous but safe flight back.

On his arrival in Tobruk, Godwin-Austen reported to Ritchie: 'Corridor to Tobruk perfectly secure and open to passage our troops and will be kept so. Have arrived without incident. Press may now be informed that Tobruk is as relieved as I am.' He may have been relieved personally at having reached the secure haven of Tobruk, but his statement that Tobruk as a besieged garrison had been effectively relieved was a trifle premature. During the next two days, attempts were made to move the one remaining brigade of 1st South African Division up to join Freyberg, whose 6th Brigade at Sidi Rezegh was under constant atttack. Before this was achieved the Italian Ariete Armoured Division intervened, separating Freyberg's from Norrie's forces to the south. Godwin-Austen urged Ritchie to get Norrie to protect Freyberg from these constant attacks, saying that, if this could not be done, he would be forced to withdraw both Freyberg and Scobie's troops back to the original perimeter of Tobruk. He had already refused a request from Freyberg for his battered 6th Brigade to move in, all hopes still being pinned on Pienaar's 1st South African Brigade, which Norrie was leading in person to join Freyberg.

Ritchie flew in to see Godwin-Austen early on 1 December while Rommel, well aware, from intercepting the wireless conversations between the widely scattered British commanders, that Norrie's and Freyberg's forces were trying to join, had already launched a strong attack to finish Freyberg off. In spite of the intervention of 4th Armoured Brigade, 6th Brigade was pushed off Sidi Rezegh and Freyberg decided that he could no longer hold the rest of his position. At this time there was some confusion as to whose command he came under, accentuated by the poor communications, partly due to the fact that Freyberg's headquarter was in the thick of the battle. He had reported at 10 am that his division had been cut in two and that he hoped to extricate the remnants that night. His signal was addressed to Norrie but copied to 13 Corps, and Godwin-Austen appears to have raised no objection, while Norrie also accepted it as inevitable. Ritchie does not appear to have been consulted. Freyberg withdrew that night back to the frontier area, leaving Godwin-Austen and Harding shut up in Tobruk with Scobie. There they remained until Norrie, having gathered his forces together again and been reinforced by 4th Indian Division, began an outflanking attack on Bir Gubi on 6 December, which led to a general withdrawal of all Rommel's forces back to Gazala. Tobruk was at last relieved.

On 9 December Ritchie handed over all the forces in the forward area to 13 Corps and Harding found himself faced with much the same situation as he and O'Connor had been after the capture of Tobruk the previous year, although the forces on both sides were now much larger. Rommel was meanwhile engaged in furious arguments with the Italians. He wished to withdraw all the way to El Agheila, while they refused to abandon Cyrenaica. Godwin-Austen's plan was for 5th New Zealand Brigade, which had not been engaged with Freyberg at Sidi Rezegh, assisted by the Polish Carpathian Brigade, to push along the coast, while Messervy's 4th Indian Division carried out a left hook to reach the coast at Tmimi and 7th Armoured Division made for that well-known spot, Mechili. These moves finally got Rommel his way, but only after a heated meeting at which Kesselring, Cavallero, Bastico and Gambara all tried to dissuade him. His intention to withdraw was now clear to Godwin-Austen and Ritchie, and all hopes were pinned on Gott to get round his southern flank and cut him off. Unfortunately a combination of refuelling problems and misunderstandings prevented this, and on 17 December Rommel slipped away, and did not run the risk of lingering in the 'Bulge'. Gott sent his Support Group, led once again by the 11th Hussars, across the desert to Antelat, but 15th Panzer Division held them off while the Italian divisions got away down the coast road. After giving 22nd Armoured Brigade a bloody nose near Agedabia on 28 December, Rommel held off the pursuit until he had established a firm position at El Agheila in the first few days of January 1942.

For his contribution to the victory of *Crusader,* as victory indeed it was, Harding received a bar to his DSO. The citation, written by Godwin-Austen, read:

Brigadier Harding's services throughout the operations for the expulsion of the enemy from Cyrenaica have been outstanding. His energy, fighting spirit and relentless determination to savage the enemy have inspired all formations under my command. All orders and instructions drafted by him are imbued with offensive spirit. He is that invaluable asset: a fighting

Staff Officer. His advice is invariably sound; his speed of Staff direction quite exceptional. His organization of Advanced Headquarters has ensured rapid movement and aggressive direction of operations. His personal example has been priceless not only from the point of efficiency, but also of gallantry when, on three successive occasions on Nov. 27, 28th and 29th Advanced Headquarters seemed about to be overrun by the enemy, Brigadier Harding's complete imperturbability and vigorous organization of offensive action impressed all.

I can think of no more meritorious example for immediate recognition.

The situation at the turn of the year bore many resemblances to that which Harding had faced the year before. Logistic difficulties severely restricted the size of force that could be maintained in the forward area, Benghazi not immediately being available as a supply port. The newly arrived 1st Armoured Division, which Messervy, replaced by Tuker in 4th Indian Division, had taken over when Lumsden was wounded in an air attack, was, except for the battered 22nd Armoured Brigade, new to the desert and restricted by petrol supply in its training. It was thought that Rommel would be in no position to take the offensive for a long time; but, if he did, he was to be held at Agedabia. Godwin-Austen's wish to station 4th Indian Division there, with 2nd Armoured Brigade in the desert to the east of them, was not agreed by Ritchie on the grounds that to keep that size of force so far forward would prevent the build-up of supplies for a future renewed offensive. The only troops forward therefore were those of 1st Armoured Division, its Support Group and 200 (ex 22nd) Guards Brigade near Agedabia and 2nd Armoured Brigade thirty-five miles behind at Antelat, where Godwin-Austen had his advanced headquarters.

Once again however the intelligence forecast, based on what was reasonable, did not hold good for Rommel, who had received fifty-four new tanks and crews and more fuel in a convoy which reached Tripoli on 5 January. His staff told him that this and another convoy, due on 17 January, would give him a local superiority in the forward area, which would disappear as 8th Army's logistic situation improved with the development of Benghazi as a supply port. Rommel, who knew that his superiors would not approve, therefore decided on a spoiling attack to take place on 21

ABOVE Rock House, South Petherton, Somerset

RIGHT Harding's father, Francis Harding

BELOW Aged one (right), with his mother and his sister Dorothy

BELOW RIGHT At Ilminster Grammar School

In India, 1925: the officers of the 2nd Somerset Light Infantry. Harding, the Adjutant, is second from the right in the front row

Mary Harding, newly married, in 1927

At the army point-to-point, Arborfield, 1929

In Libya, 1941: Harding (right), with Generals O'Connor (left)
and Creagh (back view)

Major-General, 1942

With Leese, Alexander and Airey,
Italy 1944

Knighted by George VI at
Lake Bolsena, Italy, June 1944

Harding with Major-Generals
Roberts (left) and Whistler,
all triple DSOs

With Mary in Germany, 1952

The Chiefs of Staff at the
Coronation, 1953

With Head and Mountbatten,
at the CIGS conference, 1955

With Montgomery and Mary, 1964

1964: Harding meets an old friend, Joe Guthrie, at the Finsbury
Rifles reunion

With Mary on his eightieth birthday, February 1976

January. When it was launched, the forward columns of 1st Support Group and the Guards withdrew to Agedabia as planned, but lost several vehicles and guns on the way, stuck in soft sand. Meanwhile Messervy ordered his armour up to an area twenty-five miles east of Agedabia. Rommel had now decided to take the bit between his teeth again and envelop Messervy's troops, not from the desert but from the coastal flank, and this he proceeded to do on the 22nd. Sensing that this was his intention, Godwin-Austen told Tuker to block the coast road south of Benghazi and to be prepared to cover its evacuation, while Messervy was to make certain that Rommel did not capture the supply dump at Msus on which he depended. The enemy's advance was actively supported by the German and Italian air forces, while the RAF was being forced to evacuate the forward airfield at Antelat.

Ritchie, returning in the afternoon from a visit to Cairo, took a robust view of the situation and thought that Rommel was 'sticking his neck out and would not be able to operate in force much beyond Agedabia'; but by a night move Cruewell had placed both his panzer divisions behind Messervy's brigade, and when they began to withdraw towards Antelat on 23 January the two sides became thoroughly mixed up. While this was going on, Kesselring and Cavallero flew to see Rommel and told him to withdraw to Mersa Brega, which he refused to do. Messervy's tank strength had been reduced as a result of two of his regiments becoming engaged separately in the day's fighting, but he had managed to extricate his troops from the net which Cruewell had cast around him. Godwin-Austen now feared a repetition of the previous year's experience, not being confident that Tuker could hold Benghazi or Messervy keep the enemy off Msus as well as off Tuker. Early on 24 January he signalled Ritchie, explaining this and asking for permission to withdraw, if necessary, towards Mechili. Ritchie took the same line as Wavell had with Neame, and said that 13 Corps must stand at Msus and cover Benghazi, but he did authorize him to make plans and preparations for a withdrawal if it became necessary, including preparations for demolitions in Benghazi harbour. Ritchie reported all this to Auchinleck, emphasizing that the permission he had given was only an insurance. Much of this was overtaken by events as the combined action of 15th and 21st Panzer Divisions, converging on Msus on the 25th, drove Messervy's weakened division northwards to the southern edge of the Jebel, sixty miles east of

Benghazi. This persuaded Godwin-Austen and Harding that a withdrawal from Benghazi could not now be avoided, and Godwin-Austen ordered Tuker to abandon it and Messervy to move to Mechili.

Auchinleck and Tedder were with Ritchie when he heard of this and, backed by them, Ritchie countermanded these orders at 8.30 pm. Tuker, instead of withdrawing, was to send columns against Rommel's lines of communication northeast of Agedabia, while Messervy was to protect Tuker's left flank and stop any enemy advance northwards towards his own position at Charruba. 'The most offensive action is to be taken together with the greatest risks', he wrote. Godwin-Austen, speaking to Ritchie by wireless, formally objected to this. With only forty tanks he did not believe Messervy could carry out his task. Ritchie was unmoved and assumed command over Tuker himself. Godwin-Austen issued orders as directed, but made a formal protest both at the orders and at the lack of confidence in himself. Ritchie soon found that both Tuker and Messervy confirmed Godwin-Austen's view of what they could achieve, but he insisted that his orders must stand. Dust-storms and Rommel's supply difficulties led to little activity during the next two days, while Ritchie continued to urge offensive action. On 28 January Rommel moved again, his main force striking northwest from Msus to the escarpment east of Benghazi, making a feint move towards Mechili, which was unfortunately seen by the RAF and led to Messervy being ordered eastwards to deal with it, thus taking him well away from Tuker, who now realized that he was in danger of being cut off in Benghazi. He insisted that he must withdraw at once and Ritchie agreed. He managed to get most of his division away that night, but the road was blocked by the time the 7th Indian Brigade's turn had come. They turned round and made good their escape by a wide sweep south and east behind all Rommel's formations.

Once again Harding found himself organizing at short notice a hurried withdrawal through the 'Bulge', and by 6 February the whole army was back on the line Gazala-Bir Hacheim, from which they had driven Rommel only seven weeks before. By then Godwin-Austen had asked to be relieved, to which Auchinleck had agreed, appointing 'Strafer' Gott in his place. (Freyberg's comment was: 'When the butler and the footman fall out, one of them's got to go, and it's usually the footman.') Harding stayed on for another two weeks and then himself left to take over the post of Director of Military Training at GHQ in Cairo, handing over to Brigadier 'Bobbie' Erskine. He had supported Godwin-Austen throughout the latter's disagreement with Ritchie, with whom Godwin-Austen had never been able to establish an easy relationship.

Harding liked Godwin-Austen and admired his courage, determination and robust, optimistic and cheerful attitude in times of considerable difficulty. He had had no previous experience of operations in any way resembling those he had had to command, and had leaned heavily on Harding's advice and calm counsel. There had been times when it was clear to Harding that Godwin-Austen needed both guidance and support, and he had never himself felt any doubt about what it should be. High in his priorities had been the need to keep control of the battle in the forward area, even at the risk of prejudicing communication to the rear, and to take a cool, calm and collected view when others were indecisive or even at times on the verge of panic; also to see that the tasks given to 13 Corps were commensurate with its resources.

Harding's own departure was not a result of this: quite the reverse, as it meant promotion for him. Apart from the six-monthly ration of five days' leave, he had been continuously in the desert in a post of great responsibility and strain for over a year. He needed a change, and GHQ sorely needed his first-hand and extensive experience of desert fighting. What those who had worked under Harding at Headquarters 13 Corps thought of him is well described by Sir (then Captain) David Hunt, who was GSO3 Intelligence:

> He was a man of the greatest physical and intellectual courage, strong-willed and persistent in all he did; but the vigorous impression he made on me was by reason of his sheer intellectual capacity. He had one of the most lucid and clear thinking brains that I have ever known. He was not outstandingly rapid or intuitive in his apprehensions, but he was quick enough to seize the elements of a problem and from that point on his mind worked like some beautifully oiled machine to deliver the brilliant and inevitable solution. He had a reputation for bad temper, which he would sometimes half humorously accuse himself of, but I never saw it.[1]

[1] Sir David Hunt, *A Don at War*, p. 69.

CHAPTER SEVEN

GHQ AND SEVENTH ARMOURED
1942–3

1942 was a difficult period for GHQ Middle East. The setback in Libya coincided both with the fall of Singapore and the consequent threat to India and the Indian Ocean, and with the threat to Iran, Iraq and Turkey posed by the German advances into southern Russia. Auchinleck took these very seriously and clashed with Churchill in suggesting that to make provision to meet them was of higher strategic priority than launching an early offensive in the desert, primarily for the sake of Malta. In Auchinleck's view Malta's importance lay in its possible contribution to the desert campaign, not the reverse.

By February 1942 Auchinleck had three armies to deal with, 8th in the desert under Ritchie, 9th in Syria under Wilson and 10th in Iraq under Quinan, responsibility for this area having been transferred to Auchinleck's command from Wavell in India in January. The problems which Harding faced as Director of Military Training were therefore immense and varied. Many of the troops and their commanders, particularly the divisions from India, were totally untrained in the requirements of mechanized warfare and were not well equipped to embark upon it. At the same time Auchinleck's conclusion from the desert war was that the armoured divisions had too much armour, the infantry divisions too much infantry and that the close cooperation between the two, and between all arms within both types of division, needed considerable improvement. The German panzer divisions appeared to be much better integrated operational formations. As a step to achieving this, the armoured division was to consist of only one armoured brigade, and its support group to be enlarged to become a motorized infantry brigade, both containing their own units of field, anti-tank and anti-aircraft artillery. In the infantry division a similar distribution of artillery and engineers to the brigades was to take place; but at this stage he did not contemplate incorporating tanks in the division. The army tank brigades with their Matildas and Valentines, would be allotted as the operations demanded. Harding therefore had a dual task, to redirect training to suit this reorganization, benefitting from all the experience gained to date, and to bring up to scratch the new formations and units arriving in the theatre. In addition to this there was a large number of training establishments throughout the command concerned with training individuals in all aspects of their profession, as they could not be sent back to the United Kingdom for this. Harding threw himself into the task with his characteristic energy, enthusiasm and clarity of mind.

At the time he took over the post of Director of Military Training, Auchinleck was engaged in an exchange of letters concerning the appointment of an armoured corps major-general to his staff to coordinate the re-equipment and reorganisation of the armoured divisions and tank brigades, and to provide him with general advice on armoured matters. This was being pressed on him by Alan Brooke, who proposed to send McCreery, then commanding an armoured division at home. Auchinleck accepted him, but reluctantly, partly because he had been pressing in vain for other posts at GHQ to be upgraded to major-general, partly because he suspected, rightly as it turned out, that McCreery might not like some of the ideas that, prompted by Dorman-Smith, Auchinleck was proposing for a closer merger of armoured and infantry formations, and partly because he found heads of arms and services inclined to treat their own arm or service as a private empire to the frustration of himself and the general staff. Harding's post as Director of Military Training would clearly be much affected by this, as McCreery would expect to have the last word in supervising the training of armoured units. The problem of co-ordinating the action of tanks and infantry, the degree to which the actions of one should be subordinated to the needs of the other, the tactics to be employed and the part that artillery should play in them were matters of keen controversy which affected both training and organization. Harding was later, as DCGS at GHQ, to become responsible for the latter as well as the former and to find himself at the heart of the disputes which raged in this field.

Very soon after he had arrived at GHQ, General Arthur Smith, who had been Wavell's popular and respected Chief of Staff from the very beginning, left. Brooke had suggested that he be replaced by Ritchie and that Beresford-Peirse should take over the 8th Army, but Auchinleck did not wish to remove Ritchie and did not consider Beresford-Peirse of the calibre of an army commander. Brooke then suggested Pownall, who had been Chief of Staff to Wavell's ill-fated ABDA (American British Dutch Australian) command in the Far East, but Auchinleck pressed for and obtained Corbett, an Indian Army Officer then commanding 4 Corps in Iraq. It was an unfortunate choice. He had no experience of a large headquarters like GHQ, nor of modern warfare, and Harding, in common with many others, thought little of him.

Auchinleck fell increasingly under the influence of Dorman-Smith, who had been commandant of the Middle East staff college at Haifa since Wavell's time and whom Auchinleck had known well when he had been Director of Military Training in India. When 8th Army had been pushed out of most of Cyrenaica, Auchinleck had sent him up to the desert to make a personal report on the state of the army in the light of recent events. On his return Dorman-Smith had recommended that Ritchie should be replaced and return to GHQ as deputy chief of the general staff; but Auchinleck felt that he could not sack Ritchie only three months after sacking Cunningham. Not only would it be unfair to Ritchie after the victory of *Crusader,* but it would affect the morale of 8th Army. So Dorman-Smith himself became DCGS instead. Harding, who knew Dorman-Smith well, had considerable reservations about the soundness of the advice he gave and distrusted the growing influence he acquired over Auchinleck. Like many others, he respected Dorman-Smith's brain and his ability as a critic to analyse the faults in the actions and ideas of others; but he had no respect for Dorman-Smith's appreciation of the realities of the battlefield. Auchinleck was determined not to appear a blimp and tended to favour any idea of Dorman-Smith's that appeared unorthodox. Harding found this situation particularly difficult when, later on, he took over responsibility for organization as well as training and became a second DCGS, Dorman-Smith covering operations and intelligence. Harding was excluded from the operational conferences on security grounds, and found it difficult to get what he wanted done through the vast and cumbrous base organization to which Auchinleck paid little attention. To try through Corbett was a waste of time.

One of the principal problems that arose towards the end of

Auchinleck's time resulted from his desire to go further with abolishing the distinction between armoured and infantry divisions. The disasters of the summer fighting round Tobruk and his experience in command in the battles of July on the Alamein line had persuaded Auchinleck that all divisions should consist of one armoured and two infantry brigade groups, apart from a light armoured division which should be created out of the cruiser tanks, unsuitable for close fighting, and armoured cars. McCreery was strongly opposed to this and found himself, as he had done for most of his time as 'Major-General AFV', at odds with both Dorman-Smith and Auchinleck. Harding, who got on well with McCreery, even if he did not always agree with him, acted as a go-between. Auchinleck's proposal had not been implemented at the time of his dismissal, and was not to be, except in the case of the New Zealand Division.

In the controversy which subsequently arose over the degree to which Montgomery's first successful battle, that of Alam el Halfa at the beginning of September, depended on plans made by Auchinleck before he left, Harding played a crucial part. Montgomery, having taken over command of 8th Army on 13 August, two days before Auchinleck had authorized him to do so, had spent the 14th touring the area and decided that he must have an additional division to hold the Alam el Halfa ridge in the left rear of the line. He knew that the 44th Division, which had recently arrived from England, was training in the base area and wished it to be sent up to him. In his memoirs[1] he wrote : 'We had a little trouble with the staff at GHQ when de Guingand telephoned these requests that night. I then got on direct to Alexander and he agreed to everything; I do not know if he consulted Auchinleck who was due to go the next morning.' Harding's account differs. The staff had told de Guingand that they would try and get some parts of the division moving in a few days' time, but that the division as a whole could not be complete in the forward area earlier than already planned. Montgomery then himself rang Harding, who said that he would see what he could do, adding : 'In any case they're not properly trained', a remark which Montgomery did not like as they had been under his own

[1] Montgomery of Alamein, *Memoirs*, p. 105.

command in England. Harding then went to Corbett, who said they were not fit to go and not properly equipped; but added 'You'd better go and see the C-in-C'. 'Who is the C-in-C?' asked Harding. 'You'd better see the Auk first. I think he's with Casey' was the answer. Harding found Auchinleck, who said : 'Have you asked Alex?' 'No', said Harding. 'Where is he?' 'I think he's at the embassy', said Auchinleck. Harding found him there, discussing pictures with Sir Miles Lampson, the ambassador. 'If that's what Monty wants, let him have it,' was Alexander's reply, no doubt one that was to be repeated many times thereafter. Harding rang Montgomery and told him the answer, and said that his advice was that the division should only be used in a defensive role and that he personally would do all he could to get the division ready, which he devoted the whole of the following day to doing.

Much has been made of Montgomery's impact on 8th Army. Little is ever said of the impact that Alexander and his Chief of Staff, McCreery, made on the base organization, which Harding had found so cumbrous and on which Auchinleck and Corbett had made so little impression. Harding noticed the rapid transformation that came about under the new management, which saw its principal task as that of seeing that 8th Army got what it needed. Harding welcomed the new brooms, although he felt sorry both for Ritchie and for Auchinleck. The former he recognized as a sound and gallant officer, but considered his real level to have been that of a divisional commander. Auchinleck he admired as a man of the highest principles and integrity, by no means stupid, but certainly not clever. He felt that he had no real concept of armoured warfare in the desert, and that he achieved results 'more by guts than by skill'.

As soon as Rommel's attempt to defeat Montgomery, which started on 31 August and came to an end on 6 September and is known as the battle of Alam el Halfa, had clearly failed, Montgomery wasted no time in setting in hand the reorganization, re-equipment and retraining he required for the battle which, to use his own words, was to 'see off' Rommel once and for all. One of the measures was to continue the process he had already started of replacing old desert hands as commanders by new brooms. One of those to be replaced was the commander of the oldest of all the groups of desert hands, 7th Armoured Division. Its commander was the one-armed Major-General Callum Renton, who had commanded 2nd Battalion The Rifle Brigade in O'Connor's campaign against the Italians, and later 7th Motor Brigade, until taking over command of the division when Messervy was dismissed after the debacle round Tobruk. He and Horrocks, who had taken over 13 Corps from Gott when he was killed, had clashed both before and during the battle of Alam el Halfa, and he was considered, not without justification, as being too imbued with the spirit of sacrificing ground for the sake of preserving the force. On the El Alamein line there was no more ground left to sacrifice. Harding was chosen to replace him, and no better choice could have been found. To have imposed one of the white-skinned new brooms from England on the 'desert rats' would have been greatly resented. Harding had more experience of the desert war than any other senior officer in Egypt, and all the qualities to revivify, inspire, drive and lead a division which, although its tail was well up as a result of the success of Alam el Halfa, in which it had played the major part, took a somewhat patronizing view of the new arrivals.

Harding assumed command on 17 September and the situation explained to him by his GSO1 (the author) posed certain problems. Although Rommel's attack had failed, he had not been driven back to where he had started from, but had been left in possession of the three minefields and defences which had formed 7th Armoured Division's front line before the battle, the southern end of which included the dominating hill of Qaret el Himeimat, overlooking the whole area. Not only was it necessary to lay new minefields, covered by new positions, overlooked by Himeimat, but any future attempt to attack the enemy in this sector would have to pass through these and then force its way through three successive minefields, which we had ourselves laid and which would certainly be strengthened by the enemy forces occupying them, the Italian Folgore Division, one of their best. There was much to be done in order to get ready. Montgomery was under considerable pressure from Churchill to attack in the full-moon period in September, less than three weeks after the end of the Alam el Halfa battle, in order to engage the attention and resources of the enemy at the eastern end of the Mediterranean before the launching of Operation *Torch*, the Anglo-American invasion of North Africa, which it was hoped would take place not later than mid-October. But Montgomery was adamant in insisting that he could not be ready until the full-moon period of October, and he got his way.

Even this period of just under seven weeks seemed all too short to Harding and his staff, as an almost complete change round of brigades had to take place. The 7th Motor Brigade left on 23 September to join 1st Armoured Division. As a partial replacement the division was to receive Brigadier-General Koenig's 1st Free French Brigade, of which only the two Foreign Legion battalions were really fit for active operations; but they did not arrive until 18 October. Meanwhile 4th Light Armoured Brigade had to look after most of the front and could not itself be released for training until the Free French arrived. The 22nd Armoured Brigade, which under the brilliant command of 'Pip' Roberts had contributed so decisively to the victory of Alam el Halfa, rejoined the division and was able to devote itself to re-equipment and training, the latter concentrating on the task of forcing a way through the minefields. For this a special minefield task force had been formed, largely based on the reconnaissance battalion from 44th Division, which came under its command. The detailed planning and preparation of a major attack on fixed defences was something quite new to the desert rats, and Harding's clear and practical mind, allied to his experience and dynamic energy, proved invaluable.

In Montgomery's plan the main thrust of the battle was to be in the north, by Lumsden's 10 and Leese's 30 Corps. It was made clear to Horrocks that the task of his 13 Corps in the south was a subsidiary one, designed to produce sufficient of a threat to tie down 21st Panzer Division for as long as possible. The attack was not to be persisted in at the expense of casualties which would cripple 7th Armoured Division's ability to participate in the final stages of the battle or the pursuit which was expected to follow. The main problems that Harding faced in developing his plan for the battle were formidable : the dominating position of Himeimat; the long approach to the enemy's easternmost minefield, clearing and marking four separate lanes through three successive minefields, defended by troops who would have had seven weeks in which to prepare and strengthen their defences; and finally the passage of a brigade of tanks through four narrow lanes to face, perhaps, 21st Panzer Division in an area in which, even if Himeimat had by then been captured, the enemy would still have observation over the whole area from the higher ground further west. If possible, all was to be accomplished in one night, for the longer it took, the greater the difficulties. Fortunately Harding

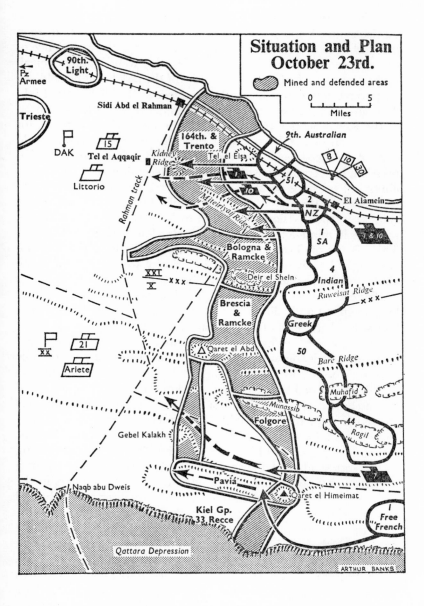

Situation and Plan
October 23rd.

Mined and defended areas

0   5
Miles

90th. Light
Pz Armee
Trieste
Sidi Abd el Rahman
DAK
15
Tel el Aqqaqir
Littorio
164th. & Trento
Kidney Ridge
Tel el Eisa
Rahman track
Miteiriya Ridge
9th. Australian
8   10   30
51
10
2 NZ
El Alamein
1 SA
1 & 10
Bologna & Ramcke
XXI
X
XXX
Deir el Shein
4 Indian
Ruweisat Ridge
XXX
Brescia & Ramcke
Greek
21
XX
Ariete
Qaret el Abd
50
Bare Ridge
Muhafid
Munassib
Folgore
44
Ragil
Gebel Kalakh
7
Naqb abu Dweis
Pavia
Qaret el Himeimat
Kiel Gp.
33 Recce
1 Free French
Qattara Depression
ARTHUR BANKS

97

combined the qualities of down-to-earth realism with an optimistic determination and resolution. There was no facile reliance on platitudinous exhortations towards which, after the experience of the summer, the men of the division tended to be wholly cynical. Appreciating to the full the difficulties of the task he set his soldiers, he nevertheless planned clearly for success. Roddick's 4th Light Armoured Brigade was to be kept in hand, except for the squadron of the Royal Scots Greys allotted to the minefield task force, for exploitation of 22nd Armoured Brigade's battle at the minefield exits. A further special task for the division was to create the impression, in accordance with the overall deception plan, that, as on almost all previous occasions in the desert, the main thrust would be made on the outer or desert flank. Every move and every activity in the division's area had to be planned and controlled with this in mind, a factor familiar to Harding both from Allenby's Third Battle of Gaza and from O'Connor's Battle of Sidi Barrani. Although the division was low in priority for equipment of all kinds and had none of the new Sherman tanks, yet it was with confidence and resolution that it faced, under Harding's inspiring leadership, a totally different task from any that it had faced in its two and a half years of desert warfare.

At a quarter to seven in the evening of 23 October, 22nd Armoured Brigade set off in bright moonlight on its ten-mile approach march to *January* minefield. There were some hitches and delays caused both by lamps marking the route going out and by patches of soft sand. The first gap, the most southerly one, was cleared by half past midnight, the two centre ones by a quarter to two, and the most northerly not until half past four; but the two southerly gaps could not be used by wheeled vehicles owing to the soft sand, and the most northerly was under fire from a strong enemy position. Both the infantry and the sappers in the minefield task force had suffered heavy casualties and only had enough men left to clear two lanes in the next minefield, *February*. Roberts ordered the attack to do this to start at half past five, but dawn broke before the minefield itself had been reached and, as it was impossible to clear the mines in daylight, it was called off. Daylight found Roberts's brigade crowded into a constricted area on both sides of *January* minefield. Their position was made more vulnerable as the two Free French Foreign Legion battalions, which had reached a position just west of Himeimat during the night, were driven off it in the morning, their gallant Georgian commander, Colonel Amilakvari, being killed. They lost all their vehicles and suffered severe casualties while trying to withdraw on orders from Koenig.

Horrocks visited Harding in the morning of 24 October to discuss whether or not a renewed attempt to get through *February* minefield should be made. They agreed that it should, and Brigadier Stainer's 131st (Queens) Brigade of 44th Division, one battalion of which had attacked on the right of 22nd Armoured Brigade during the night and suffered heavy casualties in doing so, was to be placed under Harding's command for the attack. The plan was for 1/5th Queens on the right and 1/6th on the left to attack through *February* minefield, two lanes then being cleared for 22nd Armoured Brigade to pass through, to be followed by Roddick's 4th Light Armoured Brigade. Warning orders were issued at midday for the battalions to join up with the minefield gapping parties at six, but there were delays in this, and, after two postponements, the attack started at half past ten. Both battalions reached their objectives beyond *February* without great difficulty, but the ground was hard, making the digging of slit trenches a slow business, and when they came under heavy fire they began to suffer severe casualties. The minefield gaps were through on both routes by half past two, but were under intense fire, which, in the northern gap, had prevented the sappers from marking the sides of the gap with wire as well as lights. 4th County of London Yeomanry lost twenty-six tanks trying to get through, their colonel, second-in-command, adjutant and one squadron leader being among the casualties. Some of the tanks had blown up on mines before they had been knocked out, which led to reports that the gap had not been properly cleared. The 1st Royal Tanks on the left had similar difficulties from an 88mm gun firing along the edge of *February* minefield. The account written in the author's own book *El Alamein* describes what followed :

Harding, down in the area of the minefields himself, had abandoned his tank and taken to a jeep, driven by his ADC who was killed beside him. At a quarter past four he decided to postpone further attempts to get on until it was light, when he hoped to deal with the anti-tank guns by observed artillery fire and get the engineers to clear the gaps again.

The minefield gapping parties could not be reassembled till seven, when it would be broad daylight. Before this Lieutenant-

Colonel Withers, the Commander Royal Engineers, convinced that they were already clear, said it could not be done in daylight. Harding told him to supervise it personally. Having made a formal protest, he went to the southern gap, called for volunteers and set off with them escorted by three tanks. At the entrance to the northern gap he found the fire so heavy that he ordered the rest of the party to withdraw, while he himself got into a tank and the Commander of 21st Field Squadron into another. They then set off to drive through the gap. The first tank was hit five times but not penetrated, emerged on the far side, turned round and came back. When almost back again, one of the tanks had a track blown off and had to be abandoned.

Withers was now able to tell Harding that the tanks which had been blown up on mines were outside the lane, and that there could be no doubt that it was the very accurate anti-tank fire at the exits which had caused the casualties. The fire was so heavy that it was out of the question to lift mines by hand. Harding accepted this and decided to abandon further attempts to get the tanks forward. The Queens had no option but to stay motionless where they were. Roberts was told to keep his tanks between *January* and *February* to support them, except the battered County of London Yeomanry, who were allowed to move east of *January*.

Horrocks confirmed this decision when he met Harding and Roberts at eight o'clock. Back at his own headquarters he tried to get on to Montgomery, but the latter was busy with Alexander. He spoke to de Guingand instead and told him that there was no sign of enemy withdrawal. Two alternatives presented themselves: to use the last remaining reserve, Whistler's 132nd Brigade, in a further attempt to break through *February*, or to abandon it and attack the western end of Munassib east of the minefields with Nichols's 50th Division, supported by Roddick. He preferred the latter. Even if Whistler was successful, the problem of getting the tanks forward would remain and 7th Armoured Division might lose heavily in the process. The other plan ran less risk, but might perhaps lead to finding another way through. Half an hour later de Guingand rang back to say that Montgomery preferred the second alternative. He realized that some casualties were inevitable, but wished to emphasize that 7th Armoured Division must be kept 'in being'.

Harding had been lucky to survive the battle. He had taken a tactical headquarters down into the minefield area, consisting of a Crusader tank which carried himself and the GSO2, Major Robin Hastings, while his ADC, Captain Cosgrave, followed behind in a jeep. In the congestion and darkness Harding found the tank an awkward method of movement and transferred to the jeep, from which he could speak to people, but the tank had to follow for him to maintain communication by wireless. He was driving the jeep himself and Cosgrave was sitting on the bonnet, watching to see that the tank was following, when a shell landed nearby, killing Cosgrave instantly, Harding was unhurt.

50th Division's attack on the western end of Munassib on the night of 25 October was a costly failure, and it brought offensive operations by 13 Corps in the south to an end. 44th Division took over the whole corps front with the Free French under command, and 7th Armoured Division was withdrawn into reserve with seventy Grant, twenty-seven Crusader and fifty Stuart tanks left in Roberts's and Roddick's brigades.

The 26th and 27th of October saw a major attempt by 1st Armoured Division to break out in the north thwarted by Rommel, who had now returned from sick leave in Austria, while 9th Australian Division tried to force its way northwards to the coast road. In the morning of 28 October Montgomery conferred with Lumsden and Leese. It was by now clear that 21st Panzer Division had moved north, and Montgomery decided that 1st Armoured Division should be withdrawn to rest and reorganize, while the Australians continued the pressure, Lumsden being prepared to exploit it with all his remaining tanks. 7th Armoured Division, leaving Roddick behind, but retaining 131st Brigade as a lorried infantry brigade, was to move north to near El Alamein station as a reserve. The attack which followed that night did not succeed in breaking through, and on 29 October Alexander and McCreery, prompted by messages of concern by Churchill, came up with Casey to see Montgomery, who was still intent on continuing his main thrust in the coast road area, adding the New Zealanders to the Australians. However, seizing some new intelligence of enemy dispositions as the reason, he changed his mind and planned instead that Freyberg, reinforced by brigades of 51st Highland Division, should attack westward, south of the Australians, on the night of 31 October under Leese's command. Briggs' 1st Armoured Division was to pass through Freyberg when the latter had reached his objectives beyond the enemy's defences. This was expected to lead to a major battle with Rommel's remaining tanks, after which Briggs would advance northwestwards to the coast to cut off the enemy in that area. Armoured cars would lead the pursuit in the centre, in which 7th Armoured Division would take part, moving up in reserve on the night of 31 October.

Freyberg persuaded Montgomery to postpone the attack twenty-four hours to the night of 1/2 November. As so often happened, the night attack reached its objectives, but in daylight the tanks found themselves under intense fire, their numbers already reduced by breakdowns and by tanks going astray in the minefields on the way up. Briggs was unable to exploit Freyberg's attack as soon as, or to the depth, intended, and the day was spent in battles between Briggs and all that was left of the Afrika Korps on the line of the Rahman track round Tel el Aqqaqir. However an attack by the Highlanders south of Kidney Ridge had revealed weaknesses in the enemy's defences which Montgomery decided to exploit. Leese was ordered to put in a further attack there on the night of 2/3 November; Harding, under Lumsden, was to move his division as far forward as possible behind the attack, ready to exploit by breaking through to the open desert and then swinging north to cut the coast road near Ghazal station; Roddick was also brought up to join in the pursuit. The attack that night did not greatly alter the situation, but made it possible for one armoured car regiment, the Royals, to slip through into the enemy's rear. It did however persuade Rommel to order a withdrawal of fifty miles to Fuka, an order countermanded by Hitler himself, as well as by Mussolini. Rommel compromised by ordering the German and Italian infantry to stand fast, while permitting the armour to make a partial withdrawal. He then sent a long signal to Hitler explaining how desperate was the situation of his army. This was followed on the morning of 4 November by a further signal requesting permission to withdraw to Fuka, a request which was largely overtaken by events.

Montgomery was now determined to break out to the south of where Briggs was still battering away round Tel el Aqqaqir. His orders, issued in the evening of 3 November, were that Freyberg, reinforced by Roddick, should lead the breakout south of where Wimberley's Highlanders had pushed forward south of Briggs. He was then to be prepared to make straight for Fuka to block Rommel's retreat. Lumsden to the north was to swing Briggs

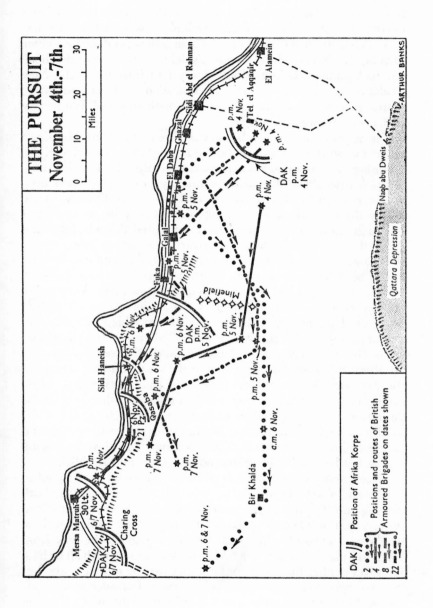

THE PURSUIT
November 4th.–7th.

Miles
0   10   20   30

Mersa Matruh
90 Lt.
6/7 Nov.
DAK
6/7 Nov.
p.m.
7 Nov.
Charing
Cross
Sidi Haneish
21 P.z.
6 Nov.
p.m. 6 Nov.
p.m. 6 Nov.
DAK
p.m.
5 Nov.
Qasaba
p.m. 6 Nov.
p.m.
7 Nov.
p.m.
7 Nov.
Fuka
p.m.
5 Nov.
p.m. 5 Nov.
Minefield
p.m.
5 Nov.
Galal
p.m.
5 Nov.
p.m. 5 Nov.
a.m. 6 Nov.
Bir Khalda
p.m. 6 & 7 Nov.
El Daba
Ghazal
Sidi Abd el Rahman
Tel el Aqqaqir
p.m.
4 Nov.
p.m.
4 Nov.
El Alamein
DAK
p.m.
4 Nov.
p.m.
4 Nov.
Qattara Depression
Naqb abu Dweis
ARTHUR BANKS

DAK)| Position of Afrika Korps
          Positions and routes of British
2   Armoured Brigades on dates shown
4
8
22

103

round northeastwards and push Harding through to the left of him to cut the coast road near Ghazal station, a few miles behind Rommel's defences on the coast road. These orders produced a tighter turning movement behind Rommel's defences than Lumsden himself had planned before Montgomery had introduced the New Zealanders into the picture. If Lumsden had had his way, Harding would have led the breakthrough south of Wimberley and been followed by Briggs.

The night of 3/4 November saw the breakout at last. Harding's desert rats started their move before last light and halted at eight, planning to move on again at a quarter to three, but this was twice postponed to allow Wimberley's infantry to complete their task. It was not until well after dawn, half past eight, that they were finally through, Harding exerting continuous pressure on everyone to get moving. Soon after 22nd Armoured Brigade, following the 11th Hussars, had started westwards through the open desert, they came up with a large column of enemy. Harding told Roberts not to be delayed by it but to thrust it aside or go round it; but, as he leapfrogged his regiments round its southern flank, more opposition was met. It was in fact the Italian Ariete Armoured Division. They put up a stubborn resistance which continued all day until they had been totally surrounded and destroyed. Meanwhile Roddick, leading the New Zealand Division, had pushed on fifteen miles westwards further to the south, and by the end of the day was the same distance south of Daba. Briggs had made little progress during the day and Lumsden had decided to send Custance's 8th Armoured Brigade during the night round to the south of Harding, directed on Daba, instead of between him and Briggs as had been planned; but Custance was slow in moving and at last light was still behind both Roberts and Roddick.

Montgomery's first orders were for Freyberg to be directed to Fuka, and Custance to Galal, between Fuka and Daba, both moving through the night, while Briggs and Harding remained stationary. But when the RAF reported during the night that there was a solid mass of vehicles on the coast road all the way from Daba to Fuka, Lumsden was told to push on boldly with all he had. However neither Freyberg nor Custance for one reason or another had managed to move very far before dawn. Lumsden meanwhile had told Briggs to stay where he was until first light, while Harding on his left was to make for some high ground west of Ghazal and southeast of Daba, Custance to his left moving as ordered to Galal, where he was to be joined by the rest of Gatehouse's 10th Armoured Division, from which he had been detached. When Montgomery's later orders were received, new orders were given at 4.45 am on 5 November for Gatehouse, joined by Custance, to make for west of Fuka, Briggs directly on Daba, and Harding to cut the road and railway between the two. Later in the day, Freyberg, transferred to Lumsden's command, was to capture the landing grounds west of Fuka.

Harding, knowing that neither Freyberg nor Custance had made the progress they had been expected to, pressed Lumsden not to add his division to the series of short left-hooks which had been ordered, but to release him, switching Roddick back to his command from Freyberg's, to move due west through the desert until he was west of Mersa Matruh; but this did not meet with approval. Had it done so and Harding been given first priority for petrol supply, he might have succeeded in cutting off all Rommel's remaining armour and put even more of his forces 'into the bag'. As it was, Custance's brigade was the only one to cut off a sizable force, most of what remained of the Italian 20th Mobile Corps. By the time Roberts had reached the area to which Harding had been directed, it was clear that the birds had flown. There was a long delay in issuing fresh orders as Montgomery was struggling through a tangled mass of vehicles to reach Lumsden. Harding did not wait, and, anticipating orders, began to move southwestwards. When the orders came at 1.40 pm, he was ordered to capture the landing grounds between Fuka and Matruh, west of those towards which Freyberg was moving, while Briggs was to get first priority for petrol and make a wide sweep south and then west to encircle Matruh, starting immediately and moving through the night. Harding, who was already on the move southwestwards, was in fact better placed to lead the pursuit, but pressure from the RAF to secure landing grounds and to open up the coast road to reach them took priority over attempts to cut the enemy off. At the time these orders were received, Freyberg was held up by a minefield and Roberts had to divert his brigade southwards to clear the tail of his division. When 11th Hussars, ahead of Roberts, came up against the same minefield, they found it to be a dummy one, laid by ourselves during the withdrawal in the summer. All this imposed a delay of some three hours, and the division halted after dark, when in any case it was running out of fuel, twenty miles short of its objective.

Rommel had intended to stand at Fuka, but realized he was being outflanked and gave orders that night for a withdrawal to Matruh, while Briggs, who had been delayed by petrol supply and other troubles, had only reached an area twenty miles west of Roberts by dawn on 6 November. At first light Roberts, accompanied by Harding, set off northwest and by half-past ten was in action against Rommel's rearguard south of the coast road. After a brief skirmish, the pursuit continued, although the tanks were getting low in fuel. This brought Roberts in the afternoon up against 21st Panzer Division on the reverse slopes of the escarpment above the landing grounds. They had run out of fuel, although this was not known to Harding. It now began to rain heavily and Roberts, taking advantage of the reduced visibility, tried to work round their western flank, but did not succeed in encircling them before it was dark, and those vehicles which could still do so got away.

Harding had received orders to set off as soon as he could on a wide outflanking move of 170 miles to the familiar ground of Sollum and Halfaya, but the torrential rain made it impossible to get the petrol vehicles up to the tanks, which even themselves had difficulty in moving. He was unable to start his move until two o'clock the following afternoon and only managed to cover twenty miles before it was dark. By then Rommel, with the advantage of a metalled road, was well on his way to Sollum, and there was no hope that Harding, whose tanks had all been old before the battle had started, could catch him. He felt intensely frustrated that he had not been let loose earlier. In retrospect he considered that Montgomery tried to get too many formations, more than was either necessary or desirable, out at the same time. They only got in each other's way and aggravated the problem of petrol supply, which was itself made worse by the traffic congestion and confusion in passing through the battle minefield areas. Harding had been greatly impressed with the skill and resolution with which Roberts had handled his brigade, another partnership of two small, lively and courageous commanders. As it was the wheeled vehicles that had the greatest difficulty in moving in the rain-soaked desert, Harding decided to leave 131 Brigade, now commanded by 'Bolo' Whistler in place of Stainer, and continue with 11th Hussars and Roberts, now reduced to forty-seven Grants and Shermans, fifteen Stuarts and thirty Crusaders.

The armoured cars crossed the Libyan frontier on 9 November and they and the Rifle Brigade entered Bardia on 11 November after engaging a train west of Capuzzo, the rest of the division moving up behind but held up for lack of petrol. The pursuit continued next day, and on 13 November the leading armoured cars entered Tobruk. 4th Light Armoured Brigade now returned to the division, while 22nd, its tanks completely worn out, was left at El Adem and 131 Brigade occupied Tobruk. Harding therefore continued the pursuit with Roddick on the coast road through the Jebel, and the armoured cars, both 11th Hussars and the Royals, once more cutting across the desert to Soluch, followed by a composite regimental group of 1st Royal Tanks, equipped with all the remaining fit tanks that Roberts could scrape together. Rain imposed some delay, but by 20 November Benghazi had been entered and contact made with a force defending Agedabia. Before they could be surrounded as Harding planned, they withdrew to the position at Mersa Brega, covering El Agheila, at which Rommel had decided to make a stand. By now Harding had outrun his supplies and was out of reach of the RAF, his headquarters suffering a severe attack from the Luftwaffe in which his chief signal officer, Colonel Maxwell, was killed. A pause followed while Benghazi was opened up as a supply port and 8th Army's strength built up. Harding had the satisfaction at this time of receiving a letter from Montgomery in his own handwriting which read :

Eighth Army

2-12-42

My dear Harding

I would like you to tell the 7 Armd Div from me that I am quite delighted with the way in which it has carried out the operations it has been engaged on since it was launched in the break-through on 2 November. The Division has done magnificently. It has shewn the whole Army how to fight the pursuit battle, how to worry a retreating enemy, and generally how to fight the mobile battle in desert areas and in Jebel country. I would be very grateful if you will tell all your officers and men that I am very pleased indeed with the way they have worked, and congratulate all ranks from me on a really fine show.

Yrs ever

B. L. MONTGOMERY

A description of Harding at this time was given by Colonel

Charles Turner, the principal administrative staff officer of the division, in a letter to his wife :

> We all think the world of him, so do the greater commanders (at Corps, Army and GHQ) tho' some may be jealous. He sleeps in the open, even when his own caravan has caught up with his constant sorties usually forrard, not even in a 'bivvy' (bivouac) tent like most commanders. Is well up before dawn. ('Charles', he once said, 'you can never catch up the hours of first light.') Often I've been at Main headquarters when he got back from an all-day reconnaissance and visits to most forward troops, after dark sensing his way and refusing offers to put up the odd Verey light to give him a line for navigation. It gave me personally a thrill of excitement these dramatic returns to Mike Carver's armoured command vehicle, where he'd at once pick up any of the information from map boards and signals which hadn't been already relayed to his Tactical Headquarters where the GSO2 and possibly ADC would have been accompanying him. Then, after making decisions and giving orders, he might condescend to have probably his first meal since before dawn. He travels always standing up in whatever it is – cut down staff car with a rail behind the driver's seat for him to clutch on to, armoured car or tank. Unless he is in a jeep when *he* always drives. He hasn't got into battle dress yet. Just corduroy trousers, cardigan and rather scruffy khaki neckerchief. Only his red hat and embroidered badges of rank on his shirt shoulder straps, which slip through holes in his cardigan, proclaim his rank. Even in the 'January' minefield days – as I call the first phase 23-27 Oct – he'd never wear a steel helmet.

During the lull the division was reorganized. Roberts's 22nd Armoured Brigade was replaced by Custance's 8th, which had been brought fully up to strength. Leese's 30 Corps took over responsibility for the front from 10 Corps, which was withdrawn to Tobruk, Horrocks replacing Lumsden in command. Montgomery's plan was for the New Zealand Division, reinforced by 4th Light Armoured Brigade (now commanded by Harvey, Roddick having been wounded), to make a wide movement south of the salt marshes which formed a feature of the El Agheila defences, to cut off Rommel, while Wimberley's Highlanders attacked Mersa Brega frontally. Harding, reinforced by one of Wimberley's brigades, was to attack south of the sand dunes, which stretched some ten miles south of the road, and swing up behind the forces facing Wimberley at Mersa Brega, but still east of El Agheila.

While Montgomery had been waiting for supplies to build up at Benghazi to support this attack, Rommel had been trying to persuade both Hitler and Mussolini that the whole of Tripolitania would have to be abandoned, if he were not to run a grave risk of losing all his remaining forces. By this time, it must be remembered, the allies had established themselves in French North Africa and their forward troops had come within fifteen miles of Tunis. At first both dictators refused to consider retreat, but eventually they reluctantly agreed to a withdrawal, if necessary, to Buerat, about two hundred miles further west and halfway to Tripoli. Montgomery had set the night of 16/17 December as the date for Leese's attack, but Rommel began withdrawing troops earlier. By 9 December signs of this were detected and it became a certainty. Wimberley and Harding were told to attack on the night of 13/14 December and Freyberg, who had already started his move, was told to hurry up.

Custance spent all day on 14 December battling against strong resistance by the Italian Ariete Armoured Division, while Freyberg, delayed by petrol supply problems, did not reach his objective near the coast road until late on 15 December, only to find it guarded by 15th Panzer Division. Harding urged Constance on 15 December to try and get round the opposition in front of him, but salt marshes and minefields, well covered by fire, prevented this and, as Custance was making no progress, Harding decided that Whistler should attack with his infantry once darkness fell. Before the attack was launched it was clear that the enemy had started to withdraw and, eluding the New Zealanders also, they got away down the coast road, leaving only 450 prisoners, twenty-five guns and eighteen tanks behind. Harding decided to face the risk of air attack and push his forces as quickly as he could head-to-tail down the road as soon as mines and boobytraps were cleared. On 17 December the division passed through the New Zealanders, picking up Harvey's brigade on the way, and taking over responsibility for the whole pursuit up to Rommel's next position at Buerat. Harding was for pushing on and believed that, given enough petrol, he could bounce Rommel out of his position by outflanking him. But Montgomery did not wish to risk a bloody nose and decided that he would pause again until he had built up enough troops and supplies to be certain of reaching Tripoli in one single stroke. So, reverting to its familiar role of patrolling and reconnoitring the enemy's defences and the desert around them, the division settled down for Christmas in an elated mood.

As at El Agheila, Rommel was trying to persuade his superiors that he should withdraw all the way to Gabes in Tunisia, while Montgomery was deliberately building up a much superior force. Rommel was reluctantly allowed to plan a withdrawal to Mareth, but told that he must take two months over it. A severe storm at Benghazi on 3 and 4 January threatened to postpone Mont-gomery's attack beyond his planned date of 15 January, but he stuck to the date and instead reduced the number of troops he planned to move forward. The plan was for the Highland Division, with Richards's 23rd Armoured Brigade, to press along the coast road, while Harding advanced south of Wimberley directly across the hilly and rocky desert to Tarhuna, on the escarpment fifty miles southeast of Tripoli. Freyberg was to be on the outside of the wheel, as before, on Harding's left. Harvey's 4th Light Armoured Brigade, although under Harding's command, would cover the New Zealanders' front and flank. Progress on the 15th, the day of the attack, was slow, the enemy putting up a spirited resistance; but during the night they withdrew and from then on it was the very rough going which delayed progress, so that only twenty miles were covered on the 16th. Contact with the enemy was regained on 17 January and the advance continued on the 18th, with Custance's brigade in action ten miles south of Tarhuna at last light.

Harding urged Custance to press on next day and prevent the enemy from establishing himself in a strong position where the road from Tarhuna to Tripoli descended the escarpment. Cus-tance set off again at dawn but made little progress. Determined to inject some vigour into his brigade, Harding went to join him, travelling in his command tank which he parked next to Cus-tance's. Finding that his radio was being jammed by Custance's, he moved his own tank away and climbed up on top of Custance's. The enemy artillery was active and Harding was standing up on top of the tank, trying through his binoculars to spot the flash of the guns in order to pass the target to his own artillery, when a shell landed in front of the tank, its fragments killing one of the crew who was standing there and hitting Harding right across his body from his left arm to his right leg, at the same time knocking him off the high Grant tank. His first reaction was to crawl under the tank, from which he was brought out when the shelling stopped and quickly placed in the hands of the nearest doctor. Harding's only memory of what then happened to him was his anger at the doctor cutting up his new pair of cavalry twill trousers. Custance immediately reported this to the author at divisional headquarters, who passed the news on to Leese. When Montgomery heard of it, he decided to send Roberts, whose 22nd Armoured Brigade was directly under Montgomery's command, moving between Wimberley and Harding, to assume command of the division.

The doctors now reported that Harding was very unlikely to survive a journey by ambulance back across the atrocious going over which the division had passed. The author therefore got on to Leese and asked for an ambulance aircraft to be sent up next day, by which time a landing strip would somehow or other be created in the forward area. Ambulance aircraft were not normally allowed so far forward, but Coningham, the Desert Air Force commander, gave special permission for an aircraft, escorted by fighters to the extreme limit of their range, to do so. The RAF landing ground reconnaissance and construction party attached to the division, supported by a whole infantry battalion, worked all night and by the morning had a strip ready. It was essential that there should be no delay in loading the aircraft, as the fighters could only stay in the area for less than ten minutes. Harding was brought by ambulance to the strip, loaded into the aircraft and away again in less than that time, while the fighters engaged the Luftwaffe and shot down two of their fighters.

Harding's departure was unquestionably a severe blow to the division, though softened by relief that his life had been saved. After the division had reached Tripoli four days later, Roberts returned to his brigade and 'Bobbie' Erskine, who had succeeded Harding as BGS of 13 Corps, now succeeded him again in command of the division. Harding had already been recommended by Montgomery for that rare distinction a second bar to his DSO, the citation for which read:

During the Battle of Egypt General Harding rendered outstanding and distinguished services. His personal gallantry in dangerous situations was an inspiration to his whole Division; his command and leadership of his Division have been of the highest order. The action of 7 Armd Div during the pursuit, and when facing up to the Agheila position, contributed largely to the success of the whole battle.

The first intimation that Mary had had of what had occurred came on the evening of 26 January. Returning from her canteen work, she was greeted by her mother's parlourmaid with the news that a telegram had been received saying that John had been wounded. Mary's mother had opened a telegram, sent off by Colonel Turner on 20 January on Harding's own instructions when Turner had seen him while he was waiting to be flown away. The telegram said 'Wounded not really seriously do not worry love John Harding'.

This was followed next day by an official telegram which said that he had been wounded in action on 19 January and that his condition was fairly satisfactory. This was elaborated in an official letter dated 26 January, detailing his wounds as 'a fractured right tibia, right radius and wrist, amputation of second, third and fourth fingers and penetrating wounds in the thigh, left chest wall and right arm.' It said that he was reported as suffering from shock, but that his condition was fairly satisfactory. A further official telegram on 30 January reported that he had been placed on the dangerously ill list, on which he was to remain until 17 February.

Mary was naturally very worried and distressed and longed for more news. A further telegram from John himself arrived on 2 February saying: 'Going on well hope John [John Charles] better and you well John Harding'. More personal news followed in the form of airmail letter cards – one from Colonel Turner, written on 20 January, went as follows:

As I am one of General Harding's staff who have seen most of him since he was wounded yesterday I feel I must just write you a line to tell you not to worry and that he will be perfectly fit in a month or so. I am afraid he has lost three fingers of his left hand and has a bit of a shell in his knee but the rest of him is all right and longing to be back with us at it. What an inspiration he has been and his name will continue to be, not only in this I think I may say famous division, but in Monty's Eighth

Army. His knowledge, brilliance and dash are alone responsible for the speed of this historic advance with so comparatively few losses. You may not know that his ADC was killed at his side on 25th October and that he was hit in an air raid in November and went on looking after his badly wounded wireless operator whilst everyone took cover. I know he will be furious when he knows I have written like this – but I think he was pleased when I said at the Main Dressing Station today, a few hours after the surgeon had operated, how much we would miss him and what an example he had been to us. His reply was typical and in a quiet voice 'I was only doing my duty Charles'. I know what Hardy felt with Nelson on the Victory.

This was followed by airmail letter cards from the matron of the 63rd General Hospital in Cairo, to which Harding had been admitted on 24 January, having been flown in a cold RAF Bombay aircraft from the New Zealand Casualty Clearing Station near Sirte, to which he had been flown on 20 January. It was not until March that Mary's anxieties were significantly lessened, as letters and messages arrived from friends and others in Cairo who had been able to visit him in hospital.

CHAPTER EIGHT

HOSPITAL, HOME AND ITALY
1943–4

Harding's wounds were severe, and he was in hospital at Helmieh near Cairo for three months. His hopes for the future were maintained by both Montgomery and Alexander. The first of a number of personal letters from the former, written in his own hand, was dated 26 January. It read:

> Eighth Army
> 26-1-43
>
> My dear John
>
> I was very distressed when I heard you had been wounded. It was a real tragedy for the Eighth Army : you have led your Division spendidly and have raised its morale to great heights. If ever a General deserved to lead his Division into Tripoli, and take part in the final success, you did. I am more sorry than I can say. I do hope you are not too bad; from the reports I have had it does seem that we shall see you back with us in due course.
>
> So get well quickly. And when you are recovered you can be quite sure of the very best job in my Army, or wherever I may be. You can have the great satisfaction of knowing that you have proved yourself a first class Divisional Commander in battle. We entered Tripoli at 0500 hrs on 23 Jan, exactly three months after we began the party on 23 October. The Eighth Army has not done too badly in the last 3 months!
>
> Good luck to you. Do write and tell me how you are progressing.
>
> Yrs ever
> B. L. MONTGOMERY

The next came a month later :

Eighth Army
25-2-43

My dear John

I often think of you these days and wish you were back with us. Your old Division is going strong and is still leading the hunt; it has been in the forefront of the battle ever since the battle began away back at Alamein. Pip[1] has gone and I fear that his successor, Hind[2], is not going to be anything like what *he* was; but then Pip was outstanding as an Armd. Bde. Comdr. Bobby[3] is well in the saddle now as Div. Comdr; and the Queens Bde have come on under Whistler to a marked degree; Bobby has awarded them the honour of having the Jerboa on their vehicles and that has raised their morale enormously. We had a great gathering of Generals from all parts of the world for our tactical discussions in Tripoli on 15, 16, and 17 Feb. A strong contingent came from England, and a party from Tunisia. I think they all learnt a very great deal.

Before that we had the visit of the Prime Minister and CIGS, which was a great event.

I have written another small pamphlet and send you a copy. It explains itself. The two pamphlets – this one and the one on 'Conduct of Battle' – really supply the answer as to why the Eighth Army is now operating in Tunisia. It may be that you have lost your copy of the 'Conduct of Battle' pamphlet; if so I will send you another; let me know.

I do hope you are not having too bad a time and that you are getting slowly better. I wish I could come and see you but I am a very long way from Cairo now and am very occupied in planning future operations; we have now got the Bosche tight up against the Mareth position proper, and once I get him out of that and I can loose the Eighth Army into the open country north of the Gabes gap – then I think his days in North Africa will be drawing to a close.

The real trouble is the low fighting value of the troops in Central Tunisia; Alexander tells me the situation there is quite frightful; there was no plan, no system, no guidance from above, no policy, and no one knew what to do. The whole thing was a

[1] Brigadier, later Major-General, G. P. B. Roberts.
[2] Brigadier, later Major-General Sir, Robert Hinde.
[3] Major-General, later General Sir, George Erskine.

complete 'dog's breakfast'. They very nearly had a real disaster, and would have done so if I had not driven forward hard and, by creating a strong thrust at Mareth, forced the Bosche to pull out from Kasserine and Tebessa. He is very windy about my intentions. He has some reason for this and he will receive a proper blow in due course – when I am ready.

Let me know how you fare. Keep up a stout heart and do not worry. So long as I have any influence in the Army, you can rest assured that you will always be looked after. There is nothing I would like better than to have you as a Corps Commander.

Freddie[1] is in good form and has recovered from his setback of last December. Matrimony has done him good.

Good luck to you.

yrs ever
B. L. MONTGOMERY

and the last from North Africa on the eve of the Battle of Mareth :

Eighth Army
20-3-43

My dear John

You may like to have enclosed copy of a message I issued today. I loose the Army tonight against the Mareth position, and we shall see what happens.

The plan is quite simple.

30 Corps with three infantry Divisions (50, 51, 4 Ind) is attacking the enemy extreme left flank, near the sea; this is on a one-Bde front and the hole made will be widened, and exploited; the tactics will be to roll up the enemy from the sea; working southwestwards; I can continue this thrust, and nourish it almost indefinitely.

At the same moment, the NZ Corps of 27,000 men and 200 tanks, will develop a movement round the enemy right (or land) flank, moving west of the Matmata mountains.

In the centre I have two full strength and complete Armd Divisions (1 and 7), holding the ground necessary to secure my vitals while the two flank thrusts are developed.

I have 5 Fighter Wings and 6 Bomber Wings.

[1] Brigadier, later Major-General Sir Francis, de Guingand.

I do not know what the enemy will do about it; he is not strong enough to hold off both flank thrusts simultaneously; they are both being developed simultaneously; if he concentrates against one, then the other will progress.

So it will be great fun.

The NZ Corps is directly under me.

I hope you are getting well.

I enclose rather a good photo of myself that you may care to have, I have given DSO to

Whistler (a bar)

Gillman CRASC, 7 Armd Div

Kidston 12 L

Smail 11 H

Herman KDG

It seemed to me that the armoured car COs were getting rather left out, and they have all done very well.

Yrs ever

B. L. MONTGOMERY

When, after the end of the campaign in North Africa, Montgomery visited Cairo in connection with planning the invasion of Sicily, he came to see Harding in hospital and sat for a long time discussing the future. His personal sympathy and encouragement contributed a great deal to maintaining Harding's morale and hopes for the future, for which he remained for ever grateful. As he gradually recovered his strength, Alexander asked him what he wished to do. Harding replied that he wanted to go home. He had not seen Mary and John Charles for four years, and he was certain that both his health and his future would be best served by his return. By the beginning of May he was considered fit to travel, and he set off by RAF flying boat. It was a long journey round by Khartoum, the Congo and West Africa. He had to get in and out of the aircraft three times a day and change the dressings on his wounds himself. It was with a great sense of relief that he finally reached Poole harbour, from which he had not far to go to join Mary at her mother's house at Long Ashton.

He was determined to get fit for active service again and applied all the strength of his formidable will to this end; but first impressions were depressing. Having been three months out of action, he reverted to his 'war substantive' rank of Colonel, and, when he went before a medical board at the naval hospital near Bristol which he attended, he was graded 'D', which debarred him from any active duty. Hopes of future employment appearing to be low, his mind and Mary's turned to thoughts of a permanent home, and they began to look around for a cottage in Somerset. His father, who had gone back to work at his old job with Poole's, heard that Lower Farm at Nether Compton was up for sale and thought it might suit them. Its 130 acres might provide an occupation as a smallholder. They drove over with John Charles in a pony trap from South Petherton. The owner was ill and the house and property in a very poor state. Mary was horrified at the thought of having to live there, but John Charles was enthusiastic and Harding himself could see that, with effort and time, it could be turned into the very attractive house that it later became. They moved in in time to spend Christmas 1943 there.

Meanwhile the gloomy view of the future that had led to the thoughts of setting up as a smallholder had been totally reversed. After the board at Bristol had graded him 'D', his old desert companion, Sandy Galloway, longing to escape from his desk in the War Office as Director of Staff Duties, had suggested that Harding should replace him. Before this could come about, he had to go before another medical board, this time in London in July. Although they would not pass him fit for work, they adopted a more helpful and understanding attitude. His main problem was the lack of movement in his lower left arm. The board decided that more could be done for it, and sent him to the Wingfield-Morris Hospital, now the Nuffield Orthopaedic Centre, at Oxford. Here he came under the care of Doctor Jim (later Sir Herbert) Seddon, who operated on his nerves and successfully restored movement to the arm. Harding found the whole atmosphere there encouraging, and it did a great deal to raise his morale. Mary came to Oxford and they spent much of the time walking round the Colleges. Oxford in summer and the sensible regime at the hospital combined to provide a feeling of relaxed freedom. Montgomery contributed with one of his inimitable letters :

Sicily
4-8-43

My dear John

I have just got your air letter of 19 July and was delighted to hear from you. I knew you were going to be DSD, and had been advocating that myself for some time, but it is quite sickening that they will not pass you fit for service. I hope the Oxford Hospital will do the trick for you.

I am enjoying this campaign. I could write a best seller about the preliminary planning stage; it was one continuous fight to try and get a decent plan, and the whole party kept on the rails. If it had been done on the original plan it might well have been a disaster. But I won my case and they accepted my plan.

The initial phase was an unqualified success. The enemy was thrown right off his balance by the strength, speed and violence of our attack and it took him some time to recover. He *did* recover in the end but by that time we had secured practically the whole island, had bagged about 90,000 prisoners, and had him hemmed in in the NE corner of the island.

He was well posted in ideal defensive country, and it was necessary to pause and regroup. This has now been done and I launched the Army again on 1st August. My main thrust of three Divisions (51, 78 and Canadian) is directed at ADRANO (or ADERNO on some maps), and when I get that place the Bosche will be in queer street. He is sitting very strong in front of Catania, so I stopped the thrust, regrouped, and put in the ADRANO thrust. Oliver[1] is in charge of that.

On the 'holding front', south and SW of Catania, I have 13 Corps (Dempsey). 10 Corps (Horrocks) is at Tripoli, waiting as my reserve corps; Horrocks is of course champing at the bit. The Bosche is getting very stretched and he cannot possibly stand up to my thrusts. One of the lessons here is that it is the 'Divisional' thrusts that pay; a thrust of less than a division is of no use.

Good luck to you and get well soon.

Yrs ever

B. L. MONTGOMERY

A fellow patient was Basil Liddell Hart's son Adrian. When visiting him, Liddell Hart asked Harding if there was anything he could do to help him. 'Yes,' said Harding, 'tell people in authority that I am fit to get back to work.' Early in October Seddon pronounced him fit, and, as a result, he went once more before a medical board, which to his delight graded him 'A', fit for any job in his rank. He went straight from the board to the office of the Military Secretary and was interviewed by a brigadier, who

---

[1] Lieutenant-General Sir Oliver Leese.

thumbed through a book and asked him if he would be prepared to be a divisional umpire, the officer at a divisional headquarters responsible for umpiring exercises. This was hardly what he had been hoping for. He had kept Montgomery informed of these developments (their correspondence was carried out by ordinary handwritten forces air mail letter card), and received the following reply :

Eighth Army
31-10-43

My dear John

The moment I got your letter saying the specialist had said you were OK, I sent an official message to the CIGS recommending you for a command of a Corps in England. You have commanded a Division successfully in battle, and you should now have a Corps command. So I hope very much this will be done. I have just got your air letter of 14 October saying the medical board have passed you Category A. That is splendid and is another reason why you should be given a Corps. I have no vacancy here at the moment; in fact I now have the Canadian Corps spare.

Let me know how things go. The weather has broken out here and our enemies are the wet and the mud; these, combined with the mountains and the difficult country, make our further advance a very slow business. I do not think we can conduct a winter campaign in this country. If I remember right Caesar used to go into winter quarters – a very sound thing to do ! !

Keep me in touch with what they do with you.

Yrs ever
B. L. MONTGOMERY

By the time this was received the good news had come. The Hardings had gone to stay with friends in Newcastle, when the same brigadier who had interviewed him rang up to say that he was glad to be the first to congratulate him on being appointed to command 8 Corps. This was good news indeed. The corps, the headquarters of which was at Maldon in Yorkshire, was perhaps the elite formation of those formed in England for the return to the Continent. It consisted of 11th Armoured, Guards Armoured and 15th (Scottish) Infantry Divisions, all to prove themselves later in northwest Europe as formations of the highest fighting quality. On 11th November, now a Lieutenant-General, Harding took over command and immediately began to visit all the units and headquarters and inspire them with his own enthusiasm, confidence and vitality. He made the same impression on them as he had as commanding officer to the 1st Battalion of the Somerset Light Infantry. In an unguarded moment, invited into the officers' mess to sing Christmas carols, the band corporal told him that his initials, AFH, were known in the battalion to stand for 'All F***ing Hurry'.

Christmas 1943 offered therefore a more cheerful prospect than had been expected when Lower Farm had been bought. It was still in a dilapidated state in December when they moved in, but the first Christmas together for five years and the upturn in Harding's future fortunes compensated for the state of the house. On Christmas Day a despatch rider arrived on a wet and windy night with a message. When Harding first glanced at it, he thought it said that one of his staff at 8 Corps Headquarters was being sent to Italy, but when he read it more carefully after the despatch rider had left, he realized that it said that he himself was to be ready to go to Italy. His first reaction was one of great annoyance, just having taken over command of 8 Corps and having thrown himself into the task with enthusiasm. Next day the local policeman called with a message for him to ring up the CIGS. When he did so, Alan Brooke indicated that his job would be Chief of Staff to Alexander and that he was to come up to London to discuss it. When they met, Brooke told him about the projected landing at Anzio and explained that Alexander had no properly established headquarters with which to control two separate armies and a further operation of this nature.

The situation in the Mediterranean at the turn of the year derived from the two conferences, 'Eureka' in Teheran, at the end of November 1943, and 'Sextant' in Cairo, which immediately followed it, at which Churchill, Roosevelt, Stalin and their advisers had decided on the strategy for 1944. Three Anglo-American armies were to invade France in May, the main operation, *Overlord*, across the Channel, and a subsidiary one on its Mediterranean coast, involving an assault of two divisions, followed up by ten sailing direct from the USA, named *Anvil*. Rome was to be captured as soon as possible, and the allied armies in Italy were to advance to the line Rimini-Pisa. Thereafter pressure against the Germans in Italy was to be maintained, subject to the requirements of *Anvil*. Mountbatten's plan to capture the

Andaman Islands was cancelled and the landing craft that would have been sent to him were to be retained in the Mediterranean. This might make possible the capture of Rhodes, but it was not essential. Sixty-eight landing ships, due to move from Italy to the United Kingdom by 5 December, could be retained until 15 January. Agreement had also been reached on changes of command. Eisenhower was to be replaced, as Supreme Commander of Allied Forces in the Mediterranean, by a Briton, Maitland Wilson, and Churchill had won his argument that there should not be one supreme commander responsible for operations both in Northwest Europe and in the Mediterranean. Alexander was to remain as the commander of what was variously known either as 'Allied Armies in Italy' or 15th Army Group, subordinate to Wilson at Allied Force Headquarters in Algiers.

Progress on the Italian front had not however come up to these expectations. 8th Army's operations on the eastern side of the Apennines under Montgomery had ground to a halt after the battles of the Sangro and the Moro, and Montgomery himself was glad to hand over to Leese and leave for England on 31 December. Mark Clark's 5th Army, which included the British 10 Corps under McCreery, had driven von Senger und Etterlin's 14 Panzer Corps back from his Bernhardt line to the Gustav line, covering the Garigliano and Rapido rivers; but it was still a long way from breaking through into the Liri valley, which had been its objective. Alexander's plan, called *Shingle,* had included an amphibious landing of one division at Anzio, which was to take place when Clark's leading troops were within thirty miles of its beaches. It was to make this possible that the date for the return of the landing ships had been extended. By 18 December 1943 it was clear that *Shingle* could not be launched in time and there was no hope of reaching Rome by then. The allied armies were exhausted and could make no further immediate progress in the face of the combination of rugged terrain, the mountain ridges running across their lines of advance, the onset of winter and the determined and skilful resistance of the Germans. On his way back from 'Sextant' and 'Eureka', Churchill had fallen ill with pneumonia and was convalescing at Marrakesh in Morocco. His presence in that area at that time had concentrated his attention even more closely than it in any case tended to be on the Mediterranean theatre, and he was most reluctant to abandon any of his pet projects, of which amphibious landings to outflank the mainland defences were one.

Harding's appointment therefore came at a critical moment.

He left on New Year's Day, flying from an airfield in North Devon to Algiers, the site of Eisenhower's main headquarters. Here he was met by Whiteley, deputy to Bedell-Smith, the Chief of Staff, whom he was taken to see. Al Gruenther, Mark Clark's Chief of Staff, was also there and offered him a lift to Naples, which he gladly accepted. From there he flew on to Alexander's headquarters at San Spirito near Taranto. On arrival he found to his annoyance that Alexander was away in Tunis, conferring with Eisenhower. Next morning therefore he flew there himself and got hold of a jeep to drive him to Eisenhower's villa at Carthage. There was no sign of either Eisenhower or Alexander there, but he finally ran them to earth in the local schoolhouse where, with the naval c-in-c, Sir John Cunningham, and Air Marshal 'Mary' Coningham, commander of the 2nd Allied Tactical Air Force, they were discussing the projected landing at Anzio. Harding listened in, and the more he heard the less he liked it. He realized that he had had no experience of combined operations, at least not since Suvla Bay, but he did not like the apparently haphazard way in which the operation was being planned, and thought little of its prospects. It was clear however that Churchill still had his heart set on it. Alexander was due to go to Algiers, after a short return to Italy, to discuss the details of the operation at the main Allied Force Headquarters, and then to Marrakesh to explain matters to Churchill. Harding accompanied him. It was the first time he had met Churchill, who was in typical mood, clad in a dressing-gown and accompanied by Lord Beaverbrook, who remained silent. Admiral Sir John Cunningham was also there with his Chief of Staff, Power. He clearly did not like the ideas proposed. There was a great deal of discussion about the allocation and movement of tank landing ships, and, more and more concerned, John Cunningham's neck sank deeper and deeper into his collar. 'It involves great risks,' he said at one stage, to which Churchill replied : 'Admiral, of course there is risk; but without risk, there is no honour, no glory, no adventure' – at which Cunningham, reduced to silence, almost disappeared into his collar.

Returning to San Spirito, Harding found that his first task was to sort out the headquarters. Both Alexander and Mary Coningham had little more than improvised tactical headquarters, and it had been decided that they would attempt to control the next stage of operations, including another major assault by Mark Clark's 5th Army, combined with a landing at Anzio, from a train at Caserta. Logistics and administration were in the hands of General Brian Robertson from an advanced Headquarters of Allied Forces in Naples. Harding had some difficulty in persuading Alexander that it was essential for him to have a proper army group headquarters which Robertson must join, and Robertson himself helped to persuade the c-in-c. The obvious place was the palace at Caserta, but this had already been earmarked for Allied Force Headquarters when it moved from Algiers. After much discussion, it was finally agreed that Alexander's staff could occupy the top floor, Alexander and Harding living in a villa nearby.

Operational problems were urgent and time was short. The plan that Harding found in existence was for a major assault on the German Gustav line, covering the mouth of the Liri valley, to be launched in the second half of January. In the centre Keyes's 2nd US Corps, after capturing Monte Porchio and Monte Trocchio in a preliminary operation, would carry out an assault crossing of the Rapido and force their way up the Liri valley. On their right Juin's French Expeditionary Corps, which had relieved Lucas's 6th US Corps, would advance through the mountains on the north side of the valley, while McCreery's 10th British Corps would cross the Garigliano and attack von Senger's right flank in the mountains south of the valley. Once these assaults had been launched on 20 January, the landing at Anzio would follow on 23 January, 1st British Division on the left, 3rd US on the right, both under command of Lucas's 6th US Corps, to be followed up by 1st US Armoured and 45th US Infantry Divisions. Kesselring, who was thought to have only two divisions in reserve, would be faced with a dilemma as to where to employ them and would probably be forced to withdraw north of Rome.

Harding's first reaction was that the forces allocated were insufficient, and one of his first steps was to prise Freyberg's New Zealand Division out of 8th Army into army group reserve. This did not please Leese, whose relations with Mark Clark were none too good, particularly as his army had already had to surrender two British divisions to 5th Army, the 1st to join Lucas for Anzio and the 5th to McCreery's 10 Corps to replace 7th Armoured Division, which had sailed for England to be prepared for *Overlord*, the cross-channel invasion. By 15 January the preliminary operations had brought 5th Army up to the Rapido, and the assault was launched five days later. Kesselring's first reaction seemed to be playing into Alexander's hands, as in the absence of any sign of a landing, he ordered his reserves south to prevent von Senger's flanks from being turned; but Keyes's assault crossing of the Rapido proved a disastrous failure and, by the time that Lucas's troops landed at Anzio, von Senger's position was less critical.

Mark Clark's orders to Lucas had not reflected the action which Churchill at least had conceived. Later the latter was to say : 'I had expected a wildcat rushing through the mountains. What do I find but a whale wallowing on the beach ?' He may have been reminded of Suvla Bay. If so he would have been unfair on Lucas, to whom historians have been kinder than his superiors were at the time. But he was certainly no wild cat, and was called Sugar Daddy by his troops. Harding attended one of his order groups and was horrified, reporting afterwards to Alexander that he would clearly play for safety, which is what he did. In retrospect it probably saved the forces at Anzio from disaster, as Hitler reacted violently to the threat they posed and rapidly reinforced Kesselring to deal with it, pinning his hopes on the boost to German morale and to his own position that flinging the allies back into the sea would bring.

After a week's fighting, in the course of which the situation at Anzio became critical, the boot was on the other foot. Instead of Anzio being a subsidiary operation to help the main blow in, and on the flanks of, the Liri valley, it now became necessary to carry out attacks on 5th Army's main front in order to prevent Kesselring from overwhelming Anzio. This was the main purpose which lay behind the operations which took place in February, known as the first and second battles of Cassino. To provide the resources for these and at the same time to reinforce Anzio, Harding had to turn again to Leese. An additional corps was formed under Freyberg, consisting of his own New Zealanders and Tuker's 4th Indian Division. McCreery sent Templer's 56th Division to Anzio and 78th British Division came over from 8th Army to replace the New Zealanders in army group reserve. Harding was concerned at the loss of initiative, and decided that it was essential to sit down and have a hard cool look at where they were really heading, which, in contrast to Montgomery's, was not Alexander's way of setting about things.

Nevertheless Harding got on very well with Alexander and greatly admired him. He saw that, having commanded everything from a platoon upwards, Alexander had an instinct for the battlefield, and was at his best in difficult and critical situations. He had no great intellect, but was a combination of dedicated professional soldier and patrician. The concept of his plan would evolve from discussion, and it was for the Chief of Staff to translate it into orders and action. The adequacy of the forces, the arrangements for command, all these were the concern of the staff. He had the highest sense of duty and in no respect more so than in being faithful to his task of doing all he could to help the future invasion of France. He saw his duty as that of pressing the Germans as hard and as continuously as he could in order to ensure that nothing was taken from Italy to reinforce Northwest Europe. He continued to batter away at Cassino in the belief that, if he did so, they were bound to remain south of Rome, in contrast to the Whitehall view that, if they were hard pressed, they would withdraw to another line. But Harding did not believe that a breakthrough could be achieved without a superiority of at least three to one in infantry and that the operation and its consequences must be clearly and thoroughly thought out. While the battles for Cassino were raging, Harding sat down and drew up an appreciation which was to form the basis of the victories which followed. Alexander having approved it, it was forwarded on 22 February to Maitland Wilson's headquarters, where it was coolly received. This was not surprising, as it contained some suggestions which would clearly cause difficulties.

There was no argument about the aim : to force the enemy to commit the maximum number of divisions to Italy at the time that *Overlord* was to be launched. But controversy arose over the method. Harding, with ruthless logic, pointed out that neither pushing back the German line nor the capture of Rome would help to achieve the aim. That must be to destroy German formations in Italy to such an extent that they had to be replaced from elsewhere in order to prevent a disastrous collapse. There were three requirements to achieve this : first, a three to one local superiority in infantry; second, good weather, so that the allies could exploit their great superiority in artillery, tanks and air-power; finally, time in which to rest, refit and retrain the divisions exhausted by the winter's fighting. An additional seven and a half divisions would be needed. They were available within the Mediterranean and the Middle East, but shipping limitations could not make them available for operations in Italy before the middle of April. This would however meet all the other criteria, including that of acting as an overture to *Overlord*.

Having considered the possibility of Alexander's 15 Army

Group's operations having advanced its line to either south of or even north of Rome by mid-April and shown it to be much less likely than that the Germans would still be on the Gustav line, Harding took the view that this in fact would be advantageous. If his criteria were met, there would be a good chance that an attack by three or four divisions from Anzio, combined with a major offensive up the line of the Liri valley, would stand a reasonable chance of encircling and destroying a considerable part of Kesselring's forces. The chances would be improved if operations could be developed up the Ausente valley, which led from the lower reaches of the Garigliano up towards the Liri valley, and if a diversion could be landed from the sea in the Gulf of Gaeta. The command arrangements should be changed. If 8th Army were restricted to east of the Apennines while 5th Army commanded everything west of the watershed, the former would have only four and the latter twenty divisions. Mark Clark had a hotchpotch of nationalities in his army, unnecessarily complicating logistics. His army should become primarily American, while British divisions and those equipped and supplied by them, like the Poles, should preferably come under Leese. This would mean Leese becoming responsible for the Liri valley, leaving his current sector to a corps directly under Alexander, while Mark Clark was restricted to Anzio and the lower Garigliano. The navy's priorities should be to get the additional divisions to Italy as soon as possible and build up supplies at Anzio to support an attack from there. The air forces should maintain the supremacy they had established, keep up their attack on the enemy's rail communications and be prepared both to deal with any further counter-attacks against Anzio and to attack targets which could have a significant effect on future operations.

The sting in the tail of this masterly appraisal was the conclusion that Operation *Anvil* – a landing on the Mediterranean coast of France – should be cancelled, as neither the troops nor the shipping could be spared, but that it should be simulated as a deception plan, the proposed landing in the Gulf of Gaeta contributing to this. For the first time since the invasion of Sicily a clear, penetrating, overall examination had been made of what the allies were trying to do in Italy and how they should achieve their aim. All Harding's clarity of mind, downright, straightforward, realistic commonsense, practical military experience, determination and courage to put forward an unpopular view shone through this example of what a military appreciation, as

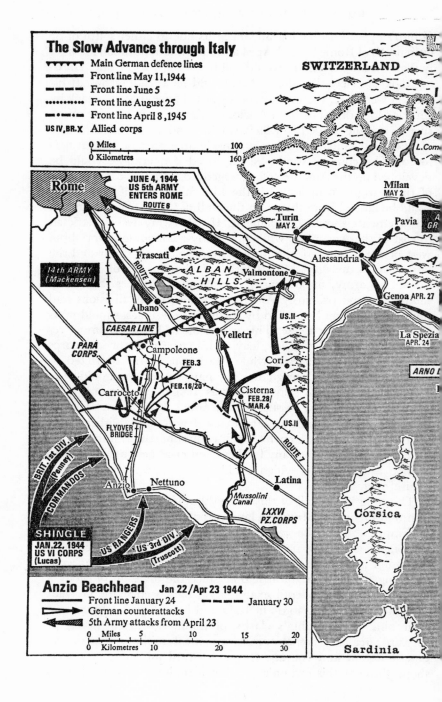

The Slow Advance through Italy

- ▼▼▼▼▼ Main German defence lines
- ——— Front line May 11, 1944
- – – – – Front line June 5
- •••••••••• Front line August 25
- —•—•—•— Front line April 8, 1945
- **US IV, BR. X** Allied corps

0 Miles 100
0 Kilometres 160

SWITZERLAND

Rome

**JUNE 4, 1944
US 5th ARMY
ENTERS ROME
ROUTE 6**

Milan
MAY 2

Turin
MAY 2

Pavia

A
GR

**14th ARMY
(Mackensen)**

Frascati

ALBAN HILLS

Valmontone

Alessandria

Genoa APR. 27

La Spezia
APR. 24

ROUTE 7

Albano

CAESAR LINE

Velletri

US. II

ARNO

I PARA CORPS

Campoleone

FEB. 3

Cori

FEB. 16/20

Cisterna
FEB. 28/
MAR. 4

Carroceto

US. II

FLYOVER BRIDGE

ROUTE 7

BRIT. 1st DIV. (Penney)

COMMANDOS

Anzio

Nettuno

Latina

Mussolini
Canal

Corsica

**LXXVI
PZ. CORPS**

US RANGERS

US 3rd DIV. (Truscott)

**SHINGLE
JAN. 22, 1944
US VI CORPS
(Lucas)**

Anzio Beachhead   Jan 22/Apr 23 1944

- ——— Front line January 24
- – – – – January 30
- ▷▷▷ German counterattacks
- ◁◁◁ 5th Army attacks from April 23

0 Miles 5 10 15 20
0 Kilometres 10 20 30

Sardinia

The Argenta Gap

- - - - - Front line April 8
◀━━ Allied attacks April 9

0　　　Miles　　　30

AUSTRIA

Brenner Pass
MAY 6

Trento

Belluno

Udine

VENETIA

Trieste
MAY 2

Verona

Padua

Venice
APR. 28

Adige

10th ARGENTA GAP
L. Comacchio

Ferrara

Reno

Argenta
Bastia

APR 1
CMDS. &
GDS. BDE.

BR.V

Bologna

Santerno

Ravenna

Imola

Serio

POL.II

R.65

US.
IV

BR.X

Forli

M. Battaglia
BR.XIII

ROUTE 9

10th ARMY

Argenta

L. Comacchio
BR.V
Ravenna

Bologna

CAN.I
POL.II

GOTHIC LINE

US.IV

M. Battaglia
BR.X

BR.
XIII

Rimini

YUGO-
SLAVIA

US.II

Coriano Ridge

Conca

Foglia

San
Marino

Pesaro

Florence

Arno

Metauro

Ancona
JULY 18

POL.II
CAN.I
BR.V

ADRIATIC

Arezzo

Siena

L.
Trasimene

TRASIMENE LINE

Perugia

San
Benedetto

SEA

Todi

POL.II

FR.
CORPS

Tiber

Terni

Pescara

US.IV

Civita

GUSTAV LINE (HITLER LINE)

POL.
II

Civitavecchia
JUNE 7

BR.
V

Rome

US II

US.VI

BR.XIII

BR.X

Valmontone

Arce

Sangro

BR 8th ARMY
(Leese)

15th ARMY
GROUP
(Alexander)

Anzio
US.VI

Ceprano

Liri

Cassino
BR.XIII
FR.CORPS
US.II
BR.X

POL.II

US 5th ARMY
(Clark)

Garigliano

Naples

taught to him by Montgomery at the staff college sixteen years before, was designed to achieve.

Wilson's objections were on two grounds, both of them no doubt influenced by the trouble they would cause in London and Washington. The first was the cancellation of *Anvil,* which would raise Anglo-American dissension all over again. The other was the postponement of further offensive operations until mid-April. Not only would this incur the wrath of Churchill, but the airmen at Algiers, mostly US Air Force, headed by Ira Eaker with Slessor as his deputy, believed that they could do the trick by a combination of extensive interdiction of the enemy's communications and direct attack by massed bombing on a key position like Cassino. Wilson also had reservations about the demands on shipping. After an exchange of views at high level between Algiers, London and Washington, a compromise, suggested by Eisenhower in London, was agreed at the end of February, by which operations in Italy should have priority over all other operations in the Mediterranean, provided that plans and preparations continued for a seaborne diversion to help *Overlord, Anvil* being first choice. The Mediterranean fleet of assault shipping could be retained until 20 March, when the situation would be reviewed. If it was then clear that nothing more than an assault by one division as a deception plan could be mounted, all amphibious shipping in excess of that needed for this would be transferred from the Mediterranean for *Overlord.*

This was agreed on 25 February by the Combined Chiefs of Staff, the day the Germans planned a second major attack on Anzio, postponed through bad weather to the 28th. It was aimed at the sector occupied by 3rd US Division, which held its ground until, as the skies cleared on 2 March, the full weight of the allied air forces could be brought to bear. Having failed to penetrate the defences, von Mackensen abandoned the attack on 4 March and withdrew his panzer divisions into reserve.

Meanwhile preparations continued for a third attempt to break through the mouth of the Liri valley. Freyberg's plan was to clear a route through the town of Cassino and then take the ruins of the monastery from below, the former the task of his New Zealanders and the latter of the Indians. The attack was to be preceded by a massive bombardment, the square mile of the town receiving 1,000 tons of bombs and 200,000 shells. For safety reasons the New Zealand front line would have to be withdrawn a thousand yards before the air force dropped their bombs. Two weather conditions were essential to success : first, three days of fine weather to dry the ground sufficiently for 78th Division to be able to pass through and thrust up the Liri valley; second, that the day of the attack should be fine and clear for the bombers to see their target. Although everything was ready for the attack by 24 February, the weather failed to oblige. Meanwhile the attack on Anzio died down and, with no activity on 8th Army's front, the Germans were able to transfer their 1st Parachute Division, tough and skilled at street fighting, to relieve the battered 90th Panzer Grenadier Division at Cassino.

An incident at this time remained clearly in Harding's memory. He wished to persuade Alexander that certain German artillery positions, tucked into the hills, must be attacked by the air force, as artillery counter-battery fire could not reach them. He therefore proposed to take Alexander up to an observation post on Monte Trocchio from which the area could be seen. They lunched with the American corps commander, General Keyes, but did not tell him where they were going. They then set off for the New Zealand Division's sector, Alexander, Harding, an ADC and two military policemen in two jeeps. They came under artillery fire and a burst landed just ahead of them, killing two New Zealand soldiers. Alexander took charge of the party just as if he were a platoon commander. By skilful use of ground they reached the observation post unseen and unharmed, Alexander being convinced by what he saw from there.

It was not until 14 March that the meteorologists predicted that the weather requirements for the attack would be met, and at 8.30 am on the 15th Alexander, Harding and several others watched the bombs fall, not all on their target, from a farmhouse not far from where the incident had occurred. It did not have the decisive effect hoped for. Not only did the Germans miraculously survive, but it made the ground almost impassable. For a week Freyberg's New Zealanders and Indians, than whom there were no braver nor more skilful soldiers, tried to struggle forward, but they could not capture the higher ground and had suffered four thousand casualties. Wilson wanted to continue, but Alexander and Freyberg decided that to do so had little hope of achieving a breakthrough and could prejudice the success of the larger scale operation Harding had proposed. Harding himself was influential in persuading Alexander to call off the attack.

CHAPTER NINE

ROME TO TRIESTE
1944–5

Although Harding's appreciation had been accepted in almost all its detail as the basis for future operations in Italy, the cancellation of *Anvil* had not. The delay in launching the third attack at Cassino and its failure had however brought Maitland Wilson round to the view that it could not be launched before *Overlord*, not in fact until the end of July. There seemed little point in launching it after that, except as an unopposed landing if the Germans collapsed or withdrew from southern France. Once it was launched, the threat of an amphibious landing elsewhere, such as on either of the coasts of Italy, could not be maintained. Eisenhower supported this view and wanted all the amphibious shipping earmarked for it to be transferred to him. The American Chiefs of Staff agreed to the transfer, but not to the cancellation of *Anvil*, which they proposed should merely be postponed until 10 July. To make this possible they were prepared to produce some amphibious shipping from the Pacific, but only if the British agreed to a definite date for *Anvil*.

While this was still the subject of a transatlantic exchange of signals, Harding was forced to throw a spanner into the works. A number of factors had made it clear that mid-April was too optimistic a date for the major in Italy attack, now christened Operation *Diadem*. Brian Robertson had always given a clear warning of the administrative and logistic difficulties in the extensive re-organization involved and in crowding so large a force into an area with such poor communications. Not until the delayed Third Battle of Cassino was over could a start be made on these detailed and extensive preparations. There were serious delays in moving the additional divisions both from the Middle East and from North Africa. It was clear that 11 May was the earliest date on which *Diadem* could start, thus postponing the earliest date for *Anvil* until August. With the Americans still insisting on *Anvil*, Churchill went ahead with a directive to Wilson reaffirming that the aim of operations in the Mediterranean was still to help *Overlord* by destroying and containing the maximum number of German formations in the Mediterranean. It was to be done by Operation *Diadem*, which was to have priority. Subject to that priority a threat was to be developed against the south of France, the amphibious shipping remaining in the Mediterranean being used to support operations in Italy or 'to take advantage of opportunities arising in the south of France'.

Planning for *Diadem* did not proceed without its troubles, at the centre of which Harding found himself. One was argument between Mark Clark and Leese about the boundary between them, particularly its projection forward past Rome. Both complained that they were not given enough room to deploy their forces or roads by which to move and supply them. Both tended to behave like prima donnas. Alexander handled them skilfully, trying to get them to put forward suggestions with which he could agree. His approach was almost feminine in its instinctiveness, a far cry from the cold, hard calculation of Montgomery; but he could also be rough at times. One occasion in which he displayed his skill at getting results arose out of a major disagreement among the air force commanders. In order to apply maximum tactical air force effort west of the Apennines, it was necessary to concentrate it under the command of one tactical air force. This clearly had to be the 12th US Air Support Command, which normally supported 5th Army. It was bitterly opposed by Broadhurst, commanding the Desert Air Force, which supported 8th Army, as it was by Leese also. Eaker supported Cannon, Alexander's tactical air force commander. Harding, unable to get agreement, told Alexander, who said that all involved should be summoned to see him. When Harding asked how he was going to deal with them, Alexander replied that he would put them in his office. He would then say that Harding had told him the problem, but that he, Alexander, had other urgent business to attend to and would leave them together to settle it among themselves and lock the door. In the event agreement was reached without recourse to this.

The plan for *Diadem* was for 8th Army to break through at Cassino, advance up Route 6 in the Liri valley, pass east of Rome and then make for Florence or for Ancona, the choice depending on whether the Combined Chiefs of Staff decided on France or Austria as Alexander's final target. The 5th Army's first task was to support Leese by capturing the Ausonia defile at the head of the Ausente valley, thereafter advancing through the mountains south of Route 6, thus cutting across the rear of the German Tenth Army. Thereafter Mark Clark was to advance through Rome to capture the airfields round Viterbo and the ports of Civitavecchia and Leghorn. The timing of the breakout from Anzio was to be decided by Alexander, Truscott, who had replaced Lucas, being placed at twenty-four hours' notice to do so from D + 4. Keightley's 5th British Corps, with two Indian infantry divisions on the Adriatic coast, was to follow up any German withdrawal on their front.

Leese's plan was for the Polish Corps of two divisions to capture or at least neutralize Monte Cassino, approaching it from the north through the mountains. The main attack was to be made by Kirkman's 13th British Corps, with two British and one Indian infantry division and one British armoured division, across the Rapido, swinging north behind Cassino to link up with the Poles, while at the same time thrusting up the Liri valley. The Canadian Corps, one armoured and one infantry division, would then be prepared to pass through and drive the Germans back before they could establish their defences on the Hitler line. On Mark Clark's Garigliano front the attack through the mountains to the Ausonia defile was to be made by Juin's French Corps, led by his Moroccan divisions. On his left Keyes's 2nd US Corps of two infantry divisions would push along the coast round the shore of the Gulf of Gaeta, to link up eventually with Anzio on Route 7. Truscott's 6th US Corps at Anzio had been brought up to a strength of six divisions, two British and four American. One US division was in 5th Army reserve, ready either to carry out a landing in the Gulf of Gaeta or to reinforce Anzio. As one would have expected with Harding as Chief of Staff, a considerable effort was devoted to deception plans, the main aim of which was to give the impression that Alexander's regrouping would not be complete before June and that the main effort would be a repetition of Anzio on a larger scale, aimed at the port of Civitavecchia. As 11 May approached, the plan seemed to be working, and Kesselring's dispositions pointed to first priority being given to meet a new amphibious assault, second to Anzio, and lowest to meet a renewed attack on the Gustav line. He did not expect an attack until the end of May at the earliest and allowed a number of senior officers to go on leave.

At 11 am on 11 May the guns thundered out and once more a fierce battle raged round Cassino. For the first two days it appeared that the pattern of earlier attacks would be repeated, the Poles failing to reach their objectives and withdrawing to their start line, having suffered heavy casualties. Below them 13 Corps struggled slowly forward and, after three days of fighting, had done no more than link up its bridgehead over the river. But success came where it was least expected, in the south. Juin's attack had surprised the Germans and thrown them into confusion. He was quick to exploit it, thrusting his Moroccan Goums through the mountains, and his success reduced the resistance to the Americans on his left, who began to advance along the coast and in the mountains overlooking it. By 15 May Juin was well on his way to the Hitler line, and thereafter renewed attempts by 13 Corps to get forward began to show results. On 17 May the Poles attacked again, while 13 Corps renewed their assault from below, and on the following morning the Polish flag was raised over the ruins of the monastery. By this time Juin had reached the Hitler line and Keyes's progress had made any idea of a landing in the Gulf of Gaeta unnecessary. Alexander therefore decided to send 36th US Division to Anzio and fixed 23 May as the date for Truscott to start his breakout, giving Mark Clark Valmontone on Route 6 east of the Alban hills as his objective.

Clark, his eyes on Rome, objected to this, maintaining that it meant Truscott advancing with his left flank overlooked by the hills on which the Germans had prepared the Caesar line; and that, even when Valmontone had been reached, there were plenty of roads to the north of it by which the Germans could escape. It had always been accepted that Rome would be within 5th Army's area, and the boundary between the armies, which had been the subject of so much argument between Clark and Leese, had been designed to allow them both to develop their full strength in the comparatively favourable country between Rome and the Apennines. Harding had borne the brunt of the dispute between the two army commanders on this issue and had only involved Alexander himself when he had finally settled the argument.

Having made his protest about the direction of the breakout, Clark accepted Alexander's direction, although in the event he did not follow it. His initial thrust on 23 May was eastward to

Cisterna, directed towards Valmontone. This coincided with the attack by the Canadian Corps on the Hitler line, which succeeded in breaking through, opening the way to the advance on Rome up Route 6. For two days all the divisions in the Anzio beachhead pushed forward, and by the end of 25 May Clark thought he detected a weakening in the northern sector, where Route 7 led straight to Rome, and a strengthening of the forces opposing the salient which had now been created in the direction of Valmontone. He therefore proposed to Alexander that he should make his main effort in the former direction. Alexander agreed, provided that he maintained his thrust towards Valmontone. Clark's response to this was to leave only the 3rd US Division heading in that direction, while he switched four divisions to the attack up the axis of Route 7. For four days they made no progress, while Churchill belaboured Alexander with advice about making scything movements with his '2,500 tanks', concluding with the words : 'I should feel myself wanting in comradeship if I did not let you know that the glory of the battle, already great, will be measured, not by the capture of Rome or the junction with the bridgehead, but by the number of German divisions cut off.' It must have been a bitter pill for Alexander to swallow. By the time he fully realized what Mark Clark was doing, he came to the conclusion that to attempt to force him to change his main thrust again would merely mean that no pressure would be exerted in either direction at a critical time, and Harding was forced to agree with him. The 8th Army was being delayed as much, if not more, by its own traffic problems as by the enemy, who, expert as ever in demolitions and rearguards, managed to escape in the hours of darkness through the mountain roads in spite of the overwhelming air superiority of the allies.

By 29 May Kesselring had managed to establish continuous defences on the Caesar line running through the Alban hills and thence up to the Apennines. Mark Clark had brought up his 2nd Corps to Valmontone and launched an attack on this line. Once more success came where least expected, and again in the centre of the hills, where his 36th Division, patrolling on the night of 30 May, found a gap and occupied high ground overlooking the defences holding up 6 Corps on Route 7 and 2 Corps on Route 6. Clark was quick to exploit this, and on the night of 2/3 June, the Germans withdrew north of Rome, which the leading troops of 88th US Division entered in the evening of the glorious 4th, two days before *Overlord* was launched, overshadowing the victory of *Diadem*, which owed so much to Harding, both in conception and in execution.

After his appreciation, which had formed the basis of *Diadem*, had been accepted and the orders to put its preparation into effect had been issued, Harding applied himself to a further appreciation to consider what should follow *Diadem*. This was also approved by Alexander and formed the basis of a signal sent to Maitland Wilson on 6 June. Once again it did not coincide with the thoughts that had been developing among Wilson's staff, in which his American deputy, General Devers, wielded considerable influence. They had been studying various possible amphibious operations to take place after *Overlord,* employing forces taken from Alexander, and had concluded that the resurrection of *Anvil* was the most profitable, and that it could be launched by 15 August. The Americans were delighted, and promised to provide the landing craft from the Pacific which they had earlier offered. Wilson had informed the Combined Chiefs of Staff of his conclusion on 15 May and warned Alexander that, after the capture of Rome, he would probably have to give up one US corps of three experienced divisions and also two French divisions.

Alexander's signal of June 6 rocked the boat again. He saw his aim as being unchanged and believed that, if he could maintain the pressure which his now experienced and well-trained army and air force team were exerting, strengthened by the high morale induced by their recent victory, he could force the Germans to reinforce Kesselring by a further eight to ten divisions (Kesselring had been sent four during *Diadem* in spite of the impending threat of *Overlord*). If this pressure could be maintained without a pause, he estimated that he stood a good chance of breaking through the Gothic line, between Pisa and Rimini, in August, thus forcing the Germans to abandon the Po valley before the winter set in. Harding's appreciation had shown that the most favourable way to do this was to develop a breakthrough in the centre, thrusting towards Bologna. Thereafter Alexander's preference was to head northeast for the Ljubljana gap with Vienna as the final target. At the same time as he sent this appreciation to Wilson, he sent a copy to Alan Brooke.

The cat was now firmly among the pigeons and feathers began to fly in all directions. While they did so, Wilson told Alexander that, pending a decision, he would have to prepare to surrender the forces of which he had been notified – the corps headquarters on 11 June, the three American divisions by the end of the month, one of the French by 24 June and the other in the first week of July. The American staff on Wilson's headquarters were prompt to act on these orders and began also to withdraw logistic units earlier. Not only did these withdrawals reduce the forces available for the advance beyond Rome, but they removed the urge to press on and take risks among both the American and French divisions. Harding was deeply disappointed as Kesselring managed to establish a strong delaying position astride Lake Trasimene, to dislodge the enemy from which involved a series of battles in the last ten days of June, the hardest fighting falling to the British 13 and 10 Corps in the centre.

By 5 July Kesselring had established a further delaying position running through Cecina to Arenzo, which he held until 15 July, when, under renewed attack, he withdrew to the Arno, covering his main position, the Gothic line. By this time the die had been cast, the argument over future strategy having escalated to the level of Churchill, who supported Alexander, and Roosevelt, who stood behind Marshall in insisting on the resurrected *Anvil,* now named *Dragoon,* even to the extent of threatening to drag in Stalin as arbiter. On 5 July Alexander had received instructions that *Dragoon* had absolute priority for all allied resources of all kinds in the Mediterranean. He was to surrender not only all the forces of which he had already been warned; but all the French divisions, about seventy per cent of his air support and a large number of important logistic units. The decisive influence in this was Eisenhower's concern at the slow progress of operations in Normandy and his hopes of loosening it up and at the same time opening up another route for American entry into France by an invasion of the south. Alexander and Harding, although bitterly disappointed, did not give up hope and proposed to continue their plan with what was left, but time would clearly be needed in which to build up and prepare for an assault on the Gothic line.

They now moved their headquarters up to a site overlooking Lake Bolsena, north of Viterbo, where they received a number of important visitors. An early one was King George VI, for whom Alexander's caravan was pitched on a rocky promontory overlooking the lake. It was very hot, and a special awning had to be erected to shade it. Harding had been made a Knight Commander of the Bath after the fall of Rome and on 25 July was dubbed a knight in the field by the King himself, an almost unique honour. In a letter to Mary dated 26 July, Harding wrote:

You will have heard and read that the King has been to see us. It was a tremendous thrill for everyone and will do a great deal of good I am sure. He dined with us the night before last and I had quite a long talk with him after dinner. He was in very good form – he hardly stutters at all in ordinary conversation. Yesterday morning we showed him round the headquarters and explained the situation and intelligence maps to him. He seemed very interested. Then all the senior officers of this HQ were presented to him and after that he knighted me and presented the CBE to Lemnitzer and Brian Robertson's American deputy Hamblen. There was a great discussion beforehand whether I should be dubbed Sir John or Sir Allan!! and in the end he said he couldn't knight me Sir John because I'd never been christened John, so it would have to be Sir Allan. I do hope you won't mind. I was so desperately disappointed you couldn't be here, but they told me you wouldn't have been able to see the ceremony if it had been done at home and that it was a great honour to be knighted in the field. The King was very charming and gracious about it all and had brought his own sword to do it. He told me afterwards I could call myself Sir John if I wanted to, but now I don't know what to do. I feel a bit that having been knighted Sir Allan by him I ought to stick to it, but I'd like to do whatever you would prefer. Will you let me know. I do wish you had been here, it would have made all the difference.

Mary favoured 'Sir John' and Harding told his solicitors to arrange for John to be added to his existing Christian names, but they mistook his intention and instead substituted John for them, which led to complications later when he was made a peer. A month later Winston Churchill came and Harding wrote of it on 21 August to Mary:

Winston has been here and for the past four nights I have been lucky enough to dine at the same table. Its been a complete education and I have enjoyed it so much, but I wish with all my heart you could have been with me and taken part in the discussions which ranged over every subject and which you would have loved. He really is a very wonderful old man and in every way typical of what I like to think is truly English. The night before last the Chief and I sat talking to him till 2.30 am!! He insists on calling me 'The Cat's Whiskers' – something to do with a remark Monty apparently made about me which he remembered. He is very attached to the Chief which is very useful. To-night we have got Brookie (Field Marshal Sir Alan Brooke, the CIGS) here, so we are having rather a flood of distinguished visitors at present.

Another visitor was Tito, who came, accompanied by Fitzroy Maclean, to discuss what would happen when Alexander's armies reached Trieste. They flew to Viterbo through some bad weather, and Tito was not a good flier. Harding was working in his caravan when Maclean arrived with a very pale Tito and a rough-looking bodyguard, including a woman with grenades hanging all round her. They asked if Tito could lie down for a rest on Harding's bed, to which he readily agreed. Harding then remembered that he had left his watch in the caravan and, fearing that the bodyguard might take it, decided to go and fetch it. Maclean warned him to be very careful of the bodyguard, who were by then firmly guarding the entrance. However Harding braved them and retrieved his watch unharmed. After lunch the talks took place in the shade of an olive tree. It was clear to Harding that Tito was not going to be at all easy to deal with when their armies met. He and Alexander spoke as one soldier to another, although Harding detected that Tito was also every inch a politician. He was stubborn and uncompromising, but a man for whom Harding felt a natural respect.

There was also a visit by the head of the Russian mission, General Bogomolov, whom Alexander had invited for the night. Three tents had been erected for him and his staff, surrounded by a protective fence, equipped with beds, washbasins and such comforts as a tented camp could offer. When they retired to bed after dinner, they were told that breakfast would be at eight next morning but when morning came there was no sign of them. The ADC went to see if they were all right and found they had gone, leaving a note saying that the general had left, having important business in Rome. It was clear that the whole party had huddled together in one tent. No message had been received for them during the night, and no explanation was ever given.

Life by the side of Lake Bolsena was not all spent receiving visitors. On the very day that Wilson's depressing signal arrived, Harding had completed a third major appreciation, setting out his conclusions on what could be achieved wtih the eighteen divisions which were all that Alexander would have left when he had sent seven to *Dragoon*. He believed that Kesselring's strength would rise to between eighteen and twenty-one divisions; that he would try to hold the Gothic line, but, if forced off it, would fight a series of delaying actions across the Po valley until he reached a final line on the southern side of the Alps. To force him back, Alexander would need six more divisions in order to have a reserve, resting, retraining and preparing for the next assault. The Americans thought that Alexander had enough troops to contain Kesselring and that to give him any more would only encourage the British to pursue their project of aiming for the Ljubljana gap, of which they disapproved both on military and on political grounds. Churchill and the British Chiefs of Staff were anxious to help, but even scraping up every possible source left in the Mediterranean would not provide this number. The only untapped source was the Italians themselves, and Alexander and Harding flew back to London later in this year to discuss how they might be equipped and organized to participate. It was a welcome opportunity for Harding to see Mary and John Charles again and discover how things were progressing at Lower Farm.

On 4 August, the day that the German 14th Army withdrew across the Arno, Alexander and Harding met Leese at Orvieto airfield and discussed with him his army's part in future operations. Contrary to the advice of his staff. Leese proposed a fundamental change from Harding's plan for a concentrated blow in the centre of the Gothic line. Leese found trying to coordinate his plans and operations closely with those of Mark Clark a frustrating business. He wished to get back to the east of the Apennines and exploit the aptitude of the Poles for hill warfare. He would leave Kirkman's 13 Corps under Mark Clark. This drastic change from the plan that Harding had proposed and Alexander approved was discussed between the three of them at length. Alexander, knowing full well the animosity that existed between Leese and Clark, realized that the former would not have his heart in a plan which involved their close cooperation, whereas he would put all the considerable drive and energy which were his best qualities, behind a plan which he had himself proposed.

Harding, who would have stuck out for his original plan if the expert mountain troops of Juin's French Corps had been available, saw which way Alexander's thoughts were tending and did not raise strong objections once all the arguments for and against Leese's proposals had been thoroughly discussed. Alexander therefore accepted it : it would give him the opportunity to employ the strategy he preferred of shifting his weight from one side to another, as one blow attracted the enemy's reserves. There were however considerable snags. All the logistic plans had been based on a build-up west of the watershed. To switch 8th Army across it by only two roads, on which the bridges had not been repaired, would present serious problems and would not be easy to conceal. Finally, the deception plan had been based on trying to persuade Kesselring that the Adriatic coast was where the next blow would fall. But these difficulties were faced and quickly overcome. Alexander's general plan for the operation, to be known as *Olive,* was for the first blow to be struck by Leese on 25 August, using the Polish, Canadian and 5th British Corps side by side, aimed at turning the eastern end of the Gothic line at Rimini. When this had drawn Kesselring's reserves in that direction, 5th Army would assault the centre of the Gothic line, aimed for Bologna. As soon as this had attracted the reserves back again, Leese would renew his attack and break out into the Romagna, the plain between Bologna and Ravenna. The change in plan also posed a problem of protocol to Harding, who had briefed the King on his visit on the basis of the original. The King had returned to England and Harding was anxious that he should not think that he had been wrongly briefed.

By the time that 8th Army moved across the mountains on the night of 22 August, Patch's 7th US Army had landed in the south of France, and by the day of Leese's attack three days later had already reached Grenoble. Kesselring took fright at this and, imagining that Patch would turn east into Italy, sent some of his reserves off in that direction. Both Eisenhower and the Russians were sweeping forward, Romania declared war on Germany on that day and Bulgaria withdrew from the war on the next day. Hungary was restive and the attraction of the strategy favoured by Alexander and Harding seemed greater than ever.

Initially Leese made good progress and pushed the Germans out of the Gothic line defences, but, as Kesselring woke up to the threat, he reinforced the area, holding Leese on the vital Coriano ridge, covering the approach to Rimini. Leese and Keightley were over-optimistic and tried to push the tanks of 1st Armoured Division through on 4 September before the time was ripe. They failed, and two days later heavy rain began to fall. Leese realized that he must prepare another set-piece assault, which could not take place before 12 September. Now it was Clark's turn. He had closed up to the Gothic line, and on 13 September 2nd US Corps began its attack to gain the Futa Pass on Route 65. For four days they fought, but made little progress against the German 4th Parachute Division at the cost of heavy casualties. Kirkman's 13 Corps on their right met less determined resistance and by 17 September had gained the Il Giogo Pass on the road to Imola. This turned the flank of the parachutists, who withdrew from the Futa Pass, opening a gap for 2nd Corps reserve, 88th US Division, guided by Italian partisans, to slip through and reach Monte Battaglia by 27 September, only twelve miles from Imola and the lateral Route 9. Meanwhile Leese had resumed his attacks and had finally broken through into the plain, but at heavy cost in men and equipment. The terrain that lay ahead was no better suited to mobile operations than the mountains left behind. Reclaimed marshland, it was intersected by rivers, streams and canals, bordered by high dykes, all running across the line of advance. The rain poured down and turned it all into a sea of glutinous mud. Across it 8th Army plodded on through October, while 5th Army did the same through the mountains, but it could not quite reach Bologna, although only nine miles away. By now both armies were exhausted, and Alexander decided that the time had come to call a halt.

While the two armies had been pushing their way gradually forward, discussions had been going on at a high level. The first of these had been the conference named 'Octagon', held at Quebec in September, which had taken a rosy and relaxed view of the situation. American objections to a thrust towards the Ljubljana gap were no longer upheld and they were even prepared to leave landing craft in the Mediterranean for an operation across the head of the Adriatic to Istria. Eisenhower had all the divisions he could handle for the moment, and there was no pressure to remove more from Italy until von Vietinghoff (who had succeeded Kesselring as the overall German commander when the latter had been seriously hurt in a car accident on 25 October) had been defeated south of the Po, which was confidently expected within a month or two. When Churchill visited Alexander on his way to Moscow in October, the latter with greater realism suggested to him that a spring offensive would be necessary, and that it should take the form of transferring the 8th Army, now commanded by McCreery, Leese having been transferred to command the land forces in Southeast Asia under Mountbatten, across the Adriatic to thrust north through Yugoslavia to Ljubljana, while 5th Army advanced across the Po valley to Venice and Trieste. For this he would need three more American divisions. Churchill relished the proposal and, bypassing both Wilson and the Chiefs of Staff, signalled Roosevelt direct asking for them.

By this time the mood in London and Washington was more sober. Arnhem had failed, and it was clear that Eisenhower's armies would be faced not only with a winter campaign, the first and most urgent priority for which was to open up the port of Antwerp, but with a much tougher spring offensive than had previously been thought. All this would make great demands on the allied stocks of artillery ammunition, which had shrunk to a critical level, the expenditure in all theatres having greatly exceeded the estimates. Brooke was no longer a supporter of Alexander's project. He took a pessimistic view of what could still be achieved in Italy and no longer thought that activity there could have any significant effect on the situation in Northwest Europe, nor did it seem possible that Alexander could reach Vienna before the Russians. His first concern was to persuade Eisenhower to adopt both what he regarded as the correct strategy and also the right command organization. He saw no point in continuing to annoy the Americans by disagreeing with them over future operations in Italy. The three divisions were refused, and Alexander modified his proposal from a major amphibious assault across the Adriatic to the introduction of light forces to secure and establish communications and facilities which could make possible the transfer of 8th Army, once the major thrust towards Venetia by 5th Army had begun to develop.

Alexander's proposals, which Harding had played a major part in developing, were influenced by the knowledge that, before his accident, Kesselring had proposed to Hitler a withdrawal, named *Autumn Mist,* to a Venetian line, based on defending the River Adige. He did not therefore expect great difficulty in pushing the Germans back to this line – it was not known until later that Hitler had refused to accept any withdrawal. The target date for the revised plan was early February. To make this possible, it would be necessary to bring operations to capture Bologna and Ravenna to an end by 15 November. It was important to secure these two key places, both in order to provide starting points for 5th Army's part in the proposed plan, and also to provide enough space in which to house the armies during the winter. The prospect of having to spend it in the mountains was not at all attractive.

Alexander's immediate plan was for McCreery to continue to press forward towards both Ravenna and Bologna, while Clark ostentatiously withdrew some of his forces. When 8th Army had drawn all von Vietinghoff's reserves towards them and had reached the River Santerno, twenty miles east of Bologna, Clark would rapidly return his forces to the front line and go for Bologna itself. Alexander and Harding discussed this plan with the army commanders on 29 October. Both of the latter pressed for an extension of time, which was agreed. Clark was to be ready to launch his attack from 30 November onwards and the operations would come to a halt by 15 December, by which time McCreery estimated that his resources would be exhausted. A spell of fine weather in November helped. By 9 November Anders's Polish Corps had entered Forli, and towards the end of the month they and Keightley's 5th British Corps were converging on Faenza, less than thirty miles from Bologna; but then the rain began again. Alexander agreed to a further deferment of target dates, Clark's resumption of the offensive being put off until 7 December, while the end of the month was to see the completion of the operation.

In the first week of December Ravenna fell to the Canadians; by the middle of the month Faenza had been captured and both the New Zealanders and Canadians were up to the lower reaches of the Senio, the last river before the Santerno, Alexander decided that he could not wait for McCreery to reach the latter and ordered Clark to prepare to attack on 22 December; but as he did so, intelligence came to hand that on Mussolini's orders, a counterattack by two of Graziani's Italian divisions from the Army of Liguria, supported by at least one German division, was imminent on the west coast, threatening the port of Leghorn on which Clark depended for his supplies. The only division in the area was the 92nd US (Negro) Division, and Clark was forced to send 8th Indian Division from Kirkman's 13 Corps to reinforce it. This involved cancelling his projected attack towards Bologna and brought the hopes of reaching the city in the current round of operations to an end, the onset of winter weather adding to all the other factors which compelled it. This was not the only cause of disappointment. Events in Greece had demanded the dispatch there first of 4th and later 46th British Divisions, until the strength diverted to defeating the communist attempt to take over the country rose to 81,000.

On 12 December 1944 Alexander had succeeded Wilson as Supreme Commander at Allied Forces Headquarters at Caserta, Wilson moving to Washington to act as representative of the British Chiefs of Staff in place of Dill, who had died there in November. Almost his first task in his new position was to accompany Churchill to Athens to deal with the crisis there. Mark Clark took over command of 15 Army Group, handing over 5th Army to Truscott, brought back from France. Churchill had pressed for Alexander to combine both appointments and Brooke had great difficulty in persuading him that to do so would be committing the very fault of which they both accused Eisenhower in Northwest Europe. Churchill and Brooke had in fact been suggesting that Alexander should be sent to join Eisenhower as overall land-force commander. For Harding it meant little change. He and key members of Alexander's staff went with him to AFHQ at Caserta, leaving the rest of the headquarters, then in Florence, to Mark Clark, who brought Al Gruenther with him as Chief of Staff and a number of other key staff officers from 5th Army Headquarters to replace those who had left with Harding.

Alexander's plan to cross the Adriatic and head for Ljubljana having been rejected, the planners now looked on the Mediterranean as a reserve from which to feed Northwest Europe. Rundstedt's counter-offensive in the Ardennes at the end of December had made them revise their ideas about the fight left in the enemy, and they estimated that by mid-April Eisenhower's ninety-one divisions would be facing ninety German and Alexander's twenty-four facing twenty-seven. To give Eisenhower the superiority he needed, six to ten divisions should be switched to him from Alexander. However, when the Chiefs of Staff met at Malta in January on their way to Yalta, they reduced this to five, two of which were to be Canadian, the whole of Foulkes's Corps. The other three were to be found from elsewhere in the Mediterranean, and Mark Clark was compensated by the arrival of 10th US Mountain Division, a Brazilian division, the American-Japanese

Division and the formation of five Italian brigades. These limitations forced Alexander to abandon his idea of crossing the Adriatic, a proposal which in any case Tito did not favour – realizing that Alexander's forces were not likely to be able to take the pressure off him, while Russian advances would do so, he became cooler towards the British and more welcoming to the Russians.

The plan that Alexander and Mark Clark evolved for the spring offensive of 1945 was greatly influenced by the course of the River Reno, which looped round Bologna and entered the sea on the southern side of the lagoon of Lake Comacchio. Alexander wished to avoid forcing a crossing of the river, at the same time using it to help trap the German 10th Army. Using a variety of amphibious craft including tracked amphibians called Fantails, 8th Army would cross the lake to seize the so-called Argenta Gap, where Route 16 from Ravenna to Ferrara crossed the Reno and ran between it and the lake. South of this, its main thrust would be westward, north of Route 9, through Massa Lombarda, thence either turning north to join up with the forces that had crossed the lake, or continuing westward to outflank Bologna from the northeast. All this was to be the task of Keightley's 5 Corps. The Polish Corps was to push westward to the south of them towards Bologna, while 13 Corps, returned to 8th Army's command, would hold the mountain front south of the Poles before the battle, and then come into reserve. 10 Corps, whose headquarters had been sent to Greece but would return for the battle, would command a special taskforce of troops to bridge the Po. Truscott's 5th Army would attack northwards west of Bologna, and then swing round eastwards to join the 8th, while thrusting northwards also to cross the Po, heading for Verona and the Brenner Pass, at the same time as McCreery would turn eastwards to Trieste. There were two problems of timing: first of the attack itself, and then between the two armies. To be certain of good weather and that all preparation could be completed in time, May or June would be preferable; but if the operations were to contribute to those of other fronts, that would be too late. After much discussion 11 April was selected.

Harding had long been chafing at the bit to get command of a corps, of which he had been deprived by his appointment as

Alexander's Chief of Staff, before the war came to an end. The opportunity came when Kirkman, whose relations with Mark Clark had been poor, when 13 Corps was under command of 5th Army, developed severe arthritis. Now that all the main planning for the future had been completed, Alexander was prepared to let Harding go, and on 6 March, to his delight, he assumed command of 13 Corps, to which in the desert days he had contributed so much, his place as Chief of Staff to Alexander being taken by General Morgan, who had been responsible for planning the invasion of Normandy before Eisenhower and Montgomery had taken over. At this time the corps was in the mountains south of Imola and had only 10th Indian Division under command. Its task in the forthcoming battle was to be in reserve initially, prepared, as the Polish Corps advanced westward towards Bologna and Keightley's 5 Corps northwestward, to come between them and drive westward on the right flank of the Poles, aiming at Budrio on the River Idice, some ten miles northeast of Bologna, while 5 Corps dealt with the Argenta Gap area. The deception plan was to simulate a landing north of the Po in the area of Venice and to draw attention to the Mediterranean coast by a preliminary attack there by the 92nd US (Negro) Division. This was successful, von Vietinghoff sending one of his only two reserve divisions, 29th Panzer Grenadier, to meet the former threat.

In a preliminary attack in the first week of April, Royal Marine units captured the 'spit' at the eastern end of Lake Comacchio and the islands in the centre. Both this attack and the American one at the other end of the front drew parts of the slender German reserves into the line. 8th Army's main attack started in perfect weather on 9 April, a day earlier than planned, and by 12 April both the Poles and 5 Corps were over the Santerno, the New Zealanders capturing Massa Lombarda that afternoon. By this time two brigades of 56th Division had crossed Lake Comacchio and were meeting stiff resistance east of Bastia. 5th Army should also have started its attack on this day, but the weather had turned bad and Mark Clark postponed it until the 14th in order that full-scale air support could be provided.

It was at this stage that Harding's corps was brought into the battle, taking over command of the New Zealand Division to drive westward towards Budrio, freeing Keightley to struggle for the Argenta Gap, which was being stubbornly defended. Harding did not wait for 10th Indian Division to deploy before starting his attack: Freyberg's New Zealanders forced a crossing of the River Sillaro during the night of 13/14 April, while the Poles to the south of them captured Imola. On the 14th the Americans started their attack in the mountains south of Bologna, von Vietinghoff by this time having committed most of his reserves, 20th and 90th Panzer Grenadier Divisions, to meet the threat posed by 8th Army in his eastern sector. On the night of 15/16 April the New Zealanders attacked again, and by the end of the 17th they had closed up to the Gaiana canal. 10th Indian Division had been brought up on their right flank, heading north for Molinella, but made slow progress, obstructed as much by mud and by minefields in the low-lying plain as by the enemy. On the night of 18/19 April Freyberg advanced again, crossing the Gaiana canal and reaching the River Idice to find the bridges blown but the river undefended. Von Vietinghoff had decided to withdraw north of the Reno to avoid encirclement.

Two days later, 20 April, Hitler's birthday, von Vietinghoff gave orders for a general withdrawal north of the Po, his previous request on 14 April to do so having been refused by the Führer. His chances of executing this withdrawal in good order were destroyed both by the swift advance of Truscott's 5th Army west of Bologna (spearheaded by the 10th US Mountain Division and 6th South African Armoured Division) and significantly, by the breakout of 6th British Armoured Division through the Argenta Gap along the north bank of the Reno towards Ferrara and Bondino on the Po, a few miles southwest of which, at a village appropriately called Finale, the two 6th Armoured Divisions joined hands on 23 April.

McCreery had originally intended to employ 10 Corps with its special taskforce to force the crossing of the Po, but General Hawksworth, its commander, had fallen sick – he died not long afterwards – and he changed the plan by leaving 5 Corps in action on the right and swinging Harding to face north on Keightley's left, keeping Freyberg under his command, but taking over 8th Indian and 6th Armoured Divisions from 5 Corps. All the bridging equipment had been allotted to Keightley, but Harding was determined to get his corps into the lead for the final advance to prevent the Germans from standing on the Venetian line. On the night of 24 April he closed up to the Po south of Bondero with Murray's 6th Armoured Division on the right and Freyberg's New Zealanders on the left. He was convinced that the Germans would not stand on the river bank and told his chief engineer, Brigadier Walkey, by hook or by crook to get hold of enough bridging material to build one pontoon bridge. He then went to see Murray and told him to have Verney's Guards Brigade ready to cross that night. When he suggested that Freyberg should also be prepared to get a brigade over the river, he found him in one of his cautious moods, very dubious about the prospects of success.

On his way back to his headquarters, Harding met McCreery, who told him that the Germans were withdrawing and that they only had a light screen of troops on the river. Harding therefore told Murray to get a brigade over and establish a bridgehead. Having done so, he spoke to Freyberg, told him what McCreery had said and that Murray was going to send a brigade over the river. He said that he hoped Freyberg would be able to do the same, although he did not order him to do so. Freyberg asked if Murray had been ordered to cross, and, having been told that he had, decided, without saying so at the time, that he could not be left behind. One of his brigades crossed that night and, reinforced by 43rd Gurkha Lorried Infantry Brigade and 14/20th Hussars, he led the advance to the Adige, which was reached two days later.

By this time the negotiations for a surrender, initiated by General Wolff as early as March and pursued more vigorously from 14 April onwards, were nearing completion. On 28 April, the day that Mussolini and his mistress were shot by partisans near Lake Como, von Vietinghoff agreed that Wolff should go to Alexander's headquarters at Caserta and sign terms which were to come into force at 2 pm on 2 May. There was a last-minute hitch on 30 April when Kesselring heard what had occurred and relieved von Vietinghoff and his Chief of Staff. It was not until the early hours of 2 May itself, after the news of Hitler's death had been announced, that Kesselring finally gave his approval.

While this had been going on, Harding's corps had been pressing on, first to the Venetian line, behind the Adige. This was penetrated on 28 April when a bridge at Este was found intact. Harding decided to stop Murray's 6th Armoured Division and give absolute priority to Freyberg's New Zealanders, who were told to send only the minimum force to Venice and concentrate their effort on getting as quickly as possible to Trieste. Led by the armoured cars of 12th Lancers, Freyberg drove his men on, and at 3 pm on 1 May D Squadron of the 12th Lancers met Yugoslav troops near Monfalcone. Harding had caught up with Freyberg at San Giorgio, twenty miles west of the Isonzo, while Freyberg was talking to the leaders of Osoppo, a right-wing Italian partisan group. Harding told him to get troops as soon as possible into both Gorizia and Trieste. At half past five that evening Freyberg met two senior Yugoslav officers. They readily agreed that Freyberg's troops should spend the night near Monfalcone and promised to arrange for him to meet the commander of the 4th Yugoslav Army at half past seven. He never turned up, and at 11 pm that night Freyberg spoke to Harding, who confirmed that he must get his troops into Trieste and Gorizia next day. The Yugoslav general had still not kept his rendezvous in the morning, and Freyberg moved on to Trieste, surrounded by Yugoslav troops and signs that they considered the area already as Yugoslav territory.

It was a fitting climax to Harding's service in the Second World War that he should be commanding the corps with which he had been associated since its formation out of Western Desert Force in the early days, when it reached the final objective of the whole Mediterranean campaign, and that the division under his command to do so should have been Freyberg's New Zealanders, who had shared with him so many of the dangers, hardships and vicissitudes of the long road from the Nile to the Isonzo.

F

CHAPTER TEN

POSTWAR PROBLEMS
1945–51

When Freyberg came to rest in Trieste, Harding's advanced headquarters was at Monfalcone and his rear headquarters back
at Padua. A few miles east of Monfalcone was the magnificent
castle of Duino, built on a promontory overlooking the sea, and
belonging to Prince von Thurn and Taxis.[1] Harding moved his
headquarters into this very agreeable site and prepared both to
celebrate victory and to deal with the problems that immediately
arose over the occupation of Trieste and the rest of Venezia
Giulia.

These did not take him by surprise. Terence Airey, then head
of Alexander's intelligence staff (shortly to become Harding's
Chief of Staff), recalls that when he went with Alexander and
Harold Macmillan in December 1944 to Greece, where they were
joined by Churchill and Eden, to deal with the crisis there,
Harding told him to make certain that Alexander took the opportunity to raise with Eden and his advisers the need to clarify the
rather vague agreement that had been reached with Tito when
he had visited Alexander by Lake Bolsena. Although Tito had
accepted that Alexander would need to use Trieste and Venezia
Giulia generally as his line of communication, if operations were
developed towards the Ljubljana gap or into Austria, no agreement had been reached as to who should exercise general authority
in the area. Harding wished it to be agreed that, at any rate in
Trieste and western Istria, the British should be the occupying
power, without prejudice to the final decision on the frontier

---

[1] The word 'taxi' is derived from an ancestor who grew rich on the
proceeds of operating stage coaches all over Europe. The chequered sign
on many taxis has its origin in his family coat-of-arms.

between Yugoslavia and Italy. Airey quoted this as an example of Harding's great qualities of foresight, of anticipating problems and attempting to overcome all the difficulties in their solution before they arose.

Foreign Office advice was that Alexander should reach a 'gentleman's agreement' direct with Tito on the subject. When Alexander and Airey visited him in Belgrade in February 1945, Tito's reply was that he would like to have an occupation force of three thousand men in Venezia Giulia, which would come under Alexander's command. As the war neared its end, it became evident to Tito that he was less in need of help from the Anglo-American forces to clear the Germans out of his country, and that the Russians were going to be in a better position to influence affairs on his borders. He began to turn towards them and to pay less attention to support to or from Alexander. On 9 April a hand-grenade had been thrown at the Yugoslav military mission in Rome, which had caused a considerable stir in Belgrade. Tito then visited Moscow and, while there, on 15 April made an official claim to the whole of Istria, that is to the frontier which had been that between Italy and Austria before 1914, and which had been changed after the First World War to give the whole of Istria, including the ports of Trieste and Pola, the former Austrian naval base, to Italy. The ethnic situation was that the inhabitants of the ports of Trieste, Pola and Fiume were largely Italian, while the sparsely populated area of the hinterland was inhabited by Slovenes.

On 30 April Tito announced that his 4th Yugoslav Army had entered Fiume, Pola and Trieste, and on 1 May that they had occupied Gorizia and stood on the Isonzo. Alexander announced simultaneously that the New Zealand Division had crossed the Isonzo and contacted Tito's troops. On 3 May, as has been told, the New Zealanders entered Trieste and the situation remained confused for the following week, and tense for the following month, although Harding's relations were cordial with the local Yugoslav commander, General Drapsin, who was a cheerful and convivial character – though this did not prevent him from placing a Yugoslav detachment, manning a captured German anti-aircraft battery, with its guns pointing straight at the window of Harding's office. The Yugoslav flag flew over the town hall in Trieste and they refused to acknowledge Harding's right to take over the administration or to do more than make use of the area for purely military purposes, while Tito continued to make belligerent noises from Belgrade.

On 19 May Alexander issued a statement saying that the allies were now waiting to hear whether Tito was prepared to cooperate in accepting a peaceful settlement of his territorial claims or whether he would attempt to establish them by force, to which Tito replied that Yugoslavia could not be tricked out of its rights, but was prepared for collaboration and agreement on a basis which should not be insulting or humiliating to her as an allied country. In a separate statement he said that the Yugoslav army, as one of the allied armies, had equal rights to remain in the territory it had liberated and the honour of his country demanded the presence of the Yugoslav army in Istria, Trieste and the Slovene coastline. This exchange was followed by negotiations in Washington, London and Belgrade, as a result of which it was announced on 9 June that agreement had been reached that :

1. The western part of Istria and Trieste, through which ran the railways and roads from Trieste to Austria via Gorizia, Caporetto and Tarvisio, as well as Pola and the anchorages of the coastal littoral were to be under command of the Supreme Allied Commander.

2. Yugoslav troops in the area, limited to a detachment of regular troops not exceeding 2,000, were to occupy a district selected by the Supreme Allied Commander and not to have access to other areas.

3. Using Allied Military Government, the Supreme Allied Commander was to govern the area in paragraph 1 as he might deem necessary. A small Yugoslav detachment would be attached to Headquarters 8th Army as observers.

4. Tito was to withdraw other Yugoslav forces in the area, which was to come under Allied Military Government by 0800 hours 12 June.

5. The Yugoslav government was to return residents who had been deported or arrested and to make restitution for property removed.

6. These arrangements were not to prejudice the ultimate disposals of Venezia Giulia either in western Istria under Allied Military Government or in eastern Istria under the Yugoslav government.

These new arrangements came into force peacefully on 12 June

1945, when the Yugoslav flag was run down on the town hall and replaced by the Union Jack and the Stars and Stripes, Harding by then having taken under command 88th US Infantry Division, which replaced 8th Indian in the Gorizia area. On 20 June a further agreement was reached between Generals Morgan and Jovanović on the demarcation line between the two areas, to be known subsequently as the Morgan line. It produced a number of anomalies, separating farmers from their fields and in one case running through the middle of a cemetery, but it was a great achievement to have reached agreement on it so quickly and it served its purpose well.

Harding could now at last relax, and he had the good sense to appreciate that this was what his soldiers wished to do also. As a reward to them and also to avoid discontent arising out of the orderly fashion in which demobilization and the rundown had to take place, priority clearly being given to the return to their own countries of troops of other countries of the Commonwealth, he paid much attention to the welfare and entertainment of the troops, combining these with military displays which also served to impress the inhabitants and the Yugoslavs. General Drapsin had been replaced by an unsympathetic character in General Dapsović, who took a hard line about everything, although this was compensated for by the goodwill of the Yugoslav liaison officer at Harding's headquarters, Colonel Benčić.

Life at Duino was pleasant and his task interesting without being arduous. He found time to take up polo and racing again in spite of his injuries. One of the first problems was to build up a police force for Trieste against a background of criticism from Yugoslavia that ex-fascists were being employed for the purpose. Harding's Deputy Provost Marshal, Geoffrey White, a Hendon graduate, was given the task. Founding it initially on a force of purely military police, he evolved an efficient civilian police force which gained much credit in later troubled times in the city. He was to serve with Harding again many years later in Cyprus.

A personal problem that faced the Hardings as the war came to an end was the future of their son, John Charles. When Harding had returned to England on duty in the autumn of 1944, he was faced with the question as to whether or not his son should apply for deferment of his conscription, the call-up for which took place when a young man was seventeen and a half. The headmaster of his school, Marlborough advised that he should do so. Harding however took the view that, if he missed the opportunity of service during the war, he would never forgive himself. In the event the war in Europe came to an end before he was called up. When Harding went home on leave soon after the war ended, he himself took his son along to the recruiting office, and, after he had returned, John Charles joined a primary training regiment run by the Green Jackets, first at Winchester and later at Retford. When he was a lance-corporal at the Royal Armoured Corps training centre, he came out to Trieste, brought out by the American General Lee who succeeded General Ridgway as the titular Allied Commander in Italy. Joining the General's party at Claridges as a lance-corporal was an experience he did not forget. He had seen very little of his father since 1939, when he was only eleven, but had always found him most sympathetic and interested in all he did, and a most faithful and regular correspondent.

In the spring of 1946 wives were allowed to join their husbands and Mary came out to Duino. Their rooms were in the same passage as that of their ADC, John Joicey, and Terence Airey recalled that, after Mary arrived, he warned the duty officer, a tough parachuting Yorkshire gunner, that if anything occurred during the night which required the General's attention he should not wake him directly, but wake the ADC instead. It happened that an urgent message did come in, and the duty officer, mistaking the Harding's door for that of the ADC, banged on it and shouted as he opened it: 'Wake up John, you lazy b***r, I've got something for you', to find himself faced with the other John and Mary sitting up in bed laughing their heads off.

Changes in the command organization naturally took place after the war. The first, soon after it ended, was the departure of Alexander, who was succeeded by Morgan, 8th Army having been converted into Central Mediterranean Force, until in November 1946 the latter was merged with Harding's own headquarters and he became its commander. The Allied Headquarters to which he reported for allied matters was then at Leghorn, first under General Ridgway and later under Lee. The Trieste situation began to darken again in March 1946, when it was announced that the four powers, the USA, Britain, the Soviet Union and France, had appointed a commission to make recommendations for a boundary between Italy and Yugoslavia in Venezia Giulia. On 1 April Tito, in a general review of foreign policy, demanded the return of the whole of Venezia Giulia and accused Allied

Military Government of admitting twelve trains and seventy lorries of 'fascist bandits armed like d'Annunzio's and Mussolini's in order to intimidate the inhabitants into giving evidence to the commission, and of disbanding the local police and introducing fascists in their place. This was a build-up to the visit of the commission itself, which took place in a tense atmosphere. They left the area on 5 April to report to the Foreign Ministers' Conference, which met in Paris at the end of the month to prepare the peace treaties. All four ministers put forward different lines as the frontier, Molotov proposing the 1914 frontier, giving the whole area to Yugoslavia, the others proposing variations of the 'Wilson' line of 1919 with some concessions to Yugoslavia, although eventually Britain and America dropped their proposals in favour of that of the French; but no decision was reached and a proposal for a plebiscite was rejected.

At the end of May the British and American governments delivered a note to Tito protesting at Yugoslav propaganda and unfriendly acts in Venezia Giulia, and the British protested again in July at unauthorized crossings of the Morgan line by Yugoslav troops which had led to clashes between them and allied soldiers. There were two serious incidents in August: first when two US Air Force transport aircraft were shot down by Yugoslav fighters when they strayed into Yugoslav airspace on their way from Udine to Vienna; the second when two Yugoslav officers drove fast through the main street of Gorizia after a bomb had exploded during a mass to celebrate the liberation of the city by the Italian army in 1916. Their car was held up by the crowd, and the civil and the US military police had to protect them when the driver brandished a hand-grenade, further grenades and a pistol being found in the car. Fortunately General Moore, commanding 88th US Division, and Colonel Benčić sorted it out, and the latter sent the two officers packing to their side of the Morgan line.

In November Tito offered to surrender his claim to Trieste in return for Gorizia, but the Italians refused. By this time arrangements for the completion of a peace treaty with Italy were nearing finality. This would hand over most of the area occupied by the Yugoslavs to them, but proposed to establish a Free Territory of Trieste under United Nations supervision, consisting of Zone A, from Duino to the Morgan line between Trieste and Capodistria, i.e. that part occupied by the Anglo-American force under Harding's command, and Zone B, from the Morgan line down to Novigrad and the River Mirna, occupied by the Yugoslav army. This was to be a permanently Free Territory (similar to Danzig under the League of Nations between the wars), guaranteed by the United Nations and under a governor, who was to be neither a Yugoslav nor an Italian. This was approved by the United Nations Security Council in January 1947 and incorporated in the Italian peace treaty, signed in Paris on 10 February. However Yugoslavia never accepted it and no governor was ever appointed. On 1 February 1947 the Allied Control Commission in Italy had been abolished and its remaining functions vested in Allied Force Headquarters at Leghorn. On 15 June an agreement was signed with the Italian Government under which all occupation forces were withdrawn and the area of Venezia Giulia left to Italy under the peace treaty was handed over to them. This took place shortly before Harding handed over command of Central Mediterranean Force to his Chief of Staff, Terence Airey, who thereafter was solely responsible for Zone A of the Free Territory of Trieste. In fact it was not until October 1954 that the problem was solved, by handing over Zone A to Italy and letting Yugoslavia keep Zone B, and not till 1977 that the two countries finally recognized the arrangement as their mutual frontier.

It had originally been intended that Harding should leave in February 1947 to take over Southern Command in England, but his departure had been delayed because he had been the convening officer of the war crimes trial which charged Kesselring, von Mackensen and Melze of implication in the massacre of Italian hostages in the Ardientine caves as a reprisal for the death of German soldiers at the hands of partisans in Rome. Harding found the whole affair highly distasteful. It had been decided that Kesselring and von Mackensen should be tried by a British military court sitting in Venice, but that Melze should be tried by an Italian one. One of the complications was that Mussolini had abolished the death penalty in Italy, but, after an exchange of telegrams with the British ambassador in Rome, Sir Noel Charles, the Foreign Office ruled that in certain exceptional circumstances it was possible for an Italian military court to impose the death penalty. Kesselring and von Mackensen were convicted and sentenced to death, but Harding commuted their sentences to life imprisonment.

This period of two years in Trieste had been a welcome opportunity to take life at a slower tempo and to enjoy it to the full – and Harding was one who loved life and liked enjoying it – and to renew a family life which, apart from the five months when he was in England recovering from his wounds and was under considerable mental and physical strain, he had been unable to enjoy since he left for India in 1939. At the same time the highly political atmosphere of Trieste and the problems of Venezia Giulia had been of interest and were to be of value to him in the responsible posts which lay ahead.

Southern Command had superseded Aldershot Command as the plum home command, containing as it did, the majority of operational units based in the United Kingdom. It had the added advantage of including Harding's own home, the headquarters at Salisbury being only about an hour's drive from Nether Compton. Lower Farm was let furnished and the Hardings lived in Clive House, Tidworth, originally built to house the commander of the Cavalry Brigade. The original Commander-in-Chief's house in Salisbury had been turned into an officers' mess and the divisional commander's house, Bulford Manor, into flats. The Hardings were happy in Clive House, from which they could easily ride out into the open spaces of Salisbury Plain. They both took up hunting again and John shooting also.

Pleasant as life was, Harding did not find his job easy. The army was both running down and in a rundown state. There was no clear plan for the future and it was not easy to give national servicemen a sense of purpose (national service took the place of wartime conscription in 1948). Harding concentrated on the field of training, at which he had always been expert and enthusiastic, one aspect of it being assessment of the lessons of the war and inculcating them among those who, for one reason or another, had not experienced active service during the war. Montgomery was CIGS at the time, but in November 1948 he handed over to Slim. Soon after the latter had taken over, Harding, at a conference for all Territorial Army commanders and association chairmen, stressed the importance of retaining the Territorial Army because of the threat of militant communism. This was leaked to the press and Shinwell, Secretary of State for War, was furious. Slim rang Harding and passed the rebuke on. He said that Shinwell had wanted to send for Harding and rebuke him personally, but Slim had advised him not to, 'as Harding might lose his temper and bite you.'

It was at this time that an incident occurred which caused considerable amusement. Mary was accompanying him to a ceremonial parade and, in order not to crease her skirt, had removed it and wrapped a rug round her. On arrival she had forgotten this and, when the door of the car was opened, she stepped out, flinging the rug aside, clad only in her petticoat. As usual she was as amused as everyone else.

At this time John Charles, who had been commissioned as a national service officer into the 11th Hussars in October 1947, came to the end of his conscript time and, feeling that life in the army was not for him, went up to Oxford in 1948 to read PPE. When he came down in 1951 he joined Churchman's in Ipswich, a subsidiary of Imperial Tobacco, but decided that the indoor life was not what he wanted. He returned to the army, his father having persuaded the 11th Hussars to take him back as a regular officer after he had passed the regular commissions board, although he naturally forfeited seniority. He served with his regiment for another fifteen years, reaching the rank of major and retiring in 1968 two years after he had married Harriet Hare, granddaughter of Harding's divisional commander at the First battle of Gaza.

In July 1949, after two years at home, Harding was off abroad again. Slim had chosen him to succeed Ritchie as Commander-in-Chief Far East Land Forces with overall command of the army in Malaya and Hong Kong. In those days there was no joint service commander, the activities of the three services being coordinated in the British Defence Coordinating Committee Far East under the chairmanship of the Commissioner-General South East Asia, then Malcolm MacDonald. MacDonald's position was a curious one. After the end of the war a Governor-General for the British territories in Malaya and Borneo had been appointed, as well as a Special Commissioner for South East Asia, to coordinate British government policy in all fields in the area. Malcolm MacDonald had been the Governor-General and, when Lord Killearn retired in 1948, he had absorbed the post of Special Commissioner also. However he no longer had any executive authority over the High Commissioner in Kuala Lumpur, who was *de facto* Governor-General of Malaya, nor over the governors of the colonies in the area – Hong Kong, Singapore, North Borneo, Sarawak and other island dependencies. Nevertheless he exercised considerable influence. Harding's colleagues when he was appointed were Admiral Sir Patrick Brind and Air Marshal Sir Hugh Pugh Lloyd, to be succeeded respectively by Sir Guy Russell and Sir Francis Fogarty.

Harding's arrival came at a crucial time. A state of emergency had been declared in Malaya in June 1948, and the state of affairs there, in spite of an atmosphere of euphoria in official circles, was not at all satisfactory. To understand it one must hark back to the situation in Malaya when the war came to an end. The only effective resistance to the Japanese, and that had been very limited, had been centred on the Malayan Peoples' Anti-Japanese Army, consisting largely of communists among the Malayan Chinese. They had been supported by Force 136, the Far East branch of the Special Operations Executive, and one of their young leaders, Chin Peng, received the OBE for his services and took part in the victory celebrations in London. Force 136, working under the direction of Mountbatten's South East Asia Command, trained inhabitants of the Malayan peninsula of all races as resistance leaders and infiltrated them back into the country by submarine or parachute. One of their tasks was to contact the Malayan Anti-Japanese Army and act as the radio link to Force 136 to arrange supplies. One of those infiltrated, unfortunately captured soon after his arrival, was a future chief of the Malayan forces, General Ibrahim, whose prime task in the 1970s was, ironically, to direct the campaign against the communist forces of Chin Peng, still holding out on the Thai-Malay border.

In contrast to the situation in Europe, the inhabitants of Malaya did not see the enemy driven out by the allies. The war ended before this could happen, and their memories were rather of the British rout before Singapore fell. British administration had been discredited and, in a loose federation of eleven states, over which British authority had never at any time been anything but light, it was not easy to re-establish it. Police morale was at an all-time low and banditry was rife. Britain's answer to this was to attempt to introduce a centralized government embracing all racial elements, the so-called Malayan Union. It was hotly opposed by all Malays, and in 1947 the British government had backed down and reverted to the more traditional structure in which it was recognized that the country was Malay and that authority rested basically on the Malay sultans of the separate states. This came as a great disappointment to the Chinese, Indians, Tamils and others whose hopes of being accepted as full citizens of the country were dashed.

The situation offered considerable opportunities to the almost wholly Chinese Malayan Communist Party. However it was itself in difficulties. Its leader, Loi Tak, was in fact an agent of the Singapore police. He came from Annam and had been acquired by them in the 1930s in Saigon, where his useful life as a French agent had come to an end when he was 'blown'. When Singapore fell, he became a Japanese agent and was undoubtedly responsible for some of the blows which the Singapore and Malayan communists suffered under their occupation. He did not come under serious suspicion until 1948, when he went into hiding in Singapore. He was probably done to death by a communist murder squad in Thailand some years later. There is no doubt that he fostered dissensions that split the Malayan Communist Party at this time, dissensions that reflected those within China itself, principally over the question of whether to embark on an armed struggle, which some thought should have been taken up as soon as the war ended, or to concentrate on infiltrating the trade-union movement and overthrowing imperialism by ruining the economy and undermining the authority of the government in that way. Throughout 1947, and increasingly in 1948, the communists were active and successful in pursuing the latter policy, and the authorities were ambivalent in dealing with it. Accusations that the trouble was caused by communist conspiracy tended to be dismissed as reactionary exaggeration, the blame being laid at the door of unsympathetic employers. As the situation deteriorated in the first half of 1948 there was a general feeling, which Malcolm MacDonald shared, that the colonial government of the Federation, and in particular the High Commisioner himself, Sir Edward Gent, leant too far towards this view, underestimating the threat to law, order and good government, and failed to take sufficient steps to counter it. MacDonald had prevailed on the Colonial Office to relieve Gent and to replace him by a tougher figure, when matters came to a head in June 1948.

It is not easy to say clearly who started the 'Long, Long War', as Richard Clutterbuck has described it, but the principle steps which preceded the declaration of an emergency on 17 June 1948 are clear. One was a communist youth conference in Calcutta in

February of that year; a second was the disappearance of Loi Tak and his deposition as secretary of the Malayan Communist Party in March, to be replaced by Chin Peng, who was naturally inclined to think in terms of armed struggle and to resuscitate the Malayan Peoples' Anti-Japanese Army through its old comrades' association; finally there was the action of the government itself in reaction both to the internal developments within the MCP and to the increasing number of strikes and incidents. The MCP clearly knew that consideration was being given to banning the party, arresting its leaders and either detaining or 'banishing' them. As a defensive measure therefore it was prudent of Chin Peng to go underground and turn to the armed struggle.

The critical incident was the murder of three European rubber estate managers near Sungei Supit, a communist area of Perak, on 16 June 1948, which itself may have been a reaction to the deployment of Gurkha troops in that area. A state of emergency was declared the next day and, as seemed typical of colonial struggles of that time, all the principal authorities responsible went away. Sir Edward Gent, after a stormy meeting with MacDonald on 22 June, flew back to London on 28 June and was killed when the RAF York in which he was travelling collided with another aircraft near London. His successor, Sir Henry Gurney, previously Chief Secretary in Palestine, did not arrive until October. The Commissioner of Police, Mr Langworthy, who had been in bad health for some time, promptly resigned and was succeeded in August by Colonel Gray, previously Inspector-General of the Palestine Police. The General Officer Commanding Malaya, Major-General Wade, had left a few weeks before and been replaced by Major-General Boucher. It is not surprising therefore that no very firm grip was taken in the early days. The same could be said of the opposition, which tended to give the authorities the impression that matters were improving. At this stage the emphasis by everyone, including the army, was that responsibility lay primarily with the police, the task of the rest of government and of the military being to help them where and when they asked for it; but when the army was asked to help by assuming responsibility for guards, its reaction, as always, was to say that this was no task for trained soldiers, who should be used to engage the enemy's armed men by offensive operations, based on information which it was the responsibility of the police to provide. One of MacDonald's complaints, as it was also of the army, was that such information was totally lacking.

Towards the end of 1948 terrorist bands in considerable strength roamed the worst affected areas of Perak and Johore, carrying out acts of murder and arson, terrorizing the labour of rubber estates and tin mines and the Chinese inhabitants of squatter communities that had settled down on the edge of the jungle. Both Gray and Gurney realized that both the methods and the resources employed by the police and the government were incapable of dealing with the situation, and they looked to the military to help them out while they put their own machinery in order; but they did not want the military to take over. Nor indeed did the military wish to do so. The army in Malaya and Singapore had been reduced at the end of 1947 to its lowest level ever, three British and six Gurkha infantry battalions, two battalions of the Malay Regiment and one field artillery regiment. The British battalions were not only under strength, but a proportion was always ineffective owing to the continual changeover of national servicemen. The army regarded its primary task as being prepared to meet major communist aggression by Russia or China and regarded support of the civil power in Malaya as secondary. It was also inclined to regard the base in Singapore as a higher priority in this respect.

The operations which the army did carry out, mainly in Johore and in Perak, consisted principally of 'sweeps' through areas in which incidents had been occurring and where communist strength was known to be dominant. These were in fact effective in disrupting activity by the larger gangs of terrorists and in causing them problems over supply. They also helped to maintain the morale of the population who were threatened by the terrorists, but they did not remove the threat of murder and terrorism which, once the soldiers had departed for another field of action, resumed its previous sway. Unfortunately these operations gave an impression of a greater degree of success than they in fact attained, and a dispatch by Gurney to the Colonial Office in January 1949 assumed that the end of the year would see the final defeat of the militant communists as an effective force, the following two years being concerned with a general improvement of internal security to the stage at which 'imperial troops would no longer be permanently deployed on operations in aid of the civil power'. Ritchie at this time expected to be able to reduce the number of troops so employed by the middle of 1949, when he was due to leave.

A dispatch by MacDonald in April did not dissent from this forecast, although he did stress the need for a great improvement in intelligence; but he also took the line that restoration of law and order was a police task and that 'militarily the bandits were already beaten in the sense that they could not hope to succeed in their objective.' He, like Gurney, felt that the turning point of the campaign had already been reached. A paper prepared jointly by Gray and Boucher on the security situation, dated 5 April 1949, also took the line that the initiative had passed to the security forces, but it did lay emphasis on the need to develop more forces capable of harrying and pursuing the terrorists in the jungle, into which they thought the terrorists would withdraw.

Harding might therefore have expected on his arrival to find the situation improving and the task of the army diminishing; but this was far from being the case. Almost as soon as he arrived the number of incidents began to increase. From the start of the emergency to the end of 1948 they had averaged a little over two hundred a month; by the time of his arrival they had dropped to one hundred a month; but by the end of 1949 they had surpassed the 1948 average and in 1950 were to reach a rate of over four hundred a month. A large number were ambushes, which from the terrorist point of view had the double advantage of inflicting casualties and providing weapons. In one of these in November four Seaforth Highlanders were killed. Trains were held up as well as road vehicles. Attacks on European estate managers increased and the problem of guarding them became a major one. This raised the question of differential treatment between European-owned and Chinese-owned estates. The labour on the latter was generally totally intimidated and many of the managers and owners were suspected of paying protection money to the terrorists. To supply them with armed guards was tantamount to presenting arms and ammunition to the enemy. This dilemma highlighted the basic problem of giving the Chinese community the feeling that they had a stake in supporting the government and the security forces, and that the latter were not just defending the interest of the Malays and the British. This was not easy when the security forces of all natures contained practically no Chinese, when Chinese squatters were being forcibly removed, and when all the counter-terrorist actions of government and of the security forces appeared to discriminate against the Chinese. Malcolm MacDonald's main theme and principal activity was to try and involve all races. This had been one of his points of disagreement with Gent, who, having persuaded the Colonial Office to drop its project of Malayan Union, supported the policy of Malay supremacy.

Harding spent his first six months in visiting all the troops engaged in operations and as many of those concerned with the emergency in Malaya as he could without overmuch 'breathing down the neck' of Boucher, or interfering in the latter's direct responsibility to the High Commissioner. By the end of the year, at which time he was promoted to the rank of full general, he had come to the clear conclusion that far more radical steps were needed than had hitherto been considered. In spite of some successful actions, such as that of the Gurkhas at Labis in January 1950, terrorist strength was not being effectively reduced, incidents were increasing and the intimidation they exerted on the Chinese population continued. Harding's view was that the problem was not primarily a military one, but one of providing an effective and strong administration, capable of maintaining order, which would give all elements of the population confidence that it could and would protect them against the terrorists and further their interests generally. All operations of government, including security force operations, needed to be not just coordinated but directed by a more effective organization than that of the High Commissioner, his officials and a series of committees, leaving the overburdened Commissioner of Police responsible for operations against the terrorists. Malcolm MacDonald was of the same view.

Meanwhile Harding accepted that the army would have to assume responsibility in various fields from which it might have preferred to keep clear, in order to make it possible for government and the police to build up the organization and effectiveness needed to transform the situation. More troops would be needed for this, although the reinforcements sent since the emergency had started had raised the forces available to Boucher to a strength of seventeen battalions of which three were Malay. No more were available from outside his command and, in spite of concern about the Communist Chinese threat to Hong Kong at that time, 26th Gurkha Brigade was transferred from there to Malaya in March, as Boucher was succeeded by Urquhart.

On the eve of his departure Boucher had written a somewhat

gloomy but nevertheless realistic appreciation of the situation, one of the principal themes of which was the need to have enough troops to provide a framework all over the country, in order to ensure that the situation did not revert to its original state of lawlessness once troops involved in major operations were moved elsewhere. The infrastructure of administration and police was not capable of fulfilling this function. He assessed the requirement as being for six additional battalions (this was before 26th Gurkha Brigade arrived), allowing three battalions at a time to be withdrawn into reserve for rest and retraining. Largely based on this, Harding produced his own appreciation for the Defence Coordinating Committee in April, laying great emphasis on the need to improve intelligence, improve the police and reinforce the army. In his own words :

> For lack of information an enormous amount of military effort is being necessarily absorbed in prophylactic and will o'the wisp patrolling and jungle bashing and on air bombardment. Information services must depend on the confidence of the people, especially the Chinese, and the civil administration generally and its power to protect them, and on a thoroughly efficient Special Branch organization at all levels. Until the police, including the frontier force, has been built up to a much higher degree of efficiency and confidence in itself, and civil administration has been effectively established throughout the country, troops are required for protective duties, screening operations and other defensive tasks ... therefore the need for more troops, in addition to 26th Brigade, must now be seriously considered as being the only means of giving the breathing space required by the civil and police authority to put in hand the decisive measures that they alone can take.

Again no troops were forthcoming from any other command, and again therefore they had to come from Hong Kong in the form of 3rd Commando Brigade Royal Marines, their move to Malaya being completed in July. By this time the direction which would make good use of them had been provided, for London had acted on the recommendations of MacDonald and Harding even before a joint visit at the end of May of the Colonial Secretary, James Griffiths, and the Secretary of State for War, John Strachey. Gurney had agreed to the suggestion that a Director of Operations should be appointed with authority to coordinate and direct all measures concerned with the restoration of law and order. On Slim's advice Lieutenant-General Sir Harold Briggs had been appointed. He was an Indian Army officer, well known to both Slim and Harding, who had commanded a division both in North Africa and in Burma, and, having commanded the troops in the latter after the war, had retired to Cyprus. He arrived in April 1950, and did not have an easy time establishing himself in a novel appointment which inevitably involved taking authority and responsibility away from those who had held it hitherto and asserting his own. However his clarity of mind, strength of character, sound commonsense and handling of sensitive personalities stood him in good stead.

Brigg's first task was to assess the situation and, after only a week, he had sketched out in a report to Gurney eight points which remained the essence of the 'Briggs Plan', the foundation on which the success that followed was built. This was further developed in a report made to Harding and his colleagues in the Defence Coordinating Committee on 24 May. The key to it was the appreciation that the terrorists, the Malayan Races Liberation Army as they called themselves, depended on support and supply from the 'Min Yuen', the population at large, which aided them, either because they were in sympathy or were intimidated. The responsibility for defeating and eliminating the former should rest on the army, the latter with the civil authorities. He argued that in the long run security could only be established:

1 by demonstrating Britain's firm intention to fulfil her obligations in defence of Malaya against both external attack and internal disorder;

2 by extending effective administration and control of all populated areas, which involved : (i) a large measure of squatter resettlement in compact groups; (ii) a strengthening of the local administration; (iii) provision of road communications in isolated populated areas; (iv) setting up of police posts in these areas;

3 by exploiting these measures with good propaganda, both constructive and destructive.

Within this general policy, his plan was to clear the country area by area from south to north, dominating the populated areas first, breaking up the Min Yuen and thereby isolating the terrorists, who would be forced to attack the security forces to obtain their supplies. The police were to concentrate on their normal functions, particularly the intelligence-gathering activities of its Special Branch. The army was to maintain a framework in all the states, deployed in cooperation with the police, primarily to cover the areas where the police were weak, and was to establish strong points as patrol bases. The administration was to intensify its strength and activity in all areas. Superimposed on this framework, the army was to provide striking forces in each state capable of dominating the jungle in areas up to five hours' walking distance from potential areas of terrorist supply, supported by the RAF both with strike and supply. To put all this into effect and to direct it, a Federal War Council was established, consisting of the Director of Operations, the Chief Secretary, the GOC and the AOC Malaya, the Commissioner of Police and the Secretary for Defence, which acted through similar executive committees at state level.

It was a remarkable feat on Briggs's part not only to have thought and worked all this out in so short a time, but also to have it actually in action within two months of his arrival. Harding gave him his full support – and there were times when he badly needed it. One way in which he did so was in persuading the War Office to resurrect the Special Air Service, which had been disbanded after the war, and to deploy it to Malaya, bringing in also a Rhodesian squadron commanded by David Stirling. In the early months of the emergency a force called 'Ferret Force' had been raised by ex-Force 136 officers, employing Dyaks from Borneo, but the difficulties of keeping it going on a permanent basis had led to its demise. July 1950 saw the start of operations under the Briggs Plan in South Johore, and from then on Harding could afford to pay less detailed attention himself to the needs of the Malayan emergency, his main effort in that field being to lend his support to Briggs in the latter's attempt to put more drive behind the civil administration of Malaya, persuading it to approach the emergency more in the spirit of conducting a war than of administering a colony.

One of Harding's major concerns outside Malaya was the outbreak of the Korean War in June 1950. He was anxious that Britain should make a significant contribution and considered that it should be of at least brigade strength, which he was prepared to provide, although he could only do so at the expense of either Malaya or once again Hong Kong. The British government was at that stage only prepared to provide two British battalions from the latter, and these, the First Battalions of the Middlesex and the Argyll and Sutherland Highlanders, were moved to Korea in August, and Harding went to Hong Kong to see them off. On the return journey with Malcolm MacDonald, who had been visiting the Governor, they were having tea in the aircraft when the 'Fasten seat belts' notice lit up. MacDonald obeyed, and noting that Harding did not, drew his attention to it. No sooner had he replied : 'I can't be bothered', than the aircraft hit an air pocket and MacDonald recalled with pleasure the sight of Harding, his teacup and his saucer all airborne separately. The two battalions were under Brigadier Coad, whose command was later built up to a brigade group from the United Kingdom and finally incorporated in May 1951 into the Commonwealth Division.

Harding later met MacArthur in Japan on his way to visit the British troops in Korea. He was astonished at the regal atmosphere in which he lived and found him aloof and unsympathetic. It was clear that MacArthur, in common with many other Americans, had written off South East Asia as already lost to communism, although at this stage within China itself Mao had not fully established his authority south of the Yangtse. It was the possibility that he might do so that caused such anxiety in Hong Kong. To compensate for the withdrawal of troops from the colony, where Festing was in command, Harding instituted a policy of building defences and improving communications in the New Territories in order to make better use of the troops that were there, and of placing greater reliance on air support. The construction of Sek Kong airfield was one of the results of this policy.

The American attitude caused much concern to Harding, MacDonald and their colleagues in the Defence Coordinating Committee. It was basically anticolonial and rested on the naive belief that perpetuation of colonial regimes was itself the prime incitement to communism. If only they could be removed, the threat would disappear. The Americans applied this as much to British regimes as they did to the French, who at this period were in grave difficulties in Viet Nam, where they had only succeeded in restoring a limited degree of authority in the densely populated areas of the Red River and Mekong deltas. At any great distance from either Hanoi or Saigon their writ hardly ran at all in Viet

Nam (the old territories of Tonkin, Annam and Cochin China), or in Laos and Cambodia, all theoretically French territory. Harding visited Saigon and was not impressed. General Carpentier, an old friend from Italy, was an improvement on his predecessor, but Harding had no confidence in his qualities of command or in his political sense. He found that the French troops were all shut up in forts and carried out no offensive operations with mobile troops, of which they had very few.

Constant changes of government in Paris and the mutual lack of sympathy and support between them and the French commanders in Indochina led to an atmosphere of hopelessness. This was dispelled on the arrival of Marshal de Lattre de Tassigny, who visited Harding in Singapore. He impressed the latter as having the right ideas, military and political. His aim was to develop national independence on the basis of separate states in Tonkin, Annam and Cochin China, as well as Cambodia and Laos, all freely associated with France. Tragically he received no support in this either from his own government or from the United States. The French were still hoping to maintain the artificial unity of Viet Nam, although the attempt to produce Bao Dai, ex-Emperor of Annam, as the head of it had failed. Their fear, justifiably, was that an independent Tonkin would mean a communist Red River delta under the rule of Ho Chi Minh, who had been recognized by both Moscow and Peking as such in January 1950.

Relations between the Defence Coordinating Committee and their Australian and New Zealand colleagues were not as close at this time as they subsequently became, when their forces were fighting side by side both in the Commonwealth Division in Korea and later in the Malayan emergency. This was in spite of the ANZAM (Australia, New Zealand and Malaya) agreement in 1949. It was a vague document, doing little more than agree that the signatories had common defence interests in the area and adopting certain principles for mutual assistance. It was concerned, as was ANZUS, with the requirements of a major war of the Second World War type and envisaged a sweeping Russo-Chinese advance southwards through South East Asia. The governments of Australia and New Zealand, after their great efforts to support the British position both in the Middle and the Far East in the war, were in no mood to get too involved overseas again. However a flight of Royal New Zealand Air Force Dakotas was stationed in Singapore in September 1949 and a squadron of Royal Australian Air Force aircraft at Butterworth on the Malayan mainland opposite Penang in June 1950. It is symptomatic of the outlook and events of the time that, in the two years he spent in the Far East, Harding never visited either country.

Malcolm MacDonald and Harding had great respect for each other and got on well. Both were devoted to the concept of racial harmony and did much to promote it by personal example as well as by official pressure. Early in his period of command Harding had suggested that Chinese should be recruited into the Malayan forces and not be restricted, as they were, to non-uniformed branches of the police; but he was told by Gurney that it was constitutionally and politically unacceptable. MacDonald confirmed that, even making allowance for the fact that it was the activities of the army which most concerned the Defence Coordinating Committee, Harding dominated his colleagues. In his farewell letter to Harding on the latter's departure on 22 May 1951, MacDonald wrote:

> We all miss you a great deal. On many matters you were the wisest as well as the most forceful member of the team, and we owed a great deal to your experience and sagacious guidance during the last two years. I have told many people – who show no reluctance to agree with me – that you are the best soldier in the British Army after Bill Slim, and that in due course you should step into his shoes. I feel sure that this is true and hope that it is recognized in the proper quarters.

Harding had found MacDonald an excellent chairman of the Defence Coordinating Committee and particularly admired his never-ceasing efforts to bring people towards independence and full responsibility for their own affairs. Harding saw clearly that, without progress in that direction, military action by itself in South East Asia would be fruitless.

Although progress was being made in Malaya on the basis of the Briggs Plan at the time that Harding left, he was far from satisfied that it was rapid enough, and sympathized with the frustration that Briggs himself experienced from the apparent lack of drive behind and within the colonial administrative machine, with its divisions and dispersion of responsibility. Harding's view was that the Federation should be placed on a war footing and that responsibility for all aspects of government should be firmly placed on the shoulders of one man, preferably a soldier, who should have access direct to the Prime Minister if he found himself obstructed by the Colonial Office and the Secretary of State. He put this view to Slim on his return, and it undoubtedly influenced the appointment of General Templer as High Commissioner after Gurney had been killed in an ambush on his way up to the hill resort of Fraser's Hill in October 1951.

In that month the Conservatives had returned to power, and they were naturally more inclined to favour such a solution. When the new Secretary of State for the Colonies, Oliver Lyttelton, visited Malaya before the end of 1951, a solution on these lines was pressed upon him by many of the settlers and the European business community, although Malcolm MacDonald was not in favour of appointing a general as High Commissioner. However Lyttelton himself was convinced and, after trying in vain for General Brian Robertson and then Slim himself, he accepted Slim's suggestion of Templer, who arrived in February 1952 after yet another seemingly inevitable colonial interregnum, Briggs by this time having been replaced by General Lockhart and both Gray, Commissioner of Police, and Jenkins, head of intelligence, having been replaced.

Although Harding had enjoyed his two years in the Far East (which among other things had provided him with the opportunity to take up playing polo again) and had found his task intensely interesting, he was glad to return to Europe. The climate had not agreed with him, and he had been under considerable strain, working hard and travelling endlessly, with the result that his wounds and their effect on his general state of health had caused him trouble and at times intense pain. He had never allowed this to affect the performance of his duty in any way, but it was a relief to return to a less demanding climate and a post which also appeared to impose less of a strain, that of command of the British Army of the Rhine in Germany, which he assumed at the end of August 1951, his predecessor in the post, General Charles Keightley, having succeeded him in the Far East. General Colin Callender, another old boy of Ilminster Grammar School from much the same background as himself, had held the fort in the interim.

CHAPTER ELEVEN

GERMANY AND CIGS
1951–5

As so often in Harding's career, his arrival in a new post occurred at a critical time, giving him the opportunity to make a significant contribution. Germany in 1951 was no exception. The Berlin crisis of 1948–9, following on the communist coup in Czechoslovakia, had produced the North Atlantic Treaty, signed in April 1949, and the alliance and organization based on it. The military organization under Eisenhower as Supreme Allied Commander Europe, with Montgomery as his deputy, did not set up its headquarters, SHAPE (Supreme Headquarters Allied Powers in Europe), near Paris until April 1951. It took over, as a subordinate headquarters, the staff at Fontainebleau which had served Montgomery as Chairman of the Western Union Commanders-in-Chief Committee, renamed Headquarters Allied Land and Air Forces Central Europe, the Commander-in-Chief of the former being in theory Marshal Juin. He however remained in Morocco, General Guillaume acting for him. Under this headquarters two army group headquarters were formed, one, called Northern Army Group, based on the headquarters of the British Army of the Rhine, then at Bad Oeynhausen, not far from Minden, the other based on the US Army Headquarters at Heidelberg, named Central Army Group

At that time the British Army of the Rhine had been run down to an occupation force whose principal activity was training national servicemen up to the level of battalion training. Only one division, the 2nd, was maintained as an operational force, more or less capable of taking the field. In 1950, partly as a reaction to the formation of NATO and partly to that of the outbreak of the Korean War, the Labour government of the day had embarked on an ambitious rearmament programme, the army's target being to form ten active divisions, four of which were to be stationed in Germany. At the time the number of units there amounted to the equivalent of two and a third divisions only. The three additional operational divisions were all to be armoured, and their formation involved the resurrection of the 6th, 7th and 11th.

One of the first steps taken by the Americans after the formation of NATO and the outbreak of the Korean War was to demand the rearmament of Germany. They even went so far, when the French raised objections to this at the NATO Council meeting of September 1950, as to threaten to refuse to take part in European defence unless a way could be found for Germany to contribute to the defence of Western Europe, which the Americans saw with realism could not be achieved without them. This demand went hand in hand with the pressure, which they took the lead in exerting, for a German government to be formed which would become responsible for governing West Germany free of the shackles of the Allied Control Commission. The first attempted answer to this was a hastily concocted proposal, known as the Pleven Plan, for a European Defence Community, more popularly known as the European Army. Britain was not prepared herself to consider joining this, although she was prepared to be as closely associated as possible. Both the Labour government and that of the United States would have preferred the solution, which was eventually to be adopted, of direct membership of NATO by the West German government, but at this stage the French were not prepared, only six years after the end of the war, to see a rearmed independent Germany, even though it was a truncated one.

For the next three years, under a Conservative government, Britain's line was, in cooperation with the USA, while refusing to participate itself, to exert all the pressure it could on the French (and on the Dutch, who needed some persuading also) to accept the Pleven Plan as a means of providing a German contribution to Western European Defence. In the political field some steps had already been taken. In March 1951 the Occupation Statute was revised to give greater freedom to the West Germans to run their own affairs, including the formation of a Foreign Affairs Ministry. On 9 July the formal state of war was brought to an end, and in September the Foreign Ministers of Britain, America and France instructed the Allied High Commission to negotiate with the Federal government, headed by Chancellor Konrad Adenauer, to put relations 'on a contractual basis' in the hope that these negotiations would culminate in an agreement that Germany would 'participate in Western Defence through the European Defence Community under NATO Supreme Command'. The negotiations were successful, and on 26 May 1952 the agreement was signed in Bonn bringing occupation to an end.

Harding therefore found himself in August 1951 facing a number of urgent problems. On the one hand his army was to be increased and reorganized into operational formations, and his whole military organization transformed from a peacetime occupation force, supplied by the most economical means by sea through Hamburg, into an operational force ready to take the field to face a possible invasion from the east, with his headquarters capable of taking under command a Belgian and a Netherlands force, each of corps strength. This inevitably involved changes in locations and increased demands on buildings, existing or new, rights to use land for training, storage, building and other purposes and the need generally to increase demands on the German civil authorities. But this came just at a time when the political aim of the Allied Control Commission was to reduce such demands, not only for their own sake, but also to free resources so that the Germans could raise their own armed forces within the EDC. Major demands arose out of the pressure from NATO for the British to realign their line of communications to a more realistic one through Antwerp and for the Americans also to switch theirs from Bremen to one through France and its western ports. The expense of doing this caused the War Office to drag its feet for a long time, but Harding's determination prevailed and he pushed through the planning which led to the creation of the base at Antwerp as well as the move of the headquarters from Bad Oeynhausen (which made little sense when the operational plan was to defend the Weser, only two miles away) to its present site near München Gladbach, west of the Rhine.

Harding left the training of the operational troops to his corps commander, General Dudley Ward, while he struggled with these major strategic and administrative problems, all with strong political overtones. His ability rapidly to grasp the essentials of the problem, to see the other man's point of view, not to be swayed by all the objections that could be and were raised by his own staff as well as by others, to lay down the main lines clearly and then trust his subordinates to carry them out as far as they could until unsurmountable obstacles had been reached, were all seen at their best in the one crowded year he spent in this appointment. He showed himself tactful and cooperative but also firm and determined in the many problems that arose between his staff and that of the Control Commission, succeeded toward the end of his time by the British Embassy. He would not intervene in a dispute between them unless it became essential. He therefore remained on good terms with Sir Ivone Kirkpatrick, and the two between them managed to solve their problems without acrimony. The same went for his relations with the Germans, and he was helpful and sympathetic to Generals Heusinger and Speidel when they came to discuss with him the problems they faced in resuscitating the German army. With his allies there were also problems, notably in trying to persuade the Dutch to strengthen their forces deployed forward in Germany and to improve their reinforcement plans. He managed to persuade their Chief of Staff, but the latter failed to move his government.

When the Hardings arrived in Germany, the United Nations had decided to hand over the UNRRA camps for displaced persons to the German authorities for them to administer, withdrawing the welfare workers from various voluntary bodies who had worked there. Prominent among these was Sue Ryder. She and her colleagues approached Mary Harding and asked if British service wives could form committees to visit the camps and concern themselves with their welfare. Knowing that service families had many commitments of their own, Mary was hesitant to ask them to do more, but after consulting John, she launched an appeal which met with an excellent response. Mary devoted much personal effort to this good work, which for many years remained one of the principal concerns of British service families in Germany.

In the summer of 1952 Harding was summoned to London to lunch with the Prime Minister, Winston Churchill, clearly to be vetted as successor to Slim as CIGS. While they were waiting for Churchill to arrive, Harding told Alexander, then Minister of Defence, how impressed he was with the enthusiasm of young national servicemen on exercises in Germany. When Churchill appeared, Alexander told him this as an opening gambit to the conversation over lunch. 'Ah, sham fights,' replied Churchill, and went off on a long train of reminiscence about his days in the Harrow School Officers Training Corps. When this eventually came to an end, Harding told him about the plans for establishing a base at Antwerp and said that, of course, Churchill would know Antwerp well from his days with the Royal Naval Division in the First World War. This set the Prime Minister off on another seemingly interminable train of reminiscence which had not ended when Churchill had to leave to cast his vote in the local elections. Harding had hardly spoken a word and had certainly given no indication of his views on any subject, military or political. However he appeared to have made a good impression, and the news that he was to leave Germany in September, handing over his command to his fellow captain of 12th Machine Gun Battalion days, Richard Gale, and succeed Slim as head of the army on 1 November was announced shortly afterwards. The 'lovely little pink-faced lad', Second Lieutenant of the Finsbury Rifles in 1914, had come a long way, and all on his own merits.

Eden, then Foreign Secretary, was annoyed that he had not been consulted, and objected to the removal of the Commander-in-Chief of the British Army of the Rhine after only a year in the post at such a critical period when the whole future of German rearmament was a delicate issue. The Foreign Office had favoured Brian Robertson for the post of CIGS. They thought that he would be more attuned to political issues than Harding. Antony Head, the Secretary of State for War, was certain however that Harding was the better choice from the army's point of view. Robertson had left the army as a major between the wars and had only held administrative staff posts since his return, whereas Harding's fighting record was impeccable.

Harding's next meeting with Churchill took place not long after he had taken over as CIGS. He was told that the Prime Minister wished him to go to Chequers and lunch with him there, no indication being given of any particular reason for the invitation. Harding asked Head if he had any idea what had prompted it. Head said that he had no idea, but advised the CIGS to take plenty of maps. No clue was given during the lunch itself, but afterwards Churchill asked Harding if he had any maps with him. They were fetched from Harding's car and, when Churchill asked for a map of Africa, he was able to produce one. Placing a finger on the Sudan, Churchill recounted how he had shot a white rhinoceros at a place with an unpronounceable name which, to Churchill's delight, they eventually identified on the map. The Prime Minister was pleased with his new CIGS.

The burden on the CIGS at the end of 1952 was as heavy as it could ever have been in times of what was meant to be peace. He was already familiar with the developments within NATO, which affected the army in Germany. There was a tendency to leave these largely to the care of Montgomery as Deputy Supreme Commander at SHAPE, where General Ridgway, whom Harding had known when he was in Trieste and Ridgway had been the Allied Commander in Italy after Morgan, had succeeded Eisenhower. He and Montgomery predictably did not get on well together and a watchful eye had to be kept for signs of a storm there until Ridgway left in July 1953, after only just over a year in the post, handing over to Al Gruenther, Harding's valued old friend and colleague from Italy days, who had been Chief of Staff at SHAPE since its foundation. He knew exactly how to handle Montgomery and got on very well with him. From then on the affairs of NATO caused Harding little worry, although in the political field the problem of how to provide the German contribution remained unsolved. This was however a matter primarily for the Foreign Office, although excitement was caused at one stage when Montgomery who had consistently poured scorn on the concept of a European Army, surprised a visiting delegation of British parliamentarians by putting the blame for the lack of progress towards achievement of the European Defence Community on British refusal to take part. Participation formed no part of the government's intentions, and not one moment of Harding's time as CIGS was spent on making any plans for it.

Nor did he at this period have to devote much attention to the problems of Malaya, although the campaign absorbed the greater part of Britain's defence effort, with 40,000 soldiers deployed there, 25,000 from the United Kingdom. This might not seem at first sight a large number from the army's total at that time of 442,000. The problem was that half of this total consisted of national servicemen on a two-year engagement, a high proportion of whom were either in training or on their way to and from stations overseas. With Gerald Templer as High Commissioner Harding could be confident that no prodding was needed from the CIGS to see that soldiers were being properly and effectively employed. But his problem was to keep Templer supplied with soldiers when the calls from elsewhere were so heavy. The Korean War had been in a state of stalemate since the middle of 1951, and the armistice was not signed until July 1953. It was still therefore a potential if not a very active commitment. New commitments had arisen in Kenya and in the Suez Canal Zone, the first as a result of the outbreak of the Mau Mau rebellion, the second from Egyptian agitation against the continued British presence, partly linked to Arab hostility to the emergence of Israel after the departure of Britain from Palestine in 1948.

The most immediate problem was the situation in Kenya. The rebellious mood among the Kikuyu had been building up since Jomo Kenyatta's return to the country in 1946, and the anxiety of the European population, particularly that of the settlers affected by the attitude of their Kikuyu labour, had been growing. Sir Philip Mitchell, who had been Governor since 1943, had taken a relaxed view of the threat until his retirement in the summer of 1952, in spite of warnings from a number of different sources more in touch with the true feeling in the Kikuyu reserves than he was. As a result of the pernicious Colonial Office system by which a new governor could not take over until his predecessor had completed the period of leave due to him on leaving his appointment, there was the usual interregnum in which the Chief Secretary, Mr Potter, acted as governor. During this period there was a serious deterioration in the situation, and when the new Governor, Sir Evelyn Baring, later Lord Howick, arrived in October, it was clear that declaration of a state of emergency was essential if the situation was to be brought under control. As in Malaya, it is difficult to determine whether or not the knowledge that this was about to happen drove the terrorists to take refuge in the forest and take up arms against the government. They were certainly ill-prepared for an effective campaign, and 120 of their leaders, including Kenyatta himself, were arrested when the state of emergency was declared on 28 October 1952, and the colony, which had only three battalions of the Kings African Rifles as its garrison, was hurriedly reinforced by one British battalion and later by the KAR battalion from Uganda, the 4th, and from Tanganyika, the 6th.

Lieutenant-General Sir Alexander Cameron was GOC East Africa, having previously been the major-general in charge of administration in the Middle East, under whose command East Africa was placed, and of which General Sir Brian Robertson was the Commander-in-Chief. Cameron took the lofty view that this was purely a Kenyan affair and that the Brigadier in Kenya should act as adviser to the governor, who was himself theoretically also c-in-c of the forces in Kenya. Cameron saw his task as looking after the rest of the command, which included Uganda, Tanganyika, Northern Rhodesia, Nyasaland, Mauritius and the Seychelles, while the brigadier and the governor dealt with the tiresome trouble in Kenya. True to his usual form, Harding decided that he must go and see for himself. He had already sensed that the military advice given to the governor and the organization for giving military support to the civil power was not satisfactory, and he had sent Major-General Hinde to Kenya as 'Military Adviser and Chief Staff Officer' to the governor. 'Loony' Hinde was an unconventional cavalryman of renowned courage, who during the war had commanded an armoured brigade in 7th Armoured Division and since then had gained considerable political experience, first as Deputy Military Governor in Berlin from the end of the war to 1948 and then as Deputy Commander in the Allied Control Commission in Lower Saxony. Since 1951 he had been commanding the British troops in Cyrenaica. His brother was a settler in Kenya and his appointment was welcomed by that community. In that post, and later as Director of Operations, his contribution to the success of the campaign against the Mau Mau was as remarkable as it was modestly and discreetly given.

Harding went out at the end of February 1953, and did not like what he found, either on the military or on the civil side. It seemed like Malaya all over again, but worse, although the problem was much simpler. The terrorists were not communists and had no support from other tribes, let alone from outside the colony. Their level of sophistication was well below that of those in Malaya. But in the military, police and the civil administration there was no firm grip and direction, no intelligence and little sense of urgency. None of the lessons of Malaya seemed to have been learned, or indeed even been heard of. It was clear that more troops were needed, and also that Cameron was not the right man for the job. While Harding was there a crisis arose in Khartoum and the Vice-CIGS General Redman, sent him a signal suggesting that he call in there on his way back and help sort it out. This he did and, soon after his return on 10 March, a Cabinet meeting was held to consider the Kenya situation.

Fresh from the scene, and with his ideas clearly thought out, Harding convinced the Cabinet that his proposals should be accepted. They were that General Erskine – his successor both as BGS 13 Corps and as commander of 7th Armoured Division, until recently Commander-in-Chief Middle East and at the time GOC-in-C of Eastern Command in England – should take over as Commander-in-Chief East Africa, relieving Baring of his titular title as C-in-C as far as Kenya was concerned. Cameron should become his deputy to deal with the rest of the command, Hinde his Director of Operations on the Briggs model, and Kenya should be reinforced by a British infantry brigade. One of the changes that Harding insisted on while he was in Nairobi was that the African soldiers guarding Government House should be replaced by British. If the settlers marched on Government House a second time, they would not be able to rely on the reluctance of African soldiers to oppose them.

Harding's proposals were soon put into effect. Erskine arrived in June 1953 and soon found that Cameron's presence was an embarrassment rather than a help. He left in December, his place being taken by Major-General Heyman as Chief of Staff to Erskine for every aspect of his task and command. Hinde had, even before Erskine's arrival, set up a Colony Emergency Committee and similar committees at province and district level on the Malayan pattern. However when Harding accompanied the Colonial Secretary, Oliver Lyttelton, to the colony in March 1954 the situation had not only not improved, but appeared to have deteriorated. Intimidation was rife in the Kikuyu reserve, on its borders in the coffee and sisal estates, among the labour in the settler areas and in the native township of Nairobi. Terrorist incidents were increasing. Although few of them involved Europeans, the horror and alarm they aroused had a serious effect on the morale of the ten thousand Europeans in the colony and undermined the authority of the government. Harding sensed that the fundamental fault lay, as it had in Malaya in his time, in the failure of the civil and police authorities to shake themselves out of a traditional colonial administrative pattern and put the colony on the equivalent of a war footing. The Europeans were demanding this and Lyttelton was sympathetic. He discussed with Harding during the visit whether or not Baring, who was much criticized by the Europeans, should be relieved, but decided that he should stay.

While they were still there, a War Council was formed, of which the members were the governor, the C-in-C, the deputy governor, Sir Frederick Crawford, a man of clarity of mind and determination, and Michael Blundell, who was given the title of European Minister without portfolio. The council was given a joint military and civilian staff and, perhaps most important of all, provided with a secretary from the Cabinet Office, George Mallaby, whose task was to see that action was taken on the decisions of the War Council. His influence was electric. The dilatory ways of colonial administration were replaced by 'action this day' minutes from Mallaby with the authority of the War Council behind them. A further result of the visit was the replacement of the Commissioner of Police by Arthur Young, who had succeeded Gray in Malaya in 1952. He carried out a much needed reorganization of the colony's police, although he set about it in a somewhat high-handed manner which eventually brought him into conflict with Baring. As a result he resigned before the end of the year, his greatest contribution being to introduce his successor, Richard Catling, who had been both in Palestine and Malaya and was to remain as Commissioner for ten years. Lyttelton's and Harding's visit was closely followed by a major screening operation *Anvil,* in Nairobi, where a large Kikuyu population harboured the Mau Mau equivalent of the Min Yuen. It proved to be the turning point of the campaign, although the emergency did not come to an end with the withdrawal of troops from operations for another two years. After this visit, Harding had little need to devote much of his attention and concern to the affairs of Kenya.

One of the most agreeable duties that he had to undertake between his two visits to Kenya was his attendance at Queen Elizabeth's coronation in June 1953. The three Chiefs of Staff, all small men, Admiral Sir Roderick McGrigor, Harding himself and Marshal of the Royal Air Force Sir William Dickson, rode in the procession. Harding was at home on horseback, but his colleagues were not. As McGrigor rode through Trafalgar Square, a voice was heard shouting: 'Mind out, Admiral, Nelson's watching yer!' Another agreeable occasion was his own promotion to Field-Marshal and the presentation of his baton by the Queen on 19 November 1953. Antony Head was present, and in a personal note to Harding on that day wrote: 'It marked the achievement of a wonderful career in the Army and one which will provide a fine example of courage and straight dealing to every soldier.'

G

There is little doubt that the area which absorbed most of Harding's time and attention as CIGS – and indeed that of the Chiefs of Staff as a whole at that time – was the Middle East. The westward expansion of communism had been held and halted in Europe with the formation of NATO. In Korea it had also been held, but in the rest of the Far East the struggle was widespread and its outcome uncertain. In the Middle East there was no firm barrier. Its oil supplies, the aspirations of Arab nationalists and Russia's traditional interests and ambitions in the area seemed to the Conservative government that came to power in 1951 to make it urgent to erect defences against both direct military aggression and indirect influence and subversion. Turkey had already joined NATO; Nuri es Said, the real ruler of Iraq with its young Hashemite king, was friendly to Britain, but there were elements of instability in the country and the Anglo-Iraqi treaty of 1930 was due to expire in 1957. The other Hashemite king, the young Hussein in Jordan, was also friendly. The problem countries were Syria and Egypt.

British troops had been in Egypt since 1882, when they came under the command of Lord Wolseley to deal with the revolt of Colonel Arabi of the Egyptian army against the arrangement by which France and Britain, having deposed the Khedive, set about trying to put the finances of the country in order so that the holders of Egyptian bonds could be paid. France having refused to join Britain in intervention against Arabi, Britain alone occupied the country, always protesting that she would leave as soon as she had put the country straight. In 1936 Eden – then, as in 1952, Foreign Secretary – had signed the Anglo-Egyptian treaty under which Britain agreed to withdraw its troops into a small garrison on the west bank of the Suez Canal near Ismailia. This had not been done when the Second World War broke out, and by the end of it a huge base had been constructed near Tel el Kebir, the site of Arabi's defeat. After the war British troops were withdrawn into this area, but both the numbers stationed there and the extent of the area occupied were much larger than had been agreed under the 1936 treaty, which was due to expire in 1956.

Attempts by the Labour government to negotiate a new treaty with Nahas Pasha, Prime Minister and leader of the Wafd party, traditionally supporters of the demand for independence and signatory of the 1936 treaty, met with no response. Events in Iran, where, as a result of the agitation of Mossadeq, the British Petroleum refinery at Abadan had been forced to close down, had their repercussions in Egypt, and the garrison of the Canal Zone had been increased by two brigades. A further source of dispute with Egypt arose over the Sudan. In theory sovereignty lay in an Anglo-Egyptian condominium; in practice it had been exercised by Britain alone, and she was preparing to grant the country independence. Egypt tried to insist on its own sovereignty over the country, which was to the liking neither of Britain nor of Sayed Abdul Rahman, leader of the Sudanese.

In October 1951, on the eve of the general election which returned Churchill to power, Nahas denounced the Anglo-Egyptian treaty. There had already been a series of incidents in the Canal Zone, including attacks on soldiers and on British army property, and these increased. The worst incident occurred in Cairo in January 1952 when several buildings, including Shepheard's Hotel and the Turf Club, were set on fire, several British subjects killed, and damage estimated at three or four million pounds inflicted on British property. This was followed by a serious clash between British forces and Egyptian police in the Canal Zone. Considerable pressure was exerted by the United States for concessions to Egypt both over the Sudan and over the Canal Zone. Their ambassador in Cairo, Mr Jefferson Caffrey, was a strong supporter of the anti-colonial line. Nevertheless there were other American interests, particularly in the Pentagon, anxious to find some formula by which we could maintain a military presence in the area. One attempt at this was made in the margins of a United Nations meeting in Paris very soon after Eden had taken over. An American proposal was agreed by Britain, France and Turkey for the establishment of an integrated Middle East Command. However it was strongly opposed by both Syria and Egypt, and no more was heard of it until it was resurrected in a different form as the Baghdad Pact.

On 22 July 1952, following in the footsteps of Colonel Arabi, Colonel Nasser and his fellow officers carried out the coup which rid Egypt not only of King Farouk but also of Nahas and his fellow politicians, the armed forces taking over the government with the agreeable and respected Major-General Neguib installed as the titular President. It was some time before the attitude of the new regime became clear, but within a month of Harding's assumption of the post of CIGS, the new Conservative administration's policy had been sketched out, influenced by the admission of Turkey to NATO. They were already thinking in terms of a reduction of the forces stationed in the Middle East in peacetime, with the result that the numbers that could initially be deployed there in war would be reduced, and had decided to transfer the army and air force headquarters to Cyprus, abandoning the concept of an allied supreme command and aiming instead only for a planning organization.

In January 1953, in preparation for a visit Churchill was to make to Eisenhower on the eve of the latter's inauguration as President, Eden set out his plan to act as a basis for future negotiations with Egypt. It proposed a phased withdrawal of British troops, but the maintenance of a military base in the Canal Zone in peace under conditions which would ensure that it was immediately available to Britain and her allies in war; an Anglo-Egyptian organization for the air defence of Egypt; the participation of the latter in a Middle East defence organization; and a programme of military and economic aid to Egypt by both Britain and the United States. In recommending these proposals to his colleagues, Eden stressed that Egyptian cooperation and participation must be real, if international confidence in the free passage of the Suez Canal was to be preserved, and that the United States also must be closely associated with a Middle East defence organization.

Churchill's preliminary talks with Eisenhower seemed to be satisfactory, Eisenhower agreeing that it was essential for Britain to maintain its base and that she could not withdraw her troops until she had achieved a satisfactory agreement with Egypt. He also agreed to American participation in any negotiations, following Churchill's suggestion that the British and American ambassadors should be accompanied by senior military men in the hope that this might influence Neguib. For this task Churchill had already selected Slim, who was far from enthusiastic, especially as he had already been chosen as the next Governor-General of Australia. In discussion with Harding on the subject, he expressed the view that he could contribute little and would merely be blamed for any failure.

When Eden went to Washington to finalize matters in March 1953, he found the American attitude, particularly that of Dulles, less enthusiastic. Eisenhower was prepared to make a General Hull available for six weeks, but insisted that the United States could only participate in the negotiations if invited by the Egyptians to do so. However Eden was successful in persuading them to support his plan, watering down the text about reactivation of the base from 'immediately available' to 'as early as possible'. Eden had explained that he envisaged negotiating for three cases: under 'A', the ideal, up to seven thousand British servicemen would remain to run the existing depots and installations; 'B', envisaged this being carried out by Egyptians under British supervision; and under 'C', the minimum that could be accepted, Egypt would run the base and Britain's role be limited to periodic inspection. 'A' would ensure that the base could be immediately available, but 'B' and 'C' would involve delays in reactivation of sixty and ninety days respectively. Soon after Eden had returned from Washington and reported to his colleagues, all this fell flat, as Egypt refused to agree to American participation in negotiations.

While Eden had been away, the American Ambassador in Cairo, Jefferson Caffrey, had been pressing strongly that Britain should make a gift to Egypt of all the warlike materials stored in the base in order to persuade her to accept the proposals. This suggestion caused a considerable stir in Whitehall, and Harding was firm in resisting it, having no confidence that it would produce the results expected or that the army would be given the money to replace it all. Rumour that the Americans themselves were about to deliver a large consignment of arms to Egypt, which the latter might use against British troops, caused an equal stir, After representations had been made, the Americans agreed not to do so unless and until negotiations had been satisfactorily concluded.

No progress was made over the next six months, during which time both Eden and Neguib were in poor health. Nasser in public speeches and in private conversation took a hard and uncompromising line, and, although Eden did the same, the British government was forced to reconsider its policy. There seemed to be three options. First, to stay on indefinitely, facing increasing hostility from Egypt; this was favoured by the right wing of the Conservative party, but it would have had little international support and could not be sustained in the long run. Second, to announce that we would depart altogether by the end of 1956 and deploy our troops and their base somewhere else in the Middle East; this would be very damaging to the whole Western position in the Middle East, and there was nowhere else to go, except

Cyprus, which was not suitable as a base, having no adequate port, although we might be able to establish facilities in Turkey. Third, to enter into negotiations without insisting on the conditions incorporated in the previous proposals and without the assurance of American support, being prepared to go to arbitration if necessary. Reluctantly the last option was adopted, and after Nasser had replaced Neguib as Premier in May 1954, negotiations proper began, conducted on the British side by Antony Head, the Secretary of State for War. Harding's old chief, Alexander was then Minister of Defence, and had supported an attempt to reach agreement. Harding backed him, having no faith that the base could be maintained satisfactorily nor reactivated effectively unless it were kept under British military control. Both he and Alexander were concerned at the drain on resources, particularly of manpower, that the need to maintain the base and to protect it involved, when the army had so many other commitments and a reduction in its size was being pressed from all political quarters.

The argument which finally convinced both the Chiefs of Staff and ministers was that the installations of the base could not be operated without Egyptian civil labour. If Egypt was opposed to its use, the labour would not be available, however many troops were deployed there. If on the other hand she had no objection, there was no need for a garrison of troops to protect it. If withdrawal of the troops removed Egyptian objections, operation of the base by a purely civilian organization would kill two birds with one stone – the maintenance of the base and a reduction of the commitment for troops. It was on this basis that Head made his proposals to Nasser. Montgomery had let Harding have his views on the subject. They were that the base was not needed once NATO had established, as it had, its South Eastern Command at Izmir. Plans should be made for a NATO base area in Turkey, and Western defence policy in the area should rest on support of Turkey, Israel and the Sudan, leaving Egypt to defend the Suez Canal as an international waterway.

Nasser had told Head that his political support had rested on the promise to get British troops out and on rearming the Egyptian Army. The first prop would now be removed and, unless he could be supplied with more arms, the only popular line he would be able to pursue would be the heightening of the Aswan dam. If the West would not help him either over arms, because of the tripartite agreement by which the USA, Britain and France limited supplies both to Israel and her neighbours, or with the dam, he would be forced to turn to the Russians. Head reported this to his colleagues on his return, pointing out that if Nasser turned sour and the base could therefore not be used, the nearest base available was Malta. The risks of this were accepted. The negotiations resulted in an agreement signed on 19 October 1954. This provided for the withdrawal of all British troops within twenty months, but the preservation of the installations of the base as British property, maintained by a British civilian organization. The right of the RAF to land in and overfly the area was established, as was the use of the Canal ports in time of war. Both parties agreed to observe the 1888 Convention guaranteeing freedom of navigation of the Canal. None of Eden's original conditions had been maintained, and Harding among others regarded it merely as a convenient face-saving operation by which the contents of the base could be gradually removed; but this was not official policy, which envisaged continuation of the base indefinitely. The fact that Egypt was still technically in a state of war with Israel was quietly glossed over. Nevertheless the fact had to be faced that Britain was technically in breach of the 1936 treaty, which in any case had less than two years to run.

Having failed to involve Egypt in a Middle East defence organization as part of the negotiations over the base, Eden did not give up hope of achieving it by other means. In this he was strongly supported by Harding. One of the results of the fall of Dien Bien Phu in May 1954 and the subsequent division of Viet Nam agreed at the Geneva Conference which lasted from April to July of that year was the establishment of the South East Treaty Organization. Eden had not been enthusiastic about this, fearing that it would alienate Asian members of the Commonwealth, other than Pakistan who agreed to join. Its other members were the United States, Britain, France, Australia, New Zealand, Thailand and the Philippines. It was intended as a means, both political and military, to call a halt to the extension of communism in South East Asia.

Harding felt strongly that a similar organization was needed to close the gap between SEATO and NATO. The opportunity to do this came at the end of 1954 when Nuri es Said, Prime Minister of Iraq, told Eden that he was working on a plan to strengthen the Arab League Pact by bringing Turkey in, and he hoped that it would have the support of both Britain and the United States. When the Turkish Prime Minister, Menderes, visited Baghdad in January 1955, he and Nuri announced that they intended to sign a pact of mutual cooperation which other states would be welcome to join, and they did so in February, under the title of the Baghdad Pact. Nasser however was strongly opposed to it; but, especially after Pakistan had also signed a mutual defence agreement with Turkey in April, Eden hoped that Egypt would join and perhaps Iran and Jordan also. He was anxious for Britain to join too, in spite of the added commitments it might entail, and Harding supported him. When Eden set off in February 1955 to attend the first meeting of SEATO in Bangkok, calling at Cairo and Karachi on the way and Baghdad on the way back, one of his objects was to strengthen and enlarge the Baghdad Pact, and Harding accompanied him on the way out.

At the Cairo stop the Ambassador, Sir Ralph Stevenson, had arranged for Nasser, Hakim Amer, the Commander-in-Chief, and Fawzi, the Foreign Minister, to discuss matters with Eden and Harding over dinner. Lady Stevenson's insistence on wives being present limited the time available for business. Harding explained the strategic views of the British Chiefs of Staff, described the threat as they saw it and suggested the remedy : that the countries of the Middle East themselves should provide the armies and the tactical air forces, while Britain and America supported them with strategic forces from outside. Nasser said that he agreed with the appraisal, but when Eden then pointed out that the logical consequence was that Egypt should join an organization designed to implement this concept, Nasser refused, maintaining that he would be accused of handing over Egypt to the imperialists. At the SEATO meeting Foster Dulles and Admiral Stump, the American C-in-C Pacific, pressed for a more vigorous policy against China and talked of the need for a showdown, without which the whole area would be lost to the West. Harding chaired the first meeting of the military commitee and came to the conclusion that the whole organization would be no more than a façade, the French attitude being to sit on the sidelines shrugging their shoulders. Agreement on strategy and practical plans would be almost impossible to achieve and everything would depend on Anglo-American cooperation. He pressed Eden to persuade Dulles to give his support to a Middle East organization on NATO lines and wrote a brief on the subject which was given to a nephew of

MacArthur's on Dulles's staff. Harding went on to Korea while Eden returned via Iraq, where the terms on which Britain might join the Baghdad Pact were finalized.

1954 was therefore an eventful year in both the Far and the Middle East. It was an eventful one in Europe also. French political opposition to the idea of a European Defence Community had been hardening at the same time as the French government itself, after the disaster in Viet Nam, was in a weak position. During 1953 the French had tried to persuade Britain to join, but they had been promised no more than 'close association' and help with training. Until the problem was solved, no start could be made with the rearmament of Germany, which had now been hanging fire for four years. The crisis came in August 1954 when the French Assembly rejected the proposals half-heartedly presented to them by the Prime Minister Mendès-France. Eden decided to act quickly to achieve what Britain had always preferred, Germany's direct membership of NATO, and decided that the solution lay in bringing Italy and Germany into the Brussels Treaty, which already incorporated both restrictions on Germany's military revival and also stronger guarantees to its members than did the North Atlantic Treaty. After intensive negotiations over most of the month of September, he was successful, the price paid being an undertaking by Britain that she would maintain on the Continent the effective strength of the British forces then assigned to the Supreme Commander Europe, that is four divisions and a tactical air force, or whatever the Supreme Commander regarded as having equivalent fighting capacity; and that she would not withdraw those forces against the wishes of a majority of the Brussels Treaty powers 'who should take this decision in the knowledge of SACEUR's views'. This was qualified by an escape clause to cover 'an acute overseas emergency' and a review by the North Atlantic Council if maintaining these forces 'throws at any time too heavy a strain on the external finances of the United Kingdom'. This succeeded in breaking down French resistance and Germany, her sovereignty restored, joined NATO on 23 October 1954, the twelfth anniversary of the Battle of El Alamein.

Mention has already been made, in the context of the Middle East, or concern over the size of the army. This arose partly for financial and partly because of the unpopularity of the length of national service. In the 1954 Army Estimates its strength was given as 180,000 regulars and 214,000 national servicemen. The Territorial Army consisted of 60,000 volunteers and its large establishment was filled by 192,000 ex-regulars and 126,000 national servicemen, both of whom had a liability for part-time service in its ranks. The Army Emergency Reserve also contained 10,000 volunteers. The National Service Act of 1948 had specified one year's full-time service, followed by six years' part-time. This was amended in the same year to eighteen months' full-time and four years' part-time. It was changed again in 1950 to two years' full-time and three and a half years' part-time. There was considerable pressure for a reduction in its length, and the Conservative party, with its eyes on an election in 1955, would clearly have liked to offer a reduction.

Harding insisted that this could not be contemplated as long as the army's commitments remained on anything approaching the scale then current. As it was, the strain on the army was great. His aim throughout his time as CIGS was to create a strategic reserve at home; but as soon as he built it up it was dispersed to meet some new or increased commitment overseas. He saw little hope of increasing the proportion of regulars as long as moves of units and individuals had to be so frequent and the opportunity for a regular soldier to live a family life was so restricted. On one occasion the need to build married quarters for troops in the Middle East was being discussed in the Defence Committee and Churchill said: 'Why shouldn't they live in tents?', to which Antony Head commented: 'How would you, Prime Minister, like to live with your wife in a tent?' Winston grunted and turned to the next item on the agenda.

It had in fact long been apparent to the War Office that, if they continued to maintain the numbers of men that the two-year universal call-up produced, they could not afford to provide up-to-date equipment; but there was universal agreement that, if national service soldiers had to be employed as far afield as Korea, Hong Kong and Malaya, a period of less than two years was neither efficient nor economic. From the time that the Conservative administration took over in 1951, when Slim was CIGS, until national service was abolished, this problem was under constant scrutiny. In Harding's day Head tried to come to an agreement with the Treasury that, if the army reduced its strength from about 400,000 to about 300,000, it would be able to retain the same financial resources but devote them instead to equipment. One of the principal difficulties of this was that a strength of 300,000 could not have been maintained by voluntary service alone and would have involved selective compulsory service, the political difficulties of which seemed great, although Churchill was prepared to face them on the grounds that Britain was a nation of gamblers. After Harding's time Eden was on the point of forcing a decision on the issue when he resigned after Suez, and Macmillan, fresh from the Exchequer, refused to play Head's game. Head, then Minister of Defence, feeling that he must keep his side of the bargain in loyalty to the Chiefs of Staff, was forced to resign and Duncan Sandys, who was not burdened with any commitment on the issue, took his place.

It was the custom in Harding's day for the CIGS to hold an annual conference at the beginning of August at the staff college at Camberley for the senior commanders of the army and for Harding's Commonwealth colleagues. Those who attended the 1954 conference recalled the impression Harding made, especially in his review of the politico-military problems world-wide. This he did with the directness and clarity for which he was renowned. He was respected as highly by his Commonwealth colleagues as he was by his fellow Chiefs of Staff. At a press conference at the end of the study period Harding announced that the use of tactical nuclear weapons on the battlefield had been discussed, including the American Corporal missile, with which British troops in Germany were to be equipped; that it had been decided to replace the Bren light machine-gun and the Sten submachine-gun by the Belgian FN self-loading rifle, and that steps were being taken to introduce a load-carrying helicopter. The latter had been the subject of acrimonious debate in the Chiefs of Staff Committee. Experience in Malaya and Kenya had convinced Harding that helicopters were essential, but the Royal Air Force was extremely reluctant to divert its money and manpower into helicopters, or into any form of transport aircraft other than that which directly served the deployment and supply of its own forces. In the end they were shamed into putting effort into helicopters by the Royal Navy, who showed themselves not only willing but enthusiastic to divert their helicopters to help the army in jungle warfare, although in principle this was the responsibility of the Royal Air Force.

Early in 1954 Harding had to handle a delicate situation that arose over the future of General Templer, who was an obvious successor as CIGS when Harding's three-year period was due to finish in November 1955. Harding thought it important that Templer should have some experience of the German and NATO scene before he did so, and therefore planned that Templer should take over command of the army in Germany from Gale in the autumn of 1954, when Gale would have completed eighteen months in command, and spend a year there. This suited the Colonial Office, as Templer's success in bringing about progress in Malaya made it, in their eyes, appropriate that things should return to normal as far as the High Commissioner was concerned and a civilian be appointed. MacGillivray, who was Templer's deputy, was their choice. The plan was frustrated by Eden who, on his way to a meeting with Bidault and Molotov in Berlin, learnt of it from Gale. Having already been annoyed by Harding's appointment as CIGS after only a year in Germany, he objected to a double repetition of such rapid changes in the appointment at a time when Germany was on the point of re-forming her armed forces and joining the Western alliance. He represented his case in strong terms to Churchill, who supported him, to the intense annoyance of Harding, whose embarrassment was the greater as it had already been announced that Templer would be leaving Malaya later in the year to take up the post.

Unfortunately, when Harding wrote to Templer in March to break the news, he speculated that the fact that Templer (when he had been Director of Military Government in Germany shortly after the end of the war) had dismissed Dr Adenauer as mayor of Cologne might have had something to do with it. Templer was ill with amoebic dysentery at the time and was far from pleased, particularly as he was certain that Adenauer bore no grudge against him. His main concern was the likely reaction in Malaya and elsewhere at his removal without the justification of another important post. Fortunately the long-standing friendship between Harding and Templer smoothed over the difficulties, and a suitable formula was found for an announcement in June when Templer returned on leave. He was then given the task of preparing a report on the future of colonial forces.

CHAPTER TWELVE

CYPRUS–THE FIRST ROUND
October 1955–March 1956

Harding's three-year period as CIGS would normally have come to an end in November 1955, and he was beginning to consider what he should do when the time came. However in April of that year trouble had broken out in Cyprus, centred on the long-standing Greek Cypriot aspiration for *enosis,* union with Greece. Although some of the colonial officials with long experience of Cyprus thought otherwise, there was a tendency, both in Cyprus and in London, to assume that this was just another manifestation of colonial nationalism of the type that had become so familiar, and Eden decided that the best way to deal with it was on the pattern that had proved successful in Malaya, by appointing a soldier as Governor, in order to unite all authority under one head. Who better for the task than Harding? Eden approached him with the proposition in late September and, confirming it, wrote on 24 September :

I quite understand how little attraction such a post can have for you at this time. After a brilliant military career there is nothing to be gained, and may be something to be lost, in undertaking such responsibilities, but equally I know how little you allow matters of that kind to weigh in the scale when national interest is concerned.

I have been profoundly unhappy about Cyprus for some time past. I do not think we could have avoided this situation. Papagos was headed for it and attempts to stop him only created resentment. On the other hand, for the Turks Cyprus is the last of the off-shore islands. What we must now hope to do is to show the Cypriots steadily and firmly rather than harshly that we mean to carry out our responsibility and that the offers we have made still stand. The sooner these last can be discussed again the better it will be for all concerned.

Harding accepted with considerable misgiving. He had been looking forward to making Lower Farm a real home at last and had turned his thoughts to how he was both to occupy himself and supplement the half-pay of a Field-Marshal. The prospect of some relief from the heavy burden of responsibility he had borne for so long, with little opportunity for leave or leisure, was welcome to him. But it was not to be : duty came first and brought with it an invigorating challenge. He had no doubt that he must accept, but he insisted that it was for a maximum of two years.

He was required to take up his new post immediately, and there was no time for the usual round of farewells. All acknowledged that he had been an exceptionally successful cigs, as good as a leader of the army, then engaged in operations all over the world, as he had been in Whitehall – within the War Office itself, in the Chiefs of Staff and Cabinet Defence Committees, and in dealings with other ministries, notably the Foreign, Commonwealth Relations and Colonial Offices, and in battles with the Treasury. His quickness and clarity of mind, combined with his direct, straightforward approach, and his capacity for hard work remained his outstanding characteristics and had served him well in the post. On his departure Antony Head wrote :

You have been an outstanding success as cigs during a difficult and arduous period for you and I have encountered nothing but whole-hearted and enthusiastic agreement in this respect. It has been a great achievement on your part and I have indeed been fortunate.

But beyond that, by your very straightforward dealing and excellent relations with all spheres of Government you have done an immense and invaluable amount of good to the Army's standing and prestige. I doubt if the Army has ever had a better Ambassador among the potentates of Whitehall. Personally I can't tell you how much I have appreciated your absolute straight dealing and candour with me or your unfailing courtesy and consideration for a much younger and less experienced man than yourself. My only regret is that more of the measures we both knew to be desirable have not been put into effect; and that was my fault.

The country has asked a lot of you now and I still feel it may be more than should be demanded of anyone after all you've given. Their excuse can only be that they have given the most vital job to the only man in whom they have full confidence.

In order to appreciate the task which faced Harding when he set off to Cyprus, one must retrace one's step to review the sequence of events which had led to the outbreak of violence in 1955. British presence in the island was a consequence of the Russian threat to Turkey in 1878. The Russian army was then on the outskirts of Istanbul, and Britain under Disraeli came to the support of Turkey, the latter agreeing to her taking over the administration of the island as a base from which to do so. However, as in the case four years later of Egypt, the island remained nominally part of the Ottoman Empire and under its suzerainty. It is said that, when Lord Wolseley landed at Limassol in 1878 with the first British troops, he was greeted by the Bishop of Kitium with the words: 'We trust, My Lord, that you have come to grant us *enosis*.' History does not record Lord Wolseley's reply. At that time the population of the island was 186,000, of which a quarter, 46,000, were of Turkish origin.

Legally, therefore, Cyprus remained Turkish until Turkey joined the Central Powers in the First World War, when Britain annexed it – in November 1914 – as she did Egypt. In October 1915 she offered the island to Greece, if the latter would agree to go to the help of Serbia against Bulgaria; but Greece would not accept. With the end of the war, the defeat of Turkey and the wholesale dismemberment of the Ottoman Empire in the Middle East, hopes of union with Greece were naturally raised, but War Office objections prevailed, although they had never made any real use of the island, and on 1 July 1920 the British government announced that 'no change in status was contemplated'. The Greek Cypriots, led by their Archbishop, refused to take any part in the administration of the island until 1923 when, after the shattering defeat of the Greeks by the Turks in their imprudent campaign based on Smyrna, the treaty of Lausanne regularized relations between the two countries, as well as the status of Cyprus as a British colony.

Pressure for *enosis* slackened off for a time, and politically-minded Greek Cypriots turned their attention to obtaining a greater degree of self-government. This period of calm was rudely broken in 1931. A combination of grievances, combined with economic hardship resulting from the world depression, were fanned by the Bishop of Kitium and led to severe riots in Nicosia, in the course of which Government House was set on fire, although its occupant, Sir Ronald Storrs, was well known for his sympathy with everything Greek. Soldiers were dispatched, order was restored, two thousand Cypriots were sent to prison, fines of up to £66,000 imposed, and the Bishops of Kitium and Kyrenia and eight other prominent clerics banished for life. All constitutional government was suspended, political parties were banned, the legislative and local councils were abolished and the press muzzled. This produced a strong reaction in Greece, but Venizelos placed a higher price on Anglo-Greek relations than on supporting the Greek Cypriots, and his government did nothing. This period of political inactivity lasted until the Second World War which brought Cyprus both prosperity and a warmer relationship, based on Britain's support of Greece while Turkey remained neutral. Many Greek and Turkish Cypriots joined the British forces in the Middle East. In 1941 political parties were again permitted, the first to register being the communist AKEL, soon followed by a pro-enosis right-wing party, KEK. From then on politics in Cyprus tended to follow the stark divisions of politics in Greece. The Turks meanwhile kept a low profile.

In 1942 a significant meeting took place in Athens between two ex-pupils of the Nicosia Pancyprian Gymnasium, a forty-four-year-old colonel of the Greek army, George Grivas, and a twenty-nine-year-old deacon of the Cypriot Orthodox Church, Michael Mouskos, who had just finished his studies at Athens University and, unable to return to Cyprus, was appointed to a church in a fashionable suburb of Athens. Eight years later, as Makarios III, he was to be elected Ethnarch, and ten years after that President of the first independent Republic of Cyprus. Mouskos was the son of a poor shepherd of Ano Panayia in the district of Paphos. Grivas came from the other end of the island, from Trikomo in the Karpas or 'Panhandle'. His father was a prosperous, devout seedmerchant, socially ambitious and strongly pro-British. George, like his elder brother, was destined for medicine; but, graduating from the Pancyprian Gymnasium in the First World War when Greece was threatened by Bulgaria, he abandoned the idea of medicine and went to Greece and joined the army as an artillery officer. He saw action in the disastrous campaign against Turkey and later attended the French Ecole Supérieure de Guerre, where he is said to have been much influenced by an eccentric British officer on the staff, Major Wintle. He fought against the Italians in Albania in 1940 and 1941 and was on the staff in Athens when Germany overran Greece. When Greece surrendered, he led a life of idle retirement until, as the rival resistance movements prepared for the struggle for power that would come with liberation, he formed a right-wing royalist private army called simply by the Greek letter KHI, which acquired an unsavoury reputation for atrocities. Largely as a result of this political activity he was not recalled to the Greek army when it was resuscitated at the end of the war, and this greatly embittered him. From then on all his energy and fanaticism, with which he was plentifully endowed, were devoted to the cause of the union of his native Cyprus with his cultural and emotional fatherland, Greece.

Meanwhile events were developing in this field. The end of the war had naturally once again raised the hopes of Greek Cypriots. These were further encouraged both by the cession by Italy of the Dodecanese Islands to Greece and by Britain's withdrawal from other territories, nearest and most significantly from Palestine in 1948. At this time the Governor of Cyprus was Lord Winster, a Labour peer, who put forward a set of constitutional proposals which gave no promise of self-government and certainly not of independence or *enosis*. They were accepted by the Turkish Cypriots, who now clearly saw the continuation of British sovereignty as the best guarantee of their interests, but they were sharply rejected by both right and left-wing Greek Cypriot politicians, and agitation for *enosis* henceforward gathered momentum. 1950 was a turning point. In January the nationalist organization and the Church organized a plebiscite among Greek Cypriots, the result of which they claimed as a ninety per cent vote in favour of *enosis*.

On 28 June the Ethnarch Archbishop Makarios II, who had been a fervent supporter of *enosis,* died after only a short time in office, and in October Michael Mouskos, who had changed his name to Michael Kykkiotis after the monastery in which he had served his novitiate, was elected Archbishop and Ethnarch at the age of thirty-seven. Nine months later, in July 1951, Grivas came to the island to advise him on the organization of PEON, the Pancyprian Youth Organization, the foundation on which EOKA was later to be based. Grivas found that Makarios had 'grave doubts' about turning to direct action, but the events of that year were to bring him closer to Grivas's thinking. In February 1952, prompted by a statement by Kenneth Younger, Minister of State at the Foreign Office, that no official demand for *enosis* had been received from Greece, the younger Venizelos, then Prime Minister, made a statement in the Greek Parliament making that demand, and in November Greece raised it in the Trusteeship Committee of the United Nations, pointing out that Libya had already become independent. In the same month, at a NATO meeting in Rome, Anthony Eden, then Foreign Secretary, had a conversation with Averoff, at that time an Under-Secretary in the Greek Foreign Ministry, in which the latter suggested that, in return for granting *enosis,* Britain should keep its bases in the island and also have ninety-nine-year leases on four bases in Greece itself. According to Averoff Eden brushed him off angrily.

At some time early in 1952 Grivas and Makarios had contacted Field-Marshal Papagos, hero of the Albanian campaign, whose Gaullist-type Greek Rally looked like coming to power, and obtained from him a qualified promise of support. In October of that year Grivas returned to Cyprus and founded a revolutionary committee of which Makarios became chairman. He then set about a detailed study on which to base his plan for a terrorist campaign, a copy of which he sent to Makarios when he returned to Greece in February 1953. Makarios's first reaction was to restrict the use of violence to sabotage, but he inclined further to Grivas's plan for terrorist action when Papagos, who had come to power in November 1952, turned out to be lukewarm in his support. When Makarios asked him to bring the matter again before the United Nations, Papagos had said that it should be discussed with Britain first. But Papagos changed his tune after an unofficial meeting with Eden, when the latter was convalescing on a cruise in the Mediterranean in the autumn of 1953. Eden, who claimed that he made clear that he was speaking only personally and not as Foreign Secretary, said that he would be totally opposed to *enosis.* Papagos took it to mean an official 'never', and reacted sharply. Greece accordingly raised the question in the UN General Assembly in November 1954.

Meanwhile Grivas had sent a shipload of arms and explosives in March by caique to Cyprus, and in June he himself applied to the British Embassy in Athens for a visa to visit the island. This was refused, and he therefore planned to smuggle himself in:

after a rough journey via Rhodes, he landed near Paphos on 10 November.

These events must be seen in the light of Britain's general aims and policy in the Middle East, which were described in the last chapter. Not only would any weakening of the British hold on Cyprus be seen as a general weakening of its position in the Middle East by all those countries that Britain was trying to rally together as a bastion against the extension of Russian influence, but an essential element of the agreement with Egypt over the Canal Zone base lay in the transfer of the army and air force head-quarters with all their communications to new sites in Cyprus. This was announced in June 1954, and reinforced not only the determination of the British military and of Conservative politicians to retain sovereignty over Cyprus after all the troubles they had had elsewhere, but also the fears of the Greek Cypriots that hopes of self-government and certainly of *enosis* would be postponed to the Greek Kalends. These fears were strongly reinforced by a statement on 28 July by Henry Hopkinson, Minister of State at the Colonial Office, that 'there are certain territories in the Commonwealth which, owing to their particular circumstances, can never expect to be fully independent'. Selwyn Lloyd, Minister of State at the Foreign Office, in the United Nations debate in November 1954 made much of the need to retain sovereignty in order to fulfil our obligations to the Arab states, NATO, Greece and Turkey and the United Nations.

At this time great emphasis was laid on the vital strategic position of Turkey, and John Foster Dulles, the American Secretary of State, was giving full support to Eden's efforts to erect a 'Northern Tier' of states to oppose communism, the concept of which in March 1955 was to be realized in the Baghdad Pact and the Central Treaty Organization, better known as CENTO. It was thought to be of particular importance to support the position of Nuri es Said in Iraq to balance the suspect influence of Nasser. Eden summed it up in his memoirs:[1]

> The action which the British Government could take was circumvented by international considerations. First came the strategic value of the island. Our military advisers regarded it as an essential staging point for the maintenance of our position in the Middle East, including the Persian Gulf. There must be

[1] Eden, *Full Circle*, p. 396.

security of tenure. It was not then thought enough to lease certain sites on the island from some future administration on whose policies we could not depend.

The failure of Greece's appeal to the United Nations at the end of 1954 encouraged further violence in Cyprus, which included a general strike, widespread demonstrations by schoolchildren and the worst riots since 1931. On 10 January 1955 Makarios returned from the United Nations and met Grivas in the Bishop's Palace at Larnaca. He told him that Papagos was now firmly on their side and suggested 25 March, the anniversary of Greek independence, as the date for the start of the campaign of violence. Grivas wanted to start earlier, but had to agree to deferment when a third caique-load of arms and ammunition was caught by the police on 25 January in the act of discharging its cargo near Paphos. On 29 March Makarios finally gave his approval for the campaign to start on the night of 31 March/1 April. A series of explosions damaged government offices, police stations and military establishments. The EOKA campaign was launched.

Three months later Eden, now Prime Minister, invited Greece and Turkey to a conference in London 'to discuss political and defence questions affecting the Eastern Mediterranean, including Cyprus', but no representatives of the Cypriots were invited in spite of Greek objections. Makarios saw it as an attempt to draw Greek teeth before the United Nations Assembly meeting due for the autumn, at which the Cyprus issue was to be raised again. Turkey's presence for the first time gave her a direct standing in the matter. She had kept a low profile hitherto, but Eden was anxious to push her forward so that it would be seen that the objections to *enosis* and independence stemmed also from Turkish objections to them and were not thought to be just because Britain wanted to hang on to sovereignty for her own purposes. The Turks took the cue handed to them and threatened to call in question the whole treaty of Lausanne if Cyprus were to become independent. The British proposals, put forward by Harold Macmillan as Foreign Secretary, were to study gradual progress towards self-government on a tripartite Anglo-Greek-Turkish basis, the Cypriots themselves participating when a constitution had been agreed and their representatives elected; but he held out no hope of Britain surrendering her sovereignty 'in the foreseeable future'. This, combined with widespread anti-Greek riots in

Istanbul and Izmir, following a bomb attack on the Turkish consulate in Salonika, was enough to wreck the conference altogether, with the result, as we have seen, that Harding was called upon to deal with the wreckage.

Before he left London, Harding had discussed the policy to be adopted with Eden and Lennox-Boyd, the Colonial Secretary. Eden explained that his government's policy was that Cyprus should be available to Britain as a base. He was prepared to see a gradual move, through greater Cypriot representation in the government of Cyprus, to eventual independence; but the original concept on which British presence was established in 1878 – that it should be a *place d'armes* for the support of Turkey – should be preserved.

Harding arrived in Nicosia on 3 October 1955 and immediately set out to see things for himself. He found the government organization totally inadequate, the ciphers for instance being kept by the Governor in a safe in his lavatory in Government House. It was in no way geared to deal with the situation he faced, and he realized that one of his first tasks was to put this right. To start with he divided his staff into two. The civil side, concerned with all government matters other than security, was headed by the Deputy Governor, George Sinclair,[1] whose previous experience had been in the colonial service in West Africa. He had been summoned at very short notice from the Gold Coast, later to become Ghana, where he was a provincial commissioner, and after an interview with Harding in London had been chosen by the latter from a short list of Colonial Office candidates. To deal with the direction of all security matters Harding acquired the services of Brigadier George Baker,[2] whom he appointed in the dual capacity of Chief of Staff and Director of Operations.

The basis of Harding's policy was to defeat terrorism while at the same time both conducting negotiations with Makarios, with whom his predecessor had had no contact, and also pursuing a 'hearts and minds' campaign to persuade the Cypriots that the British government had their interests at heart. He wasted no time in putting this policy into effect. After a rapid tour of the island by helicopter, he summoned a meeting at Government House of all

---

[1] Later Sir George Sinclair, Conservative MP for Dorking.

[2] Later Field-Marshal Sir Geoffrey Baker and CGS, 1968–71.

those concerned with security and explained what he intended to do. First came the establishment of an efficient organization to bring together the administration, the police and the armed forces. Below the central organization described above, this would be based on District Security Committees, responsible through Baker (who was to arrive on 4 November) to himself. To serve this organization, communications were to be improved and made more secure, a proper intelligence organization was to be established, and the police force, whose morale was very low, was to be reorganized, modernized and strengthened by bringing in police officers of all ranks from other colonial and home police forces. The army was to be reinforced and properly trained for the task. Before Harding's arrival there were only four army units in the island, two of which were engaged primarily in work connected with the construction of the new base at Dhekelia. They had been employed in 'showing the flag' in the country areas, using methods described by Harding himself as 'boy-scouting'. Two more battalions and two Royal Marine Commandos were added at the time Harding arrived and within the next month the total was brought up to ten units. The organization to deal with smuggling was to be strengthened and improved, the navy's patrols increased and a more vigorous Flag Officer, Rear-Admiral Miers VC, appointed. A sense of urgency in all matters, but especially in those concerned with security, was to be inculcated into all branches of the administration, and information services and public relations improved. Finally all activities of government were to be knit together to act as one under his direction. The methods which Templer had used with such success in Malaya were to be immediately applied in Cyprus.

While infusing the governmental machine with his characteristic determination and energy, Harding simultaneously applied himself to a very different task and one which required a totally different approach – negotiations with the Ethnarch, His Beatitude Archbishop Makarios. Harding thought twice before engaging in this. Although all Greek Cypriots recognized the Ethnarch as the leader of the Greek Cypriots, Her Majesty's Government did not. To them the Greek Cypriot members of the Governor's Legislative Council, the leader of whom was John Clerides, father of Glafkos, were the official advisers on the interests and desires of the Greek Cypriot community. To deal directly with the Archbishop undermined their position and was tantamount to recognizing the Ethnarchy. Although the evidence of its close association with EOKA was not then as clear as it later became, there was no doubt in Harding's mind that there was an association and that the Cypriot Orthodox Church and the Ethnarchy supported the demand for *enosis*. To enter into discussions, let alone negotiations, with the Archbishop could not only appear to be dealing at one remove with the terrorists themselves, but might seriously handicap the campaign to suppress terrorism for fear of upsetting the negotiations. However, Harding believed in recognizing realities. He knew that military action alone would not solve the problem, and that if the Cypriot people were to be persuaded not to support EOKA there must be signs of political progress in the direction of their aspirations.

On the day after his arrival, 4 October, Harding had his first meeting with Makarios. He sought, and appeared to obtain, Makarios's agreement that international communism was the major threat, against which it was necessary to provide defences, their only disagreement on this being Makarios's suggestion that Turkish fears in this respect were much exaggerated. Harding, in the straightforward, direct and honest manner for which he was universally respected, appealed to Makarios to recognize realities also : to accept that, if only he would cooperate with the British government in gradual constitutional and political development towards self-determination, peaceful progress could be made, and that in the course of time the strategic position was likely to change, removing the obstacles which the British government now saw to a more immediate grant of self-government. Finally he made it clear that he intended to use all the resources at his disposal to stop intimidation and terrorism, and appealed to the Archbishop for his cooperation. After some discussion Makarios agreed to use his influence to prevent disorders as long as discussions between Harding and himself continued.

Next day Harding, who had appealed to Makarios to suggest a way forward, received a note from him with three suggestions. First, that the British government should recognize that the right of the people of Cyprus to self-determination constituted 'the indispensable basis' for the solution of the Cyprus problem; second, that once this had been officially recognized, the Archbishop would be willing to cooperate with the British government in framing a constitution of self-government and putting it into immediate operation; and finally that the timing of the grant of self-determination would be discussed between the British government and the representatives of the people of Cyprus elected by the constitution so framed. No mention was made of any reference to the Greek and Turkish governments. This was referred to Lennox-Boyd, whose reply, though encouraging, did not go beyond the position which had been taken at the Tripartite Conference in September, reiterating that Her Majesty's Government was 'ready to proceed as rapidly as possible with the development of full internal self-government in Cyprus, subject to adequate safeguards for the minorities'.

Harding met Makarios again on 7 October, and they went through the relevant paragraphs of the Tripartite Conference document in great detail together, Harding urging Makarios to accept that, once he would agree to cooperate and a freely elected government of Cyprus was established, the Cypriot people would then be in a much stronger position to fulfil their aspirations, whereas, if he refused, the consequences for Cyprus would be tragic. After a long discussion which went over the ground all over again, the Archbishop agreed to discuss the document with his Council. Harding however was not too hopeful and, in reporting on the meeting, asked for reinforcements of an infantry brigade and an armoured car regiment to be made ready at short notice for dispatch to the island. Harding himself broadcast a message on Cyprus Radio on 9 October, the eve of the meeting of the Ethnarchy Council, in which he appealed for cooperation. However this had no effect on the Council themselves. When Harding and Makarios met again on 11 October, apart from some discussion of the exact meaning and implication of certain phrases, it was clear that Makarios would not budge from his three suggestions and Harding himself could not depart from the Tripartite Conference document.

While Grivas reacted with a number of bomb attacks round the island, Harding and his advisers assessed the situation and exchanged views with London. Their principal problem, as always for those who had to deal with Makarios, was to determine whether he was on the side of the extremists, as his critics maintained, or was one of the moderates, which was the advice that Harding received from all Greek Cypriots. The former maintained that the Archbishop's aim was to exclude Greece and Turkey from the negotiations; to arrive as rapidly as possible at a situation in which he and his followers formed the elected constitutional government of Cyprus, the powers of the British Governor being reduced to those of a constitutional monarch; then to demand the immediate grant of self-determination, which would already have been recognized as a right. This would be followed at once by the declaration of *enosis*. EOKA's terrorist organization would be ready throughout to force the hand of the British government, if there were any delay in the process. If this were a true reading of Makarios's position, there was clearly nothing to be gained by further discussion with him. The opposing view was that the hard man in the Ethnarchy Council was the Bishop of Kyrenia, supported by his secretary, Polycarpos Ioannides and a lawyer named Constantinnides. They and EOKA under Grivas put pressure on Makarios who, left to himself, would be prepared to cooperate or just stop at the stage of self-determination and not proceed to demand *enosis*. To cut off negotiations with Makarios at this stage would weaken his position and hand control over to the extremists.

Harding had gained the impression that Makarios, allowed his own way, would have been prepared to compromise on some formula which granted the right to self-determination at some unspecified time and open the way to negotiations on the form of a constitution. He was therefore inclined to give Makarios the benefit of the doubt, but he did not favour continuing discussion until the British government had something else to offer. He thought that, in the first instance, they should find a new formula acceptable to Greece and Turkey and supported by NATO. This might then cut the ground from under Makarios's feet. He himself suggested such a formula on 19 October, and it eventually led, after discussion in Athens and Ankara, to what was known from its second sentence as 'the double negative'. The wording was as follows :

> Her Majesty's Government adhere to the principles embodied in the Charter of the United Nations, the Potomac Charter and the Pacific Charter to which they have subscribed. It is not therefore their position that the principle of self-determination can never be applicable to Cyprus. It is their position that it is not now a practical proposition both on account of the present strategic situation and on account of the consequences on relations between NATO powers in the Eastern Mediterranean. They will therefore have to satisfy themselves that any final

solution safeguards the strategic interests of the United Kingdom and her allies.

Her Majesty's Government have offered a wide measure of
self-government now. If the people of Cyprus will participate
in the constitutional development, it is the intention of Her
Majesty's Government to work for a solution which will satisfy
the wishes of the people of Cyprus, within the framework of the
Treaties and Alliances to which the countries concerned in the
defence of the Eastern Mediterranean are parties. Her Majesty's
Government will be prepared to discuss the future of the
Island with representatives of the people of Cyprus when self-
government has proved itself a workable proposition and capable of safeguarding the interests of all sections of the
community.

The Archbishop had been away in Athens from 31 October to
18 November, and three days later Harding had another meeting
with him at which he tried out the new formula. Makarios's first
reaction was that some progress had been made, but he raised a
number of doubts, particularly over the various qualifying phrases
such as 'when self-government has proved itself a workable proposition'. He criticized the formula as being altogether too vague,
and remained obdurate in his attitude that the formula constituted
a denial of self-determination. They agreed to keep the meeting
and the failure to reach agreement secret, but EOKA's reaction was
immediate. A series of bomb incidents occurred all over the island,
including one at the Caledonian Society's annual ball at the Ledra
Palace Hotel in Nicosia. In spite of the implementation of Harding's security plan, the situation was deteriorating. While Grivas's
long-laid plans were maturing, Harding's were still in embryo
stage. The leeway to be made up was immense, and the task of
galvanizing the whole machine into willing and enthusiastic cooperation an uphill one, demanding great personal effort from
Harding himself, who was tireless in visiting the administration,
welfare and development projects, to which he attached considerable importance, as well as all elements of the security forces. Mary
was equally indefatigable in visiting and promoting welfare
schemes in all communities.

Harding decided that priority in security operations should at
this stage be devoted to the towns and the means of communication between them. The activities of EOKA in the countryside would

have to be left until government had ensured that life could be lived normally and its authority maintained in and between the main centres of population. His orders to the soldiers gave them as their primary objective to uphold the law, eliminate terrorism and stop intimidation. To that end the administration, police and armed forces must work together as a team. He stressed the importance of alertness, readiness and observation as an aid both to efficient counter-terrorism and security and to intelligence. He recognized the army would in certain circumstances have to act as police and must be trained to do so. Lethal weapons were only to be used in the last resort against armed terrorists or to repel armed attack. Minimum force only was to be used, but, if attacked, no matter what the odds, the security forces were to fight it out. No commander was to embark on an operation without having at his disposal or on call adequate resources to see it through.

By the end of the year the army garrison had been further increased to twelve units and their support had been much improved and increased. The troops taking part in internal security operation were organized into three brigades, 50, 51 and 3 Royal Marine Commando Brigade. For administration they were under command of Major-General Ricketts, commanding Cyprus District, whose superior officer was General Keightley at GHQ Middle East, both of whom had their headquarters in Nicosia. For operations, however, these brigades came directly under command of Brigadier Baker, Harding's Chief of Staff and *de facto* Director of Operations. It was an untidy arrangement on paper, but it worked smoothly, very largely due to Baker's skill and tact and to the understanding and tact of Keightley's Chief of Staff, Major-General Benson. If any serious difficulty arose, a word from Harding to Keightley was enough to settle it. The greatest handicap to effective operations was the almost total absence of operational intelligence, with the result that operations by the security forces tended to be limited to reaction to incidents.

In a report to the Colonial Office on the security situation at the end of the year, Harding summed it up by saying that he was satisfied that he was working on the right lines, but that it would take time and a great deal of hard work and effort both in Cyprus and in Britain to set up a fully effective security organization. He interpreted the intensification of the conflict with EOKA not as a sign of a deteriorating situation but as signifying that, in his own words 'the terrorists have been brought to battle and forced to show their hand and fight it out.' By this time the EOKA gangs had moved out into the mountains, while maintaining 'killer squads' and bombing teams in the towns. In December the Royal Marine Commandos and the Gordon Highlanders had carried out a particularly successful operation in the mountains which led Harding to impose a collective fine on the village which had been harbouring the gang they had dealt with. At about the same time Harding had moved against the communists and proscribed AKEL, on the grounds that it was foolish to leave freedom of action to an organization whose real object was to prolong dissension and turbulence in the island and to prevent a solution being reached which offered a prospect of bringing the emergency to an end. There had been considerable discussion as to whether or not AKEL posed any serious threat to security, as they had few arms and their support came largely from left-of-centre trade unionists and radicals. There were very few hard-core communists. The arguments in favour of proscription prevailed and, in a skilful, surprise operation in December organized by Baker, all the 128 AKEL activists on the list were picked up in the course of one night and detained in an old hutted army camp at Dhekelia.

Also in December an incident occurred which revealed how far the attitude of the Greek Cypriots and of the Archbishop was from cooperating against terrorism. A terrorist called Haralambos Mouskos, a cousin of the Archbishop, had been killed when he and three others had ambushed an army vehicle near Lefka, killing the driver, but not the other occupant, Major Brian Combe of the Royal Engineers, who single-handed fought back, killing Mouskos, wounding another terrorist and capturing the other two. Mouskos was given a hero's funeral, the cortege winding its way at funeral pace along the thirty miles from Lefka to Nicosia, acclaimed by crowds with Greek flags at every village, the crowd of at least a thousand attending the funeral service at the Phaneromeni Church in Nicosia to hear the Bishop of Kitium sing his praises as a heroic fighter for freedom.

Ten days after this, an attempt to make use of the Greek government as intermediaries to bring the Archbishop to a more cooperative frame of mind backfired when the communiqué issued from the Ethnarchy, after their representative left, stated that they fully supported his position. At the beginning of 1956 Harding himself was in favour of reopening discussions in secret in order to find out if there was any prospect of progress and, if not, to make sure that the blame for it rested on Makarios. Before doing so, he met Doctor Kutchuk and the representatives of the Turkish Cypriot community, reassuring them that there would be no change in the form of government without consultation with them.

Ten days later, on 9 January, Harding saw Makarios and put to him some amendments to the 'double negative' which had been made by the British government after discussion with Greece. The last two sentences of the first paragraph had been replaced by one sentence : 'It is their (HMG's) position that it (self-determination) is not now a practical proposition on account of the present strategic and political situation in the Eastern Mediterranean.' In the second paragraph, 'within the framework of the Treaties and Alliances etc' was changed to 'a final solution consistent with the existent treaty obligations and strategic interests'. The Archbishop still did not like it, arguing that 'treaty obligations' would mean that Turkey and NATO would always be able to obstruct self-determination, while the 'workable proposition' qualification should be dropped, leaving the capability to safeguard the interests of all sections of the community as the only qualification. Harding also suggested some way be found of reversing the formula in order to convince Makarios that the Turkish government would not have a final casting vote on the application of self-determination. He made the point that negotiations must not be allowed to drag on and that the Archbishop must agree that there had to be an end to violence.

Two days after the meeting the first instance occurred of an EOKA murder of a Turkish Cypriot. This led to a serious intercommunal violence in Nicosia. On 13 January Harding had another secret meeting with Makarios at which he explained some further amendments agreed in London. They argued for two hours, the Archbishop's objection centring on the words 'political situation' and 'treaty obligations', which he suspected would be used as reasons to delay or obstruct self-determination, and he was evasive in reply to the demand that he publicly denounce violence. Harding also sensed that, even if he were satisfied with a formula to cover the two offending phrases, he might raise fresh objections to other parts of the formula or insist on agreement about the form of the constitution before accepting it, a suspicion which was to prove only too valid. It seemed that the talks were heading for breakdown, and Harding went to London towards the end of

January in order to clarify the issues in dispute, to make sure that they were differences of substance and not just of wording, and of such importance that, if a breakdown occurred, it would be seen that the fault lay with the Ethnarch.

It was decided that one further major effort should be made to reach agreement, one condition of which was that, if agreement on a formula could be reached, the Archbishop must 'use all his influence to bring an end to acts of violence and lawlessness so that constitutional government may be introduced in an orderly manner'. On 27 January their seventh meeting found Makarios in a defensive mood. After covering the familiar ground of qualifications which could be employed to obstruct or delay self-determination, Makarios raised the issue of the constitution itself. He gave his own views, which relegated the Governor to the role of a constitutional monarch, except for foreign affairs and defence, which he did not consider included internal security, and argued that he could not accept the formula without assurance about the form of the constitution. He was also reluctant to denounce violence publicly, suggesting that it should be left to him to use his influence against it, but Harding insisted that he must do so in writing. The day before the meeting Grivas had distributed a pamphlet demanding immediate self-determination and warning the Archbishop that EOKA would not accept any decision reached between him and Harding and would continue the struggle 'unless and until criminals and torturers among the Security Forces had been punished'.

Harding followed up the talks with a letter setting out the position and saying that 'the details of the constitution must be a matter for discussion with representatives of all sections of the community at the appropriate time and it is therefore open to Your Beatitude and your Council to reserve your position on that point, if you should wish to do so, in your reply to this letter'. Makarios saw the letter for what it was, an attempt to put him on the spot, clearly responsible for the breakdown of negotiations, if he did not agree. His reaction was to say that he wished to consult a wide variety of Greek Cypriot organizations before replying, to which Harding reluctantly agreed. While this was going on, Harding went over the formula with the Turkish Cypriot representatives and told London that, in his view, four principles should govern future action : there should be no discussion of constitutional development with any individual or group who would not publicly denounce violence; any discussion of the form of the constitution must be public and on a basis representative of all communities and shades of opinion; this should be done by means of a consultative conference; and finally there should be no elections until the Governor could report that in his opinion conditions had been established in Cyprus which would permit elections to be really free.

The Archbishop replied on 2 February, switching the argument to the constitutional issues, refusing to commit himself unequivocally to cooperating in the introduction of self-government, and prevaricating on the issue of 'using his influence' to bring violence to an end, demanding the end of emergency measures and an amnesty for all 'political offences'. Harding saw this as a sure sign that nothing was to be gained from future discussion and that his reply to it must be carefully composed to bring the exchange to an end and put the onus for failure on Makarios. The letter took the line that agreement to go forward had been reached and that all that was needed was for the Archbishop to denounce violence publicly, after which the British government would start consultations on a wide basis about the form that the constitution would take. Before it was sent, Harding's determination not to get involved in any further negotiations was deflected by a visit from Francis Noel-Baker, acting as a private emissary from Gaitskell, the Leader of the Opposition. At first it appeared that his intervention might be fruitful, and the exact wording of the reference to the constitution in Harding's draft reply was altered slightly in the direction of his suggestions, but in retrospect Harding felt that it may only have encouraged the Archbishop to think that he could always extract another concession. On 13 February Harding showed the draft to the Turkish Cypriot leader Kutchuk, who emphasized that for his community two essential conditions must be fulfilled before any constitutional discussions could take place : the prior suppression of terrorism and recognition of the principle of equal or balanced representation of the two main communities.

Next day the letter was delivered to the Archbishop, and on 16 February his secretary explained to John Reddaway of Harding's staff that there were still four points which he could not accept, three of which were connected with references to the constitution, the fourth with the lack of any mention of an amnesty. In reporting this to London, Harding stated that he believed that Makarios sincerely wanted an agreement, and that most of the population did also and this affected his attitude, but that Makarios calculated that, with Cypriot national feeling running strongly, he was in a position to press hard and would not give up his two principal cards, his refusal to cooperate and to denounce violence, unless he could show EOKA that he had made some progress towards *enosis*. Every effort should therefore be made to see if there was anything the British government could do to meet him, although there were three points on which it was essential to stand firm; references to the constitution must not go back on what Harding had promised Kutchuk; there must be no prior agreement to grant a general amnesty; and the Archbishop must declare himself publicly against violence before constitutional discussions could begin. 'The consequences of a breakdown are not pleasant', Harding signalled. 'In the end the culmination of this affair will have to be some sort of political settlement and perhaps another opportunity may not occur again for some considerable time. Until such time we would have to pursue a policy of firmness and force which carried with it, as you are well aware, considerable embarrassment when it comes to dealing with world opinion'.

On 18 February a meeting was held between Reddaway and the Archbishop's secretary, Kranidiotis, at which fuller explanations were given of the points raised, but it was made clear that no change was possible. The meeting revealed that the bone of contention had now become the amnesty. It was followed by a further meeting two days later at which Kranidiotis explained that the Archbishop could not agree unless the British government accepted the principles he had proposed for the constitution, including an elected Greek Cypriot majority, and an amnesty for all 'political offenders' convicted before the conclusion of the agreement. By this time the Turkish Cypriots were thoroughly alarmed, and Kutchuk tried to get Harding to agree that there would be no constitutional discussions before violence had ceased, that Makarios would be required to make a clear and unequivocal denunciation of violence and follow it up with effective action, and that the introduction of a constitution for self-government would depend on the consent of all sections of the community and not merely of the majority.

Noel-Baker had now appeared on the scene once more and persuaded Harding to see the Archbishop again, which he did secretly on 24 February with Noel-Baker acting as interpreter. Makarios continued to insist that the British government must commit itself on the form of a constitution and that an amnesty was a precondition of his cooperation. Harding did not see how the British government could meet him on either of those points, but recommended to London that they should now go ahead with starting constitutional discussions without waiting for the Archbishop's agreement, but publishing the correspondence that had passed between them, and that the question of a denunciation of violence *versus* an amnesty be pursued separately.

Makarios's official reply to Harding's letter of 14 February was received on the 25th and included a sinister new point, implying that under the proposed constitution the Governor would not remain responsible for internal security once order had been restored. Harding by then had come to the conclusion that he could go no further and that Lennox-Boyd himself must now enter the act directly. Before meeting Makarios, the Colonial Secretary sent him a statement covering the constitution and promising a conditional amnesty, and he also met Kutchuk and Kaymak, who voiced their fears at length.

On 1 March Lennox-Boyd, Harding and Makarios met at the house of the Anglican Archdeacon and discussed at great length the composition of the 'elected majority', the conditions for an amnesty and the position of the Governor regarding public security. It was Makarios's new demand that responsibility for this last subject should pass from the Governor to the Chief Minister which proved the principal point of disagreement. At the end the Archbishop said that Greek Cypriot public opinion would not allow him to accept the British government's proposals, which showed little advance on those put forward at the Tripartite Conference, while he had made a considerable number of concessions. He hoped that Lennox-Boyd, now that he had heard his views at first hand, would have second thoughts. The Colonial Secretary made it clear that he intended to make a statement in the House of Commons on 5 March in which he would explain what had been in the statement given to the Archbishop, and that there could be no second thoughts on that.

The attitude of Makarios over the previous weeks, his shift of objection from one point to another, combined with the gradual accumulation of evidence of his complicity with, support of and even possibly direction of the EOKA terrorist campaign, had now

H

led Harding to cease to give him the benefit of the doubt and to realize that, as long as he was in Cyprus, whether free or restricted in some way, terrorism could not be effectively dealt with nor any real progress be made. Eden's government agreed, and on 9 March, hurried arrangements having been made with the authorities in Kenya and the Seychelles, the Archbishop, accompanied by the Bishop of Kyrenia, the latter's secretary, Ioannides, and Papastavros, the priest of the Phanaromeni church, was flown by the Royal Air Force to Mombasa and taken from there to the Seychelles by the Royal Navy. All four had been in different areas of the island, with Makarios himself due to depart by air for Athens. In a skilful and delicate combined army-police operation, which went without a hitch, they were individually picked up and brought to the aircraft at Nicosia. Harding immediately made it clear that the elimination of terrorism and the restoration of law and order were to have absolute priority and would be pursued with all the resources at his disposal. Only when this had been achieved could the problems of self-government be tackled with any hope of success.

Shortly before these dramatic events the army on the island had been reinforced by 16 Parachute Brigade, commanded by Brigadier 'Tubby' Butler, a fighting Irishman of great energy and enthusiasm. Their dispatch had been decided upon as a result of the general deterioration of the situation in the Middle East and not specifically to deal with EOKA. They were however made available to Harding, with some strings attached to their employment, and a very valuable addition to his forces they proved to be, arriving also at a crucial time. Not only were they troops of high quality, but the addition of two battalions, bringing the strength of the army up to fourteen units, at last made available a reserve for major offensive operations, not tied to a specific district.

CHAPTER THIRTEEN

CYPRUS VICTORY
March 1956–October 1957

The immediate reaction among the Greek Cypriots and of EOKA itself was much less violent than expected, perhaps because Grivas, who had moved into the mountains near Kykko monastery in January, had to think out what his plans should be in the new situation. According to his own account he had at this time seven groups totalling fifty-three men in the mountains, forty-seven totalling 220 in the main towns, two groups within the British bases of Episkopi and Polemidhia and seventy-five groups of part-time terrorists totalling 750 men, armed only with shotguns, in villages all over the island.

One incident affected Harding personally. On 20 March there was a lunch party at Government House which included the Assistant Commissioner of Police and the Commanding Officer of the Royal Horse Guards, the future Duke of Wellington. A Greek Cypriot manservant called Neophytos Sofokleos, of the same surname as the leader of the EOKA execution team in Nicosia, suggested to the housekeeper, from whom he normally took his orders, that he should take the electric carpet-sweeper and sweep out the Harding's bedroom while everyone was at lunch. He had been unable to do so before as Mary had, as was her habit, dealt with her correspondence in her dressing-gown in the sitting-room attached to the bedroom. Although the housekeeper saw him in there with the sweeper between the two beds, her suspicions were not aroused. He had in fact brought a bomb in a flat parcel, ten inches by eight inches by two inches, strapped to his stomach when he had bicycled in the day before, and at 2.30 pm had removed the safety-pin which set it to go off twenty-four hours later, provided it was kept at a constant temperature of 67° Fahrenheit.

Having placed it under the mattress of Harding's bed, he bicycled away from Government House.

It was not until eleven o'clock next morning that suspicions were aroused, as Sofokleos and two other Greek Cypriot servants had failed to appear and the remainder refused to prepare the bedrooms for a fresh lot of guests who were due that afternoon. It was then arranged that a group of soldiers, including Harding's batman, Lance-Corporal Welsh, should search each bedroom, turning up every piece of furniture. They had searched two or three rooms before they came to the Harding's bedroom, where Welsh found the bomb under the mattress of the Governor's bed. It was removed by Lieutenant Buckley of the Royal Norfolk Regiment, commanding the guard. Placing it gently in a dustpan, he carried it out to a sandbagged enclosure at the bottom of the garden, where it exploded four minutes later. Grivas's explanation of why it had failed to explode at the time intended was that the Hardings, unlike the Greeks, slept with their windows open, bringing the temperature well below the critical one. Harding maintained afterwards that on that night he had never slept better.

EOKA activity began to increase again in April and significantly so in May, after the first of the terrorists to be condemned to death had been hanged. Soon after this the army began a series of major operations against the EOKA groups in the mountains. But Harding's attention was not solely concentrated on security operations. The departure of Makarios gave him an opportunity to take stock and think things out objectively, as he had done when he had arrived in Italy as Alexander's Chief of Staff. As in that case, he had found himself initially reacting *ad hoc* to a situation to which he felt that no clear, consistent thought had been given. So, once more, he sat down to write out an appreciation of the situation. It started with the basic conflict between British military requirements, Greek and Greek Cypriot emotions and aspirations and Turkish and Turkish Cypriot fears. Some way had to be found of reconciling them, and he concluded that pursuit of some form of self-government was pointless, and indeed dangerous, until some agreement was reached on the future international status of the island, even if only an interim solution for a limited period. His first request was for a reassessment of the military requirements, particularly in terms of the length of time for which base facilities in the island would be needed. His second was for an attempt to be made, perhaps under the aegis of NATO, to find some way of bringing about a change in the sovereignty of Cyprus that would be acceptable to Britain, Greece and Turkey. The third suggestion was for a postponement for a definite period of the possibility of self-determination. When all these had been agreed, the advance towards a liberal constitution should be resumed.

This appreciation was sent to Lennox-Boyd on 4 April and at the end of May Harding went to London himself to discuss it, spending three weeks in England. One of the principal points of discussion was whether or not the government should proceed with its intention to appoint Lord Radcliffe to recommend a constitution. Harding pressed strongly his view that there should be no question of implementing whatever Radcliffe might recommend until agreement had been reached on the international status of the island. Harding's suggestion for some way to be found by which, after an interim period in which Britain should retain sovereignty, a future change in status might be referred to NATO, had met with strong opposition from Turkey, who saw it as a way in which self-determination might be achieved as a stepping-stone to *enosis*. After Harding had returned, Eden's government made a statement on 12 July saying that, as international agreement about the application of self-determination could not be obtained, they had to accept that, for the present, progress could not be made; but that they intended to proceed forthwith with the development of internal self-government and had asked Radcliffe to start work. In retrospect Harding considered that it was a serious mistake not to have pursued discussions with Turkey further at that time. If they had been, the Turks might not have come up with partition as their solution when self-determination was next discussed.

One of the factors that no doubt contributed to the failure to discuss Cyprus further with the Turks was that Ministers in London soon had other problems on their minds. On 26 July Nasser announced that he had nationalized the Suez Canal, and from then until the Anglo-French operation in November and the withdrawal from Port Said at the end of that month, the part that Cyprus could and did play in preparing for and executing the operation overshadowed the problems of its own political future. The return of the two Royal Marine Commandos to Malta and the need to withdraw the Parachute Brigade also from operations for training at the end of a successful operation in the mountains at the end of July gave EOKA a much-needed respite from the mounting and successful pressure to which they were being subjected. However, replacement units were sent out from Britain and the Parachute Brigade returned to anti-terrorist operations before it was finally whisked away on 28 October, in the middle of a large-scale operation which was going well, to take part in the Suez operation. The changeover to new units and the requirements of mounting the Suez operation nevertheless diverted attention and effort from the offensive against EOKA, forcing the army to provide security for all the extra military facilities established in the island.

A further diversion had been provided by Grivas, who issued a proclamation on 16 August offering to suspend operations 'and await the full response of England that the demands of the Cyprus people may be fulfilled, as they were set out, supported and will be discussed by its Ethnarch, Archbishop Makarios'. Harding was quick to point out that all that was promised was 'suspension' and that there would be no real hope of progress as long as EOKA was kept in being undefeated. His response was to offer generous surrender terms to those prepared to lay down their arms, and the British Government at the same time offered to get Radcliffe to accelerate his programme. This was promptly rejected by Grivas, the offer itself expiring on 12 September, no surrenders having been received. It was followed by a series of bold strokes by EOKA, one being the rescue of Polycarpos Geoghardjis,[1] a notorious EOKA leader, from the Nicosia General Hospital, another a successful raid on Kyrenia police station in which arms and ammunition were stolen.

Radcliffe was due to return to Cyprus in September and Harding was concerned at the increasingly rigid attitude being taken by Kutchuk and his advisers towards constitutional development. He also gave careful consideration to the future of Makarios. He had rejected the suggestion that he should be put on trial for complicity in terrorism on the evidence of Grivas's diaries, which had been discovered buried in glass jars in a field off the Nicosia-Famagusta road, and extracts from which had been published on 26 August. He sought to find some way by

[1] After 1960 he was Makarios's Minister of Defence and Security. In 1970 he was murdered after the unsuccessful attempt on Makarios's life in which he was suspected of being implicated.

which the Greek Cypriots could consult Makarios about Radcliffe's proposals without giving him a right of veto or the opportunity to use the need for consultation as a way of re-entering the
scene. The impending United States presidental election and the
probability that Greece would raise the situation in Cyprus at the
United Nations Assembly meeting in November also seemed to
him factors which demanded a clarification of policy. His mind
was turning towards an attempt to involve American support in
advance of a fresh approach to Greece and Turkey, but the omens
were not favourable at that time, the breach with the United
States over Suez reducing the chances of their support, and
Turkey's attitude hardening towards partition.

Harding went to London at the end of November to discuss
what was to be done about the proposals for constitutional development which Lord Radcliffe had by then evolved, and what
should be the setting within which they should be framed. He had
himself prepared detailed proposals for this, accompanied by a
memorandum on the strategic aspects of future policy, of which
one of his conclusions was that 'a base in Cyprus without single
sovereignty over the island as a whole would be of little or no
value to anyone.' His theme was to work for the support of NATO
and the Baghdad Pact and to retain British sovereignty 'at any
rate until the communist threat in the Middle East has been held
and defeated'.

Radcliffe proposed a Chief Minister and Cabinet responsible
to a single-chamber assembly of thirty-six members, six elected by
Turkish Cypriots, twenty-four by the rest of the population and
six nominated by the Governor. His proposals were accepted by
the British government and were communicated and personally
explained to the Greek and Turkish governments and to Makarios
before they were publicly announced on 19 December, the British
government stating that they would be prepared to introduce such
a constitution as soon as they were satisfied that a situation existed
in Cyprus in which genuine elections could be held free from
violence and intimidation. The reaction of the Turkish Prime
Minister, Menderes, was surprisingly favourable, somewhat to the
dismay of Kutchuk and his advisers; but it was clear that Greek
Cypriots were not prepared to commit themselves in the absence
of comment from Makarios, who took the line that, as long as he
was in detention and therefore out of touch with public opinion,

he could not express his views. The Greek government showed no sign of being helpful.

November had been a bad month for EOKA incidents, many of them perpetrated by youths of both sexes, which had led to the introduction of a nightly curfew for all between the ages of twelve and twenty-seven; but as the eventful year of 1956 came to an end and the new year dawned, there was a dramatic improvement. Geoffrey White, Harding's chief of police in Trieste, came in September from being Chief Constable of Warwickshire and did an immense amount to reorganize and strengthen the police. He had been a member of a commission of three, one of HM Inspectors of Constabulary and two Chief Constables, sent out earlier in the year at Harding's request to report on the police. They had recommended the earliest possible assumption by the police of responsibility for law and order. Major-General Joe Kendrew, a tough and vigorous personality, had taken over from Ricketts in command of the army. In January he assumed responsibility also from Baker as Director of Operations when the latter left for another appointment, and his responsibilities as Chief of Staff were taken over by Brigadier Victor FitzGeorge Balfour. Concentration of command of the troops and direction of operations in the hands of one man simplified the chain of command and prepared the way for the time when the Governor would be a civilian.

The end of the Suez affair had allowed all the army's resources, by now increased to over eighteen battalions or their equivalent, well supported by a variety of other units, to be devoted again to the campaign against EOKA. The fruits of the measures Harding had instituted on his arrival just over a year previously were ripening. In no field was this more so than in that of intelligence. As a result of the increasing number of captures, particularly of terrorist hide-outs, and of the readiness of many of those taken to talk, the snowball effect of one capture leading to another grew apace. One significant success was the unmasking of the smuggling network in Limassol in which Greek Cypriot customs officials had been involved. In January 1957 an extensive operation in the mountains against the gangs of two leading terrorists, Grivas's second-in-command, Grigoris Afxentiou, and Marcos Drakos, greatly helped by RAF helicopters flying in very difficult weather conditions, led to the death of Drakos himself, the capture of Geoghardjis and the dispersal of the gangs. Harding took a keen personal interest in the operation, frequently visiting the soldiers, who were operating under conditions of great hardship. It was principally due to pressure from Harding that helicopters had been provided by the RAF. By making it possible to place troops in areas where they were not expected, they made a very significant contribution to success, and the close cooperation between the services was a model of its kind. Pressure was maintained, and the reward came on 14 March when Grivas issued a statement saying that 'in order to facilitate the resumption of negotiations between the British government and the real representative of the people of Cyprus, Archbishop Makarios, EOKA declares that it is ready to order the suspension of its operations at once if the Ethnarch Makarios is released.'

On 26 February the General Assembly of the United Nations had passed an innocuous resolution, a compromise agreed between the British and Greek governments, calling for a renewal of negotiations, and shortly afterwards the Secretary-General of NATO, then Lord Ismay, offered his good offices. Harding was anxious to take advantage of this favourable atmosphere and, a week before Grivas's own declaration, had proposed that an offer be made that Grivas and his principal lieutenants should be allowed to leave the island without penalty and that Makarios should be set free, but not permitted to return to the island until the Radcliffe constitution had been accepted and was working. Harding went to London on 18 March for discussions, and two days later Lennox-Boyd announced in the House of Commons that the government accepted Lord Ismay's offer; that they had taken note of the EOKA declaration; and that if the Archbishop would make a public statement denouncing violence he would be released from the Seychelles, although he could not return to Cyprus. The Greek government's reaction was totally negative, but that of Makarios more favourable. He promised a statement, but when it came it was equivocal and unsatisfactory, and there was considerable argument within the British Cabinet about whether or not he should be released. Both Harding and Lennox-Boyd were strongly in favour, and their view won the day, Lord Salisbury resigning from the government on the issue. On 28 March the announcement was made and was greeted with great enthusiasm in Cyprus and in Greece, to the alarm of the Turks, who were not impressed with the Archbishop's equivocal declaration.

Harding recognized that relations between the communities and between the Greek Cypriot population and the colonial government would never be the same again. The fears and pressures generated by the EOKA campaign had caused a deterioration in both that would not be easy to heal. He was realist enough not to indulge in fancies that the clock could be put back and the good relations that had existed before 1955 restored; but, greatly helped by Mary, he did all he could to heal the wounds and was glad to find that at village and district level relations both between the communities and with the authorities relaxed more readily than at the level of Nicosia and the other principal towns. Harding now realized that the fact that the Turkish Cypriot attitude had earlier on been cooperative had led him to underestimate the strength of their feelings. As long as the continuation of British sovereignty seemed assured, they had been content; but any prospect of its weakening, particularly if terrorism had not been extinguished, led them to dig in their toes. Harding hoped that the effort he had devoted to improving the lot of all communities and the interest that he, Mary and his officials had shown in welfare and development projects would help to improve relations between the communities and between them and the government.

A new twist to the question of what future policy should be was given when Duncan Sandys, who had succeeeded Antony Head as Defence Minister in Macmillan's government (Macmillan having succeeded Eden in January), visited Cyprus in April. Sandys was the hatchet-man given the task of pruning both the armed forces and their commitments in order that national service could be abolished and the cost of defence reduced. Suez appeared to have revealed that there was no point in maintaining such a large establishment if, under modern world conditions, it could not be used; and, as far as the Middle East was concerned, the Canal Zone base had disappeared. The outcome of Sandys' visit was the suggestion that sovereignty over the whole island was no longer a *sine qua non* to meet the military requirement. From this the concept of sovereign base areas was evolved.

The other development in April was the increasingly hard line taken by Kutchuk and his associates that the two communities could no longer live together in amity and that partition was the only solution if British sovereignty were to cease : in other words, if the Greek Cypriots wanted self-determination and *enosis,* the Turkish Cypriots were equally entitled to them. Monsieur Spaak, the notable Belgian Foreign Minister, had now taken over as Secretary-General of NATO from Lord Ismay, and it seemed to Harding urgent to get him pointed in the right direction. Macmillan's government appeared to Harding to be too inclined to wait and see what would evolve, and he sent repeated warnings that there was no time to be lost if violence was not to raise its head again and all those concerned not to harden into inflexible positions. The Colonial Office still seemed to him to be obsessed with Radcliffe's proposals, which he believed to be putting the cart before the horse. On 13 June Spaak sent a note to the British, Greek, Turkish and American governments setting out his preliminary views for an international guarantee excluding both partition and *enosis*. This was rejected by Turkey, who had no faith in the power of an international guarantee to reverse an unilaterally declared *enosis*. Harding returned to London in July for a thorough review of the whole situation.

The cessation of the EOKA campaign had made the realities of the situation clearer than ever before. It appeared that Greece would never agree to a settlement which gave Turkey a recognized status and interest in the island, while Turkey would never agree to one that did not, in order to protect both the Turkish Cypriots and her own strategic interest in the island. As long as the British persisted with the military requirement, which they considered themselves as maintaining on behalf of their allies in NATO and the Baghdad Pact, no solution was acceptable which put the use of their military facilities at risk. Harding despaired of finding a final solution which would satisfy both Greece and Turkey. To try and impose one under Anglo-American pressure might precipitate a conflict between them. Turkey was of such strategic importance that Britain and NATO could not afford to disregard her firm opposition to any solution that could lead to *enosis*, an argument which had not hitherto been fully accepted by the Americans, who tended to favour the Greeks. The only sure guarantee of the prevention of *enosis* was to give Turkey a recognized status in Cyprus; but to suggest that at that time would arouse strong Greek and Greek Cypriot opposition.

The best answer seemed to be to concentrate on securing an interim solution which would associate Turkey with the affairs of the island, but not give her a right of veto on its eventual status. Harding envisaged this as being achieved by a settlement which continued British sovereignty for a limited period of perhaps five

years, associating both the Greek and Turkish governments by
inviting them to appoint assessors to assist the Governor in certain
specific areas affecting the Greek and Turkish Cypriot communities. These were his last words of advice before handing over to
Sir Hugh Foot when the two-year period for which he had accepted the post came to an end in October 1957. They proved to be
the foundation on which the settlement eventually reached sixteen
months later was based, as both Macmillan and Lennox-Boyd
generously acknowledged in personal letters to him of 20 February
1959, a fact that tends to have been obscured by the publicity
given to the performance of his successor, whose initial proposal
for a settlement met with strong opposition from Turkey and the
Turkish Cypriots. Foot then fell back on what had basically been
Harding's proposal, although the idea of associating Greece and
Turkey with the administration of the island was not a new one,
and it had been mooted in articles in the *Observer* and the
Economist in 1954.

Before Harding left he had been incensed by the declaration in
the Labour party manifesto, supported at their annual conference,
that, if they came to power, which in the aftermath of Suez some
political prophets forecast, they would grant Cyprus self-determination after an interim period of self-government. Harding saw
this as giving hope again to EOKA and all the extremists, and as
severely prejudicing the difficult task of obtaining international
agreement to the island's future status, without which, in his
opinion, any move towards self-government would carry with it
grave dangers both within the island itself and internationally.

Harding left Cyprus deeply respected by all who had had to deal
with him. Makarios himself in after years acknowledged this. The
politicians at home, the soldiers, officials, policemen and ordinary
citizens of Cyprus, whatever their nationality, recognized in him a
man of deep sincerity, great courage, mental and physical, tireless
in his devotion to duty and determination to find a just and lasting
solution. He had inspired all those who had served under him or
who had been responsible for dealing with him from Whitehall.
Hard-bitten officials, who on his arrival had resented the severe
shock he had administered to a sleepy colonial regime, were deeply
moved at his departure. Harold Macmillan wrote:

10 Downing Street
Whitehall
October 17, 1957

My dear Field-Marshal

I cannot allow the announcement of your impending departure from Cyprus to pass without letting you know personally of my feelings. Your tenure of office as Governor of Cyprus has been an extraordinary example of public service and devotion. When my predecessor asked you in 1955 to undertake this task we all admired the way in which you so readily put aside what would have been a very understandable desire to enjoy a well earned retirement. I cannot imagine a tougher assignment being given to any man nor can I think of any man who could have discharged it with greater distinction.

During the whole of your tenure of office Cyprus has been the centre of bitter political and international controversies. This has made your task doubly hard but you have steered your course with such courage, fairness and skill that I have no doubt that your Governorship will long be remembered with pride even by those who have not agreed with our policies.

We have all been filled with admiration at the way in which Lady Harding has so nobly shared in your arduous task. I do hope that you will both now enjoy to the full your delayed retirement. In sending you my good wishes I hope I have been able to express to you something of the great debt which the country owes you for what you have done.

Yours very sincerely
HAROLD MACMILLAN

Among many other letters, official and unofficial, in the same vein was one from Anthony Eden, which ran:

8th November 1957
Dear John

I want to send you these few words to try and thank you for the wonderful service you have given the Nation in Cyprus. I cannot forget the generosity with which you undertook this thankless task in a critical hour: yours was indeed a selfless action.

Maybe, when you have at last reached your farm in Dorset, you and Lady Harding will come over and have lunch with us. We should love to see you both.

Meanwhile : gratitude and every good wish.

Yours ever

ANTHONY EDEN

In the New Year Honours of 1958 his achievement was recognized by the grant of a Barony of the United Kingdom, and so the
boy born in Rock House, South Petherton, sixty-two years before
became Lord Harding of Petherton.

CHAPTER FOURTEEN

A FULL AUTUMN

Harding was now at last free to live in his own home and to choose himself what responsibilities to accept. As far as the army was concerned, apart from the special place which Field-Marshals hold as still theoretically on the active list, he was Colonel of three regiments, the 6th Gurkha Rifles, which he had accepted when he was in the Far East in 1951, his own regiment, the Somerset Light Infantry, and in April 1957 he had succeeded the late Earl of Athlone as Colonel of the Life Guards, an appointment which brought with it that of Gold Stick to the Queen, an honour he was delighted to accept. In the same year he had relinquished the Honorary Colonelcy of the North Somerset Yeomanry.

Field-Marshals, although remaining on the active list, nevertheless receive only half-pay, and the problem of how to supplement it posed itself. His first introduction to commercial life came immediately after his return from Cyprus with his appointment as a non-executive director of the National Provincial Bank, followed soon afterwards by a directorship of Micamite Insulators, a subsidiary of Associated Electrical Industries. These directorships were a useful introduction to two more demanding appointments in industry, both of which originated in 1961. The first was in the firm of Williams (Hounslow) Ltd, a small successful family business manufacturing dyestuffs and chemicals with one factory at Hounslow and one in Yorkshire and a total labour force of six hundred. The chairman, Greville Williams, was a Dorset acquaintance and wished to retire, but regarded his son, Aubrey, then in his early thirties, as at that stage too young to be left on his own. He invited Harding to take over as chairman with his son as managing director. Harding accepted and, after a short period as a director, became chairman in 1962. It proved a happy partnership. Harding made no attempt to interfere in the running of the factories, but proved of great help to Aubrey Greville Williams in his wide knowledge of the outside world, his sound judgement and shrewd assessment of personalities. The company was expanding and developing its contacts with America, and it was in dealing with outside organizations, and particularly with foreigners, that Harding made a notably valuable contribution. This involved negotiations which, in 1970, led to the takeover of the firm by an American company. A year after this Harding handed over the chairmanship to Aubrey Greville Williams, who was most grateful for the support he had received.

Harding had enjoyed the experience of presiding over a small firm with many of the characteristics of a good regiment, but it had not been his major preoccupation during that decade. That had been his involvement with Plesseys, of which he became a director in 1962. Plesseys was a major supplier of telecommunication equipment, which had expanded from a work force of six to one of fifteen thousand during the war and then employed some nine thousand. In October 1961 it had recently absorbed Automatic Telephone Electric and Ericssons. This had involved a reconstruction of the board. Towards the end of 1961 the chairman, chief executive and virtual founder of the company, Sir Allen Clark, developed cancer, and the problem of his succession became urgent. He himself was determined that his sons, John and Michael, then aged thirty-five and thirty-four, should continue to play a principal part in the management of the company, and he had appointed his son John as joint managing director with himself. The three management directors, who included the Clark brothers, found themselves opposed by three of the four outside directors, the fourth, Sir Harold Wernher, who had been chairman of Ericssons, poised between the two sides. Sir Allen died in June 1962 and Sir Harold took over as chairman, the other three outside directors resigning.

At the instigation of Lord Nathan, whose firm acted as legal advisers to the company, Sir Harold invited three distinguished men from different walks of life to replace them; Lord Kilmuir, a lawyer and Conservative politician, better known by his previous title as Sir David Maxwell Fyffe; Sir Harold Watkinson, industrialist and Conservative Member of Parliament for Woking, who had just ceased to be Minister of Defence; and Harding, known to Lord Nathan as a result of the latter's connection and keen interest in the territorials. Wernher himself did not wish to remain chairman for long, and handed over the post to Kilmuir in 1964, when Harding succeeded the latter as vice-chairman, having acted as finance director until then. Kilmuir died in 1967 and Harding, with the unanimous support of the board, succeeded him.

By that time he had gained the respect, not only of his fellow directors, but also of all the principal executives and advisers of the company. Far from being a mere figurehead, as some had expected, he took a keen interest and applied all the clarity of mind, energy and skill in dealing with his fellow men that had been his hallmarks as a soldier. One of the most refreshing characteristics they found in him was his readiness to admit ignorance in fields in which he was not expert, and to ask for enlightenment, a trait not normally to be found among the top brass in industry and commerce. John Clark developed an excellent relationship with him, admiring the speed with which he analysed the problems of organization and suggested the solutions, and his sensitivity to the quality and character of the men concerned with management. His wise, sound judgement in choosing the course to follow was as valuable as were his energy and determination in pursuing it, once the decision had been taken, and, if the exact wording of a letter was of great importance, it was to the chairman that the managing director would turn for a draft.

Harding's period as chairman, which came to an end in 1970 when he handed over to John Clark, was an active and difficult one. It involved the absorption of the marine division of Decca, fighting off a takeover bid, and the abortive attempt to acquire English Electric in competition with the General Electric Company. The company had expanded its activity by twenty per cent during his chairmanship, and there is no doubt that he left it a stronger and sounder company than it had been when he had joined it, much of it due to him personally. He had gained the respect and affection of all who had worked with him, as he had as a soldier and as a colonial governor.

At the same time as he had been an active chairman of two companies, he had also been occupied in a very different field. In 1961, as a result of the recently passed Gaming Act, the government set up the Horserace Betting Levy Board, the object of which was to raise a levy from the profits of bookmakers to be employed for the benefit of horseracing. Harding was invited to become its first chairman, and he accepted. The Board consisted of two representatives of the Jockey Club, Sir Randle Fielden and Mr Jocelyn Hambro, one of the National Hunt Club, Lord Bicester, one of the bookmakers, Mr Archibald Scott (who must have been one of the few Old Etonians in his profession), a lawyer, an accountant and the chairman of the Tote, Sir Alexander Sim. Harding had to start the organization off from scratch and realized that the first priority was to obtain a good chief of staff as secretary. He was fortunate in acquiring the services of Major-General Rupert Brazier-Creagh, who had recently retired from the post of Director of Staff Duties at the War Office and was knowledgeable about racing.

Harding himself, apart from his early ventures at the staff college in point-to-point races, was not a racing fan. However he threw himself into the task with enthusiasm, visiting racecourses up and down the country, discussing their problems with race course managers, owners, trainers, breeders, jockeys and bookmakers. It was left to the board to determine the levy and to obtain the agreement of the bookmakers to meet it. Only if the board and the bookmakers failed to agree was it to be referred to the Home Secretary, which it never was in Harding's time. He proved such a success as chairman that, at the end of his three-year period in 1964, he was asked by the Home Secretary, Henry Brooke, to continue for another three years, which he agreed to do. During this time his major achievement was to persuade Christopher Soames, then Minister of Agriculture, to hand over the National Stud to the Levy Board and to let the board close down the stud at Gillingham and concentrate it at Newmarket. There was much opposition to this, but the decision, combined with that to sell the mares and buy stallions, proved to be of considerable benefit to British horseracing. Another controversial issue was Harding's wish to close down Musselburgh racecourse near Edinburgh, a proposal which brought him into a head-on collision with that pillar of racing, Lord Rosebery. When he handed over the chairmanship to a very different character, Lord Wigg, in 1967, there was no doubt in the minds of the racing world that he had made a most effective contribution to the health of the sport, and he received a generous acknowledgement of this from Roy Jenkins, the Home Secretary at the time.

Busy as he was with these responsibilities, he was always ready to give his time, attention and personal effort to good causes. The two principal ones with which he was most closely associated were the National Fund for Research into Crippling Diseases and the Gurkha Welfare Appeal. The former had been started by its director, Duncan Guthrie, whose daughter had been crippled by polio, as the Polio Research Fund. It had been extended to support research into all forms of crippling disease. It did not directly aid the victims, but supported with grants research by doctors, scientists and engineers into means of prevention and cure and also of relief and help to those crippled. In 1960 the council of the fund was seeking a new chairman to take the place of Admiral Sir Charles Daniel, and Edward Courage, a fellow director of the National Provincial Bank and himself crippled, invited Harding to succeed him. He held the post for twelve years and was a most effective and popular chairman, as successful with the doctors, scientists and engineers as he was with the social lionesses and public figures on the council. The former were clearly impressed with his eagerness to understand their problems and the speed and clarity with which he did so; the latter were as charmed by his friendly, open and courteous handling of council matters as they were impressed by the efficiency with which he handled their business. The director, Duncan Guthrie, found him the perfect chairman, as his chiefs of staff had always found the perfect commander, not interfering in detail, but eager to be well informed, meticulous in attendance, enthusiastic to pursue the decisions arrived at at council meetings, and a miraculous smother-out of difficulties and skilful tamer of fractious lions and lionesses.

The Gurkha Welfare Appeal was launched in 1967, when the reduction of the army in the Far East involved a considerable reduction in the strength of the Brigade of Gurhkas. The Brigade had been expanded beyond the figure agreed with Nepal when India became independent, because of the Malayan emergency, and then held at that strength as a result of what was euphemistically known as 'confrontation' with Indonesia in Borneo. When it was decided that the army's presence in the Far East would be greatly reduced by the end of the 1960s, there were suggestions that the Brigade might even be totally disbanded, certain influential British infantry officers considering that this should happen before any reductions in their own establishment. Fortunately this did not occur, but the threat of it was an important spur to the appeal, which was intended to supplement, in cases of exceptional need, the pensions or redundancy payments which the Gurkha soldier received from the British government, and to help his widow or children. The instigator was Major-General Patterson, at that time Major-General Brigade of Gurkhas. Although Harding had relinquished his colonelcy of the 6th Gurkha Rifles in 1961, after ten years, he had retained a great affection for and interest in the Brigade and was ready to throw his weight behind the appeal. Because Slim, his fellow Field-Marshal and ex-Gurkha, was unable to be very active for reasons of ill-health, Harding took the lead in raising money. His support of the appeal was, without any doubt, an important factor in its success in reaching and later exceeding its target of one million pounds.

This active public life was superimposed on the happy background of a country gentleman. He was a keen and skilful gardener, to which both the flowers and the vegetables of Lower Farm bore witness. He had many friends of all kinds in Somerset and Dorset, and there were frequent calls on his and Mary's time for public appearances in both counties and for private social engagements. Both of them were naturally sociable and generous in their hospitality. Hardly a week went by that did not involve engagements in London and the Harding's little mini-traveller spent much of its time at Sherborne station. As time went by his attendance in the House of Lords diminished, as he felt that, at his age and no longer actively engaged either as a soldier or in commerce, he was in danger of being out of touch. His eyesight also caused him difficulty, and he underwent a successful operation for cataract in 1976. In that year he was one of the pallbearers at the funeral of his old master, Montgomery – no mean feat for a man of eighty to march behind the coffin all the way through Windsor, giving no sign of weakness. He appeared again in his Field-Marshal's uniform at the Queen's Silver Jubilee Review of the Army in Germany in July 1977, at which young soldiers could be seen crowding round the diminutive Field-Marshal to ask him about the long row of medals, which included the Jubilee medal itself, marking his sixty-three years of service in the army.

Nether Compton was not only John and Mary's home, it was that of John Charles and his family also. When the latter retired from the army in 1968, he and his family had moved into the house on the opposite side of the road from Lower Farm, which

Mary had bought and converted from two cottages. He had become a smallholder, his main activity being pig-breeding. His parents had built a swimming pool at Lower Farm, and the grandchildren were frequent visitors across the road. On the Field-Marshal's eightieth birthday, 10 February 1976, he and Mary received congratulations and good wishes from countless friends and admirers and could look back on a full life, lived to the full, in which, in spite of long periods of separation and one period of severe strain, each had supported the other, Mary's contribution as a soldier's, a Governor's and a public figure's wife having been as notable as it had been individual in style.

Is John Harding to be counted among the Great Captains? Had he been given the opportunity to exercise command at a higher level in the Second World War, there is little doubt that he would have been. He had all the qualities of a great commander and few of the faults that some of them suffered from. He had the sharpness, clarity and quickness of mind as well as the determination and capacity for hard work of Montgomery, without the latter's narrowness of outlook and self-centred egotism. He had the open mind and lack of prejudice of Wavell, the enthusiasm of Auchinleck, the human sensitivity and warmth of both Auchinleck and Alexander, and the latter's clear perception of the realities of the battlefield. None was braver or put his duty higher; few could rival him in his personal concern for all under his command. He was not guilty, as many popular commanders were, of a narrow enthusiasm for his own team which worked to the disadvantage of others. He was always generous and understanding of the needs and outlook of formations other than his own and ever ready to cooperate. These characteristics receive acknowledgement from all those, in all walks of life, who have ever had to deal with him from whatever level, and nobody ever hears a word of criticism. Above all it has been his direct, open and straightforward approach to his fellow men that has impressed them most, from the private soldier to the field-marshal, the tycoon, the politician. Harding himself considered that the influences which laid the foundations of his character were the moral background of his family and his education at Ilminster grammar school. The former laid great emphasis on strict regard for the truth and a direct, straightforward and open relationship with one's fellow men : the contribution of the latter, largely based on the classics, lay in the importance attached to an analytical examination of what one heard or read, and to clarity in exposition both verbally and in writing. To these one must add the self-confidence that came from a sense of belonging to one's surroundings, and an assured position, long-established, in the local community.

All three of these influences led to a strong belief in the importance of independence, of standing on one's own feet. This was inherent in his family's background of sturdy yeoman freedom, both a cause of, and a result of, their religious nonconformism. It was enhanced by his education with its emphasis on analysis, rational thought and careful observation – the last a quality he found useful in adapting himself to new circles and surroundings. Harding recalled two nuggets of advice from his father. 'Scum always rises to the top', implying that bad men and evil thoughts are superficial – no more than froth; and 'Go all out to make yourself indispensable, but never kid yourself that you are.' One of his own favourite sayings was : 'There are only two things a sane, able-bodied man is entitled to : eighteen inches in the ranks and six feet in the ground : everything else has to be earned.'

His parents were staunch Liberals in politics; but by the time that Harding himself got round to voting, which he seldom did, he felt that the Liberals no longer represented that attitude of independence and his inclinations were and remained Tory, although he never took an active part in politics. His experience of politicians in war had led him to distrust their pressure for instant, ill-considered action, generally premature, in response to immediate political pressures, and their tendency to judge the strength of armies by counting heads. His subsequent closer association with them did not change his views, although he was fortunate in generally working under, and with, political masters with whose aims and philosophy he sympathized. He had never found carrying his heavy burdens of responsibility, in war or peace, a great strain. As they increased with each step upwards, he found that his ability to cope with them developed, that he grew naturally into the new position. He never lacked self-confidence.

He was not ashamed to recognize that his views on most subjects were conventional. He would accept the conventions, military, social or political, provided that they did not transgress his basic principle that the individual was entitled to the greatest possible degree of personal freedom, as long as it did not involve the exploitation of his fellow men. As a result he always had and retains a strong aversion to bureaucracy, which he regarded as one of the greatest curses of the age.

He never resented privilege, as long as freedom of opportunity was preserved; but he would not make use of it himself. When he married, one of Mary's relations suggested to her that he should become a freemason as a help to advancement in the army. The idea of doing so for this purpose was totally repugnant to him and the invitation was not accepted.

He was an avid reader in his youth and always a rapid one. Between the wars he continued an interest in history, particularly the biographies of famous statesmen and military commanders; but in his later years it was always action rather than reflection which motivated him. He led a full and active life in which intellectual pursuits played little, if any, part. Early insistence on his singing in the chapel choir at South Petherton had set him against music and he had never taken much interest in art. In retirement, if there were spare time, which there seldom has been, the garden has absorbed most of it.

Looking back on his life, one must hope that it will always remain possible for a boy of his typically English background and sterling personal qualities to reach the height of achievement and public esteem that has rightly been gained by Allan Francis, later to be called John Harding, Field Marshal, Baron Harding of Petherton.

BIBLIOGRAPHY

Aspinall-Oglander, Official History of the First World War, *Gallipoli* Vol. II, 1932.

Barclay, *Against Great Odds*, 1955.

Barnett, *The Desert Generals*, 1960.

Byford-Jones, *Grivas and the Story of* EOKA, 1959.

Carver, *El Alamein*, 1962.

Carver, *Tobruk*, 1964.

Clutterbuck, *The Long, Long War*, 1966.

Connell, *Auchinleck*, 1959.

Eden, *Full Circle*, 1960.

Falls, Official History of the First World War, *Egypt and Palestine*, Vols I and II, 1928.

Hunt, *A Don at War*, 1966.

Jackson, *The Battle for Italy*, 1967.

    Alexander of Tunis as Military Commander, 1971.

Kay, New Zealand Official History, *Italy*, Vol. II, 1967.

Montgomery, *El Alamein to the Sangro*, 1948.

    Memoirs, 1958.

Playfair and Molony, Official History of the Second World War, *The Mediterranean and the Middle East*, Vols I II, III IV and V, 1956, 1960, 1966 and 1973.

Rhodes James, *Gallipoli*, 1965.

Shepperd, *The Italian Campaign, 1943–45*, 1968.

Short, *The Communist Insurrection in Malaya 1948–60*, 1975.

Stephens, *Cyprus*, 1966.

Verney, *The Desert Rats*, 1954.

Wavell, *The Palestine Campaigns*, 1927.

INDEX

INDEX

Dill, Field-Marshal, *61, 65, 146*
Djemal, General, *28*
Dobell, Lieut.-General, *23–7*
Dorman-Smith, Major-General, *50, 60, 61, 91–3*
Drakos, Markos, *222*
Drapsin, General, *153, 155*
Duino, Castle, *152, 155, 157*
Dulles, John Foster, *186, 190, 201*

Eaker, General, *130, 133*
Eden, Rt Hon. Anthony (later Earl of Avon), *46, 152, 178, 184–7, 189–91, 193–5, 200–3, 219, 227*
Eisenhower, General of the Army, *122, 123, 130, 132, 138, 142–4, 146, 148, 174, 179, 186*
El Adem, *55, 69, 76, 107*
El Agheila, *61, 64, 65, 107–10*
El Alamein, *see* Alamein
EOKA, *199, 205, 209, 210, 212, 214–18, 220, 222–6*
Episkopi, *217*
Ericssons Ltd, *230*
Erskine, General, *89, 111, 115, 182*
Este, *150*
Ethnarchy, *198, 199, 205, 207, 210*
European Defence Community, *175, 179, 191*

Faenza, *145*
Farouk, King, *185*
Fawzi, Minister, *190*
Ferrara, *147, 149*
Festing, Field-Marshal, *170*
Fielden, Sir Randle, *232*
Finale, *149*
Fisher, Admiral of the Fleet Lord, *7–9*
Fiume, *153*
Florence (Firenze), *133, 146*
Fogarty, Air Marshal, *161*
Forster, Brigadier, *40*
Forli, *145*
Foulkes, Lieut.-General, *146*
French, General, *8*
Freyberg, Lieut.-General Lord, *39, 75, 78–84, 88, 102–5, 109, 110, 125, 130, 131, 149–52*
Fry, Charles, *37*
Fry, Mrs Charles, *37*
Fry, Leslie, *38*
Futa Pass, *143*

Gaeta, Gulf of, *127, 134*
Gairdner, Major-General, *69*
Gale, General, *33, 34, 178, 194*
Gallipoli, *7–19*
Galloway, Lieut.-General, *47, 79, 118*
Gambara, General, *85*
Gambier-Parry, Major-General, *43, 66–8*
Gaming Act, *231*
Gariboldi, General, *61, 65, 67*

Garigliano, River, *122, 124, 127*
Gatehouse, Major-General, *73, 76–8, 105*
Gaza, *23*; 1st Battle of, *24–6*; 2nd Battle of, *26*; 3rd Battle of, *28, 29, 98*
General Electric Company Ltd, *231*
Gent, Sir Edward, *162, 163*
Geoghardjis, Polycarpos, *220, 222*
Gillman, Colonel, *117*
Godwin-Austen, Lieut.-General, *75–89*
Gorizia, *151, 154, 157*
Gothic Line, *138, 141–3*
Gott, Lieut.-General, *71–3, 77, 85, 88, 95*
Grant, Lieut.-Colonel, *5, 6*
Gray, Colonel, *163–5, 183*
Graziani, Marshal, *45, 54, 145*
Grenoble, *142*
Griffiths, Rt Hon. James, *167*
Grivas, Colonel, *199–202, 206, 217–20, 222, 223*
Gruenther, General, *123, 146, 179*
Guillaume, General, *174*
Gurkha Welfare Appeal, *233, 234*
Gurney, Sir Henry, *163–8, 173*
Gustav Line, *122, 124, 127, 134*
Guthrie, Duncan, *233*
Guthrie, Joe, *21, 31*
Gwynne, Major-General, *39*

Hakim Amer, Field-Marshal, *190*
Halfaya Pass, *71, 106*
Hamblen, Brig.-General, *139*
Hamburg, *176*
Hambro, Jocelyn, *232*
Hamilton, General, *7, 8–14, 17*
Harding, Allan Francis (later known as John), Field-Marshal, Baron Harding of Petherton: birth and ancestry, *1–2*; school, *3*; joins Post Office Savings Bank, *4*; joins Finsbury Rifles, *5*; called up, *5*; lands at Suvla Bay, *13*; goes into action, *16*; wounded, *17*; returns to Gallipoli, *17*; evacuated, *19*; promoted Captain, Machine-Gun Corps, *21*; regular commission, *21*; at 1st Battle of Gaza, *25*; wounded, *26*; promoted Major as 54 Div MG officer, *28*; at 3rd Battle of Gaza, *28*; awarded MC, *29*; at HQ 21 Corps, *30*; commands 161 Bde MG Coy, *31*; commands 54 MG battalion, *32*; returns to England, *32*; joins 12 MG battalion, *33*; called John, *33*; sails for India, *33*; adjutant 2 Som LI, *35*; returns to England, *36*; married, *38*; attends Staff College, *39*; son born, *39*; at HQ Southern Command, *39*; brigade major, *40*; at Colchester, *41*; at War Office, *41*; commands 1 Som LI in India, *42*; to Middle East as GSO 1, *43*; joins O'Connor's staff, *50*; promoted Brigadier, *54*; BGS Western Desert Force, *54*; CBE, *63*;

242